Bees in the City

Bees in the City

The urban beekeepers' handbook

Alison Benjamin
and **Brian McCallum**

guardianbooks

Published by Guardian Books 2011

2 4 6 8 10 9 7 5 3 1

First published in Great Britain by
Guardian Books
Kings Place
90 York Way
London
N1 9GU

www.guardianbooks.co.uk

A CIP catalogue for this book is available from the British Library

ISBN: 978-0-8526-5231-2

Designed and set by seagulls.net

Printed and bound in Great Britain by Clays Ltd, St Ives PLC

Mixed Sources
Product group from well-managed
forests and other controlled sources
www.fsc.org Cert no. TT-COC-2139
© 1996 Forest Stewardship Council

Guardian Books supports The Forest Stewardship Council (FSC), the
leading international forest certification organisation. All our titles that are
printed on Greenpeace approved FSC certified paper carry the FSC logo.

Contents

Acknowledgements

We would like to thank everyone who has helped to make this book possible by sharing their urban beekeeping experiences with us and giving their time generously, either by responding to our emails and phone calls or showing us around their apiaries.

In particular we would like to thank the first Co-op Plan Bee trainees at Camley Street whose insights into keeping bees on allotments, schools and rooftops proved invaluable, especially Kate Griffiths-Lambeth, Chantal Coady, Angela Richardson, Esther Coles, Ann Eatwell, Melanie Lenz and Richard Groves; the City of London volunteer beekeepers especially Sally Coryn, David Lockie and Paula Carvel for their time and patience; Rowena Young for her astute beginners' tips and advice on children and beekeeping; Sheila Jaswon for her enthusiasm and her school risk assessment; Tim Baker for his inspirational head teacher attitude; Mossie Lyons for his 'hare-brained ideas'; Professor Francis Ratnieks, for his encouragement and sharing his important work so openly with us; John Chapple for alerting us to the possible perils of increasing honeybee colonies in cities and showing us his Lambeth Palace bees; councillor Doreen Huddart and Newcastle City Council for taking a lead in making cities more bee-friendly and Peter Whewell for demonstrating the crucial role allotments can play in increasing biodiversity; Jessie Jowers for raising our awareness about solitary bees and bumblebees; Camilla Goddard for articulating many of the reasons why we and many other people have taken up urban beekeeping and for her refreshing approach to the art; the British Beekeepers' Association (BBKA) for answering our many questions and for its advisory leaflets; and all the inspiring people out there who are at the forefront of the revolution to help transform our cities into wildlife sanctuaries.

This book would not have happened without Lisa Darnell at Guardian Books who maintained that it was a subject many people would be interested in and had faith in us to deliver it in time, and our editor Lindsay Davies.

We'd also like to thank the British Library for providing the best space to write in London. And finally, special thanks to our friends and family for their support, encouragement and understanding when we didn't see them for months.

Introduction

Cities across the UK are now dotted with beehives, high up on roofs, or tucked away in parks, city farms or allotments. Even streets of terraced houses and blocks of high-rise flats hum with the sound of busy bees – if you listen closely enough – as they come and go from hives squeezed into backyards and balconies. Some of the capital's most famous landmarks host beehives, including St Paul's Cathedral, Buckingham Palace and Fortnum & Mason. And in Newcastle, Liverpool and Sheffield, city-centre locations are starting to buzz with bees.

We have kept bees in our city backyard since 2006. One hive soon grew to four or five, scattered between friends' and parents' gardens. And in 2008 we founded Urban Bees, a social enterprise dedicated to training and educating a new generation of aspiring apiarists to become responsible beekeepers in an urban environment. Two years later we set up our first training apiary in Camley Street Natural Park in London's King's Cross, sponsored by the Co-operative Group.

On our urban beekeeping journey, we have witnessed a phenomenon unfolding before our eyes as more and more young people start to pursue a hobby that until recently was associated with older country folk. In fact, the majority of our trainees have been women, ranging from students in their twenties to fifty-something professionals – a far cry from the stereotypical bearded beekeeper of old.

More than 150 people have attended our one-day taster courses to get a feel for what the pastime entails. Some travelled from as far afield as Liverpool and Durham because courses in their area were either heavily over-subscribed or their local beekeepers' association didn't run an introductory class. They wanted to know if they could keep hives in their sliver of urban space, how it would affect their neighbours and children, how much time would it take, how much it would cost, what equipment they would need and what the role of beekeeper actually entailed. Some even wanted to know about the flavour of urban honey.

We should point out that some have been put off taking up the hobby when they have better understood the commitment and responsibility involved. But many have added to the spiralling numbers of people managing hives in an urban location.

As such they are transforming apiculture from a rather staid Middle England pastime into part of a vibrant inner-city environmental movement that goes hand-in-hand with greening our urban spaces and growing more of our own food.

In writing *Bees in the City*, we wanted to take a step back and chart this recent rise in urban beekeeping, and paint a vivid picture of what it's like for the people involved. With most hives hidden from the public gaze, many people are unaware that beekeeping is being practised on their doorstep and that it is a pastime they too could enjoy. Nor are they aware of the potential benefits to their flowers, fruit trees and vegetable patch, not to mention their own state of mind as they reconnect with nature amid the hustle and bustle of city life.

By showing the eclectic mix of people keeping bees in enclosed spaces, cheek by jowl with urban society, we hope to inspire and encourage others to take up this fascinating and rewarding pastime. We had created Yeats' 'bee-loud glade' in the shadow of a tower block and we wanted others to be able to share that joy.

In our previous book, *A World Without Bees* – part eulogy, part wake-up call exploring the mysterious decline of the honeybee and what it meant for humans – we suggested that a possible way to help bees was to keep hives in cities. Following the book's success, it appears many people have heeded our call and done just that. Triggered by anecdotal stories in the press about bees doing better in cities than the countryside – due to a more diverse supply of flowers and plants in our parks, gardens and railway sidings – there has been a frantic rush for bees.

Urban beekeeping seems to tick all the right boxes. In a world where we feel increasingly powerless to change things, it allows us to make a contribution to saving a species, to increase biodiversity among the concrete and the housing estates, and to produce delicious local food, as well as satisfying a yearning to reconnect with nature.

But the more we researched the book, the more we realised that beekeeping isn't the only way to help bees in an urban environment. And that actually introducing millions more honeybees into our towns and cities may not be such a good idea without increasing sources of pollen and nectar to sustain their colonies.

As a result, this book has changed from being merely a cheerleader for urban beekeeping to investigating what else city dwellers can do to help bees, and not just honeybees. In the furore surrounding the collapse of honeybee colonies, particularly in the States where they are responsible for $14bn of crop pollination, the plight of bumblebees and solitary bees has often been overlooked.

So the book contains information about how to make cities more bee-friendly by planting suitable forage, leaving our gardens untidy and campaigning to get our councils to reduce grass cutting and ditch floral displays of annual bedding plants that provide little forage for all our bees.

We wrote most of the book between November 2010 and March 2011 when our own bees were for the most part huddled together in their hives keeping warm and eating their winter honey stores. We interviewed a selection of people who we think together give a flavour of the new face of beekeeping in our towns and cities, from the office workers tending bees in their lunch hour, to the teachers doing it at the end of the school day, the inner-city youngsters who are overcoming fear and learning new business skills, and the former drug addicts who have found beekeeping therapeutic and life-changing.

While the book focuses for the most part on London where we have witnessed the urban beekeeping revolution unfold, Newcastle, Manchester, Liverpool, Sheffield, Birmingham and Gloucester also feature.

The final part of the book provides a more practical guide for those who want to become urban beekeepers themselves, with tips about how to decide where to locate your hive, where to get your bees and how to harvest your honey. It includes blog entries that draw on our own experiences, but equally importantly it provides tips and advice from other urban beekeepers and highlights where some of us have got it wrong. And there are appendices for more detailed information on school risk assessments, allotment beekeeping and bee-friendly planting schemes.

We hope it enables you to participate in the beekeeping revolution in whichever way you choose.

PART I

The urban beekeeping revolution

Meet the urban beekeepers

On a Tuesday evening in May in London, 20 people have gathered just behind one of Europe's busiest train stations to learn about a new pastime. Dressed in white boiler suits with hats and veils, they look like a crack squad of weapons inspectors. Their activities are played out against the backdrop of gasometers and cranes, and the din of pneumatic drills and heavy traffic are a constant reminder of the inner-city environment. London's signature red buses and black cabs trundle past, their passengers unaware of the new arrivals on their route home.

This is the scene of something extraordinary that is taking place in our cities. It is being repeated in urban settings across Britain and in other countries around the world, in backyards, on rooftops and in community gardens. What is happening is that people living in cities are coming together to learn about how to keep honeybees in the heart of a metropolis.

There are four beehives located at the edge of Camley Street Natural Park in London's King's Cross. This former coal yard is a 0.8 hectare (2 acre) retreat from the urban jungle for water birds, amphibians and insects, and serves as an environmental education centre run by the London Wildlife Trust. It is now home to four new colonies of honeybees and is hosting a year-long beekeeping course with weekly classes throughout the summer at the apiary and monthly classroom sessions during the colder months.

At that first Tuesday night class there was a wonderfully eclectic mix of people from far-flung corners of the capital. They included a young financial analyst, a charity worker, a couple of museum curators, a few teachers and academic administrators, a successful entrepreneur, an HR director, a redundant company director, an eminent chocolatier, a chap who mends the organ in St Paul's Cathedral and a couple of retirees. Their ages ranged from mid-twenties through to mid-sixties. What they all shared was a passion about keeping bees in a city and an eagerness to learn how to do it. However, what none of the trainees knew was that they had been selected to go on the course out of more than 700 applicants.

If ever proof was needed that a beekeeping craze was sweeping the land, it was the volume of responses in 2009 to the Co-operative Group's offer of free urban beekeeping classes in London. People from all over England signed up in the hope of securing a place. 'It was a bit scary,' admits Naomi Davies, the Co-op's sustainability projects manager who co-ordinated the company's entry into the world of beekeeping. 'I'd given out my telephone number and the phone wouldn't stop ringing. I couldn't even check my voice mail, so we had to redirect callers to our website to register. We knew people were more aware about bees but not on that scale.'

This reaction would have been unthinkable just a few years earlier when membership of beekeeping associations was limited to a few, mainly retired gentlemen. But in just five years, beekeeping has been transformed from a rather genteel, slightly eccentric pastime enjoyed predominately by old men in country gardens to an activity carried out in city backyards and rooftops by younger, savvy, urban professionals, both male and female.

The British Beekeeping Association (BBKA) is a charity and umbrella group for more than 60 local associations and their members, who account for about half the amateur apiarists in the UK. Founded in 1874 and based at the National Agricultural Centre in Stoneleigh Park in the Warwickshire countryside, it has been as amazed as any by the surge of interest in urban beekeeping.

'I am very surprised that many more people from all walks of life are taking up beekeeping in our cities, towns and suburbs,' says BBKA president, Martin Smith. Yet in just three years, from 2009 to 2011, its membership has doubled to more than 20,000 – and Smith confirms that urban apiarists are a growing proportion among the newer members.

Nowhere is the phenomenon more pronounced than in London. Beehives now grace some of the capital's most famous landmarks, from St Paul's Cathedral to Tate Modern and Fortnum & Mason, and can be found in the grounds of Buckingham Palace and Lambeth Palace, as well as in schools, offices and community centres where staff and volunteers are keeping bees.

Courses for beginners are being run at more and more venues, from city farms to parks and workplaces, and membership of London beekeeping associations has spiralled to an all-time high. North London Beekeepers has 170 members, compared to 100 a decade earlier. But it could have even more if in 2010 it hadn't made the decision, for the first time in its history, to close its books.

'All new beekeepers want to join an association and we are left to carry the can to support and mentor them. We are overloaded with inexperienced beekeepers in London,' says John Hauxwell, a retired architect and former chair of the association.

We are sitting at a large kitchen table in his end-of-terrace Victorian villa in Tufnell Park. Hauxwell, an affable 70-year-old man sporting a short, gnome-like beard, says: 'There's a lot to learn in your second year about swarm management and disease control and we don't have enough experienced beekeepers to support and mentor newcomers, so we decided we had no choice but to stop taking any more members at that point.'

It's a far cry from when he joined the association in the mid-1980s when newcomers would meet at his house and comfortably fit around his kitchen table. 'This level of interest is unheard of during my beekeeping career,' he stresses.

It's a similar story south of the Thames where the London Beekeepers' Association has witnessed an even more dramatic three-fold increase in people joining between 2006 and 2011. It now has around 180 paid-up members, but unlike its north London equivalent refuses to turn anyone away. The scale of the transformation can be witnessed at their monthly meetings. Just a handful of members used to meet at the café in the basement of the Natural

History Museum, which also has beehives, on a Sunday morning. Now there is often standing room only as chairman John Chapple addresses a throng of people squeezed into a classroom at Walworth Garden Farm. Chapple tells us that when he became chairman in 2000, the association had just seven members and was on the verge of collapse.

In addition to the two inner-London beekeeping clubs, there are another dozen or so dotted around the fringes of the capital, in places such as Ealing, Enfield, Bromley, Croydon and Twickenham. All of these without exception have seen an unprecedented growth in membership.

No one knows exactly how many beekeepers there are now across greater London, because not all of them join an association or register with the government's BeeBase, an online registry of beekeepers and their hive locations that allows the government bee inspectors to monitor and control the spread of disease. It has been estimated, however, that there could be as many as 5,000 living within the M25, each with an average of three hives.

It is still a far cry from the heyday of British beekeeping just after the second world war when more than 76,000 people kept bees, many of them unashamedly for the sugar ration they received from the Ministry of Food to feed their bees, which oral histories reveal was mainly kept for themselves.

But were these wartime beekeepers living in cities? The history of urban beekeeping is incredibly sketchy. According to *Digging for Victory* author Twigs Way, although restrictions on keeping livestock in towns were relaxed during the war, and many urban allotments had pig clubs and kept rabbits and chickens, there were far fewer adverts for keeping bees. Way points out that many wartime diggers had little knowledge of the beneficial role of any insects, not even bees.

We do know that some of the most urban locations for present-day hives in the City of London would have hosted apiaries back in medieval times when the City was dominated by religious orders, whose presence lives on in names such Greyfriars and Blackfriars, and who would have used beeswax for church candles. Much more

9

recently, the former governor of the Bank of England, Robin Leigh-Pemberton, kept hives on the roof of the Old Lady of Threadneedle Street from 1983 to 1993.

We also know from the wills and inventories of the landed gentry, yeoman and cottagers, that before sugar became affordable in the mid-19th century, people from all classes kept bees. And records from some of the older beekeeping associations shed light on members' backgrounds and beekeeping practices 100 years ago. However, most hives were located in the countryside or suburban hinterland. Truly, urban beekeeping is still a very recent phenomenon.

Today, the rise in urban beekeeping is not simply a London trend. In 2010 in the Yorkshire city of Sheffield, more than 100 local residents joined a beekeepers' association that had been moribund for 30 years. 'Its revival was part of a wider project to encourage urban beekeeping,' explains Anna Cooper, the secretary of the association. Her day job is as project manager for Groundwork Sheffield, an environmental and regeneration charity that works in some of the poorest parts of the city. Cooper established a Groundwork urban beekeeping project called Sheffield Bee Buddies and breathed new life into the Sheffield Beekeepers' Association, providing its trainees with ongoing support.

On the roof at Weston Park Museum on the edge of the city, Jez Daughtry, a commercial beekeeper, is teaching some of the trainees what a colony of honeybees looks like when you open a hive. Daughtry founded The Sheffield Honey Company in 2009, which sells local blossom and heather honey from the moors and around the city in delis, health shops and cafés throughout the Yorkshire area. He has been contracted by Groundwork Sheffield to teach the 30 recruits on its Bee Buddies project. The museum roof site is one of four new training apiaries. Trainees receive two days of theory and hands-on learning for free, followed by a year of one-to-one mentoring by an experienced beekeeper.

Cooper says the project – which, as it names suggests, encourages trainees to pair up to support each and share the costs of buying hives and equipment – has proved so popular in its first year, that a further seven sites have been earmarked as future training apiaries, including a school with a green roof, a city farm and a housing association. Here, 50 more Sheffield residents will learn how to keep bees in the backyards and on the rooftops of the former steel capital of Britain.

Across the Pennines in Manchester, a further 100 new beekeepers have been trained on a new year-long course targeted at park keepers, allotment managers and plot holders. And in the north-east of England, Ouseburn city farm in the east end of Newcastle is the latest venue for urban beekeeping classes. Here, during a visit in 2010, Prince Charles officially opened the city farm's first hive, which is sponsored by the council.

In cities where no extra classes have been put on to meet the demand from aspiring apiarists, there are reports of long waiting lists, courses being oversubscribed by a factor of three and people travelling hundreds of miles for training. Stonebridge city farm in the St Anne's inner-city district of Nottingham reported having enough people to fill two years' worth of courses in 2010.

'I've been amazed by the number of people turning up for courses who had already ordered their hive and equipment,' says Hannah Hodgson, former secretary of Liverpool Beekeepers' Association. 'It's incredible, suddenly [in 2010] people were jumping on the bandwagon that urban beekeeping had become and buying the new plastic Beehaus hive before they had even got any training.' In the space of 12 months she says membership had doubled to 100 people and beehives were popping up on roofs across the city, disused bits of land in inner-city Toxteth and in the grounds of the Anglican church.

At 32, Hodgson is the poster girl for a new generation of beekeepers. She is young, female and when she took up the hobby she was living in a city. Her face smiles out at you from the BBKA website. A commercial airline pilot in her working life, Hannah started out as a 'DIY beekeeper' in 2009, inspired by her late apiarist grandfather, but became a member of the association when she realised the complexity of bee husbandry. She now has four hives on an allotment in the city.

You can 'adopt' Hodgson, or one of a number of other beekeepers across the UK, for just £29.50 a year. Your annual donation doesn't actually go towards the upkeep of her beehive: instead it funds research into honeybee health and education programmes for beekeepers. But in return you will receive an adoption certificate, a factsheet about the honeybee, a jar of honey, and a newsletter with an update about 'your' beekeeper and their bees. The scheme was launched by the BBKA in 2010 and allows people to participate in the nation's newfound fascination with honeybees by becoming virtual, or armchair, beekeepers. In its first year, 5,000 people adopted a hive and the scheme raised some £150,000.

The same basic principle behind 'adopt a hive' is evident in Birmingham where a bee landlord scheme allows people to contribute to honeybees' wellbeing without having to don a bee suit.

Sharif Khan, secretary of Birmingham and District Beekeepers' Association, explains how the scheme works: 'It aims to match beekeepers who feel they have too small a garden themselves to keep a hive with someone with a plot of land or a large garden who is happy to rent out the space to them,' he says. 'Standard rent is four jars of honey per hive.'

Khan, 32, now has three bee landlords on whose land he keeps a total of 14 hives. When he started beekeeping a few years ago in the backyard of his terraced house, he quickly joined his local association. 'It was like obtaining an instant pool of grandfathers all offering lots of advice, but none of it ever the same,' he recalls fondly. 'When I became secretary of the association I vowed I was going to attract younger members. None of our members were unapproachable but because they fitted so neatly into the stereotypical "bunch of retirees" category, I thought it would put some people off joining. I tried to engage [with younger members] as much as possible and make them feel welcome.' Six years on, membership has increased by almost two thirds.

Khan describes himself as white British despite his mixed heritage and says the association, like the majority around the UK, has yet to attract a diverse range of people from different ethnic backgrounds. But that is not to say they are not keeping bees. In north London, for example, the Greek Cypriot community has many bees on its allotments and in the south of the capital a mosque is planning to install hives.

So why is it that in just a matter of a few years thousands of people have decided to take up or support beekeeping in an urban environment? What has created this buzz around bees?

According to a 2010 survey of beekeepers commissioned by the Department for Environment, Food and Rural Affairs (Defra), the reasons people are taking up the hobby in ever-increasing numbers include the desire to harvest honey for personal use, a greater knowledge of environmental benefits and also concern about the declining number of bees. Of those who had started keeping bees within the last two years, the study found they were twice as likely to have been motivated by environmental factors as those with two or more years' experience.

The growth of interest in beekeeping therefore fits with people's aspirations to live a healthier and greener lifestyle by helping nature's master pollinator increase the flowers, plants and wildlife in our cities, not to mention eating pure, locally produced honey. It is also a response to the blanket media coverage in the last few years about honeybees mysteriously disappearing across the globe because of a possible combination of pesticides, parasites and modern farming methods.

It is no surprise therefore that one of the places you are most likely to find urban beehives is on the allotments that fringe our towns and cities. There are around 330,000 allotment holders in the UK and more than 100,000 people are on allotment waiting lists. They are part of the boom in the grow-your-own movement that eschews supermarkets in favour of locally produced, seasonal fruit and vegetables that are food-miles free. This movement has spawned local food groups growing seasonal produce in small urban spaces, and has seen the sales of vegetable seeds outstrip those for flowers. This same desire for self-sufficiency is also behind such initiatives as the flourishing Transition Town movement, which promotes local food growing to reduce our reliance on oil-based pesticides, energy and transport.

In Manchester, an ambitious project by a group of residents to 'create an aspirational vision for the future of Manchester as a genuine garden city' is proposing to transform the top floor of an NCP car park into a community garden growing food and producing urban honey. What honeybees offer these green-fingered diggers is their pollination service, which can increase the yield of fruits and vegetables by as much as 30 per cent.

For us, keeping bees was a way to escape the hubbub of city life and to reconnect with nature. Coming back from a long day in the office and watching our bees arrive home with blobs of pollen on their back legs was a wonderful way to unwind. But we also became more in tune with the changing seasons and aware of when different trees and flowers were in bloom.

We now realise that we were probably suffering from something called 'nature deficit disorder' – a term coined by author Richard Louv in his 2010 book, *Last Child in the Woods*, which claims that the decreasing amount of time children are spending outdoors is linked with a wide range of behavourial problems. This idea that humans (not just children) have an innate affinity with nature also ties in with Harvard University entomologist Edward O. Wilson's theory of biophilia, referring to our inherent 'love of living things'.

'How could our relation to nature, on which survival depended minute by minute for millions of years, not in some way be reflected in the rules of cognitive development that generate the human mind?' asks Wilson.

We knew that we weren't ready to move to the suburbs or the countryside to satisfy our yearnings. But by providing a haven for honeybees in an urban backyard we felt as if we were re-engaging with nature while continuing to enjoy the benefits of city life.

Moreover, all the evidence seems to point to honeybees faring better in urban rather than rural areas. 'Forage for bees is disappearing from many areas of the countryside but there's plenty of bee food left among our tree-lined streets and local parks, back gardens and allotments and on railway embankments covered in ivy and brambles,' says the BBKA's president, Martin Smith.

Anecdotally, some beekeepers say that bees they keep in urban locations are more productive, making twice as much honey as hives in more rural or suburban settings. Could this be because a patch of overgrown inner-city scrubland is said to contain more biodiversity than 16 hectares (40 acres) of cultivated arable countryside? Biodiversity means a diverse range of biological species ranging from plants and animals to insects, fungi and bacteria that are all dependent on one another in a complex ecosystem. Human activities associated with intensive farming, including planting one crop across huge swathes of land, the use of pesticides and habitat destruction, have caused dramatic losses of biodiversity and destroyed fragile ecosystems in non-urban areas.

In cities it is often the reverse. A mark of our post-industrial society is that sites that were once coal mines or heavy goods depots have been transformed into nature reserves, rich in biodiversity. Examples are Tyne Riverside County Park on the outskirts of Newcastle, a 60 hectare (150 acre) site on the former Isabella Colliery, now home to wildflower meadows, woodland and a large pond; and the Victorian coal yard in London that has been transformed into Camley Street Natural Park. Environmentalists have noted that one upside of the recession was that land earmarked for city development was being left empty for long periods of time, giving wildlife a chance to flourish. These sites, along with our public parks, tree-lined streets, railway sidings, cemeteries and small community gardens, not to mention the millions of backyards that are as individual as their owners, create a rich tapestry of flora that allow honeybees to thrive. Cities also enjoy high temperatures because of air pollution and concrete trapping heat from homes and offices, which gives bees a longer, almost year-round foraging season.

Tapping into this city beekeeping trend, a new beehive design has even been launched, aimed squarely at the urban demographic. More than 150 years after modern beekeeping was created with the invention of what is known as the moveable frame beehive – because frames can be removed from the hive without destroying the colony of bees – a sturdy plastic 'Beehaus' has been manufac-

15

tured in bright colours to appeal to today's young, city-dwelling, iPad-using beekeeper.

The Co-operative Group has been at the forefront of this urban beekeeping revolution. In 2008, the UK's largest mutual retailer launched a 10-point plan to help save the beleaguered bee. Urban beekeeping was one strand of its £500,000 Plan Bee campaign.

'We wanted to encourage people to become ambassadors for the honeybee and one way to do that was to create a new army of beekeepers,' says Paul Monaghan, head of social goals at the Co-operative Group. 'There are three elements to Plan Bee,' he explains. 'The first is education and empowerment – we want people to understand there is a problem [with the bees' decline] and to show them there is something they can do about it, from planting bee-friendly flowers to going the whole hog and keeping bees. Secondly we want to change the way we farm, and thirdly we will be pumping significant sums of money into new research and development into what's exactly behind these problems.'

The Co-op piloted an urban beekeeping project in Manchester, a city where bees, as a symbol of industry, are on its coat of arms and in the mosaic floor of its Victorian gothic town hall.

Commercial beekeeper and trainer, Paul Peacock, set up three training apiaries in different parts of the city and trained council park officers and allotment holders how to keep bees. What set the project apart from traditional beginners' courses run by beekeeping associations was its timeframe and its cost. In contrast to a 10- or 12-week course run by an association, the Co-op funding allowed Peacock to teach a six-month theory course followed by six months of hands-on experience, all for free. 'It takes real commitment to keep bees,' says Peacock, 'and it takes a whole year to really start to understand what is going on inside a hive.'

Moreover, the project provided trainees with free hives, equipment and bees to make sure that the initial start-up costs didn't deter any enthusiasts from taking up the hobby. More than 100 people attended the beekeeping training and around 60 new beehives have been installed across the city.

In 2010, the Co-op rolled out its urban beekeeping experiment to London. This is where we come into the story. A couple of years earlier we had founded Urban Bees, a social enterprise that encourages responsible urban beekeeping through education and training. By the time the Co-op knocked on our door, we had taught more than 100 people the basic principles of keeping bees in cities. We jumped at the chance to deliver long-term training and to set up a training apiary at a central London location.

We chose Camley Street in King's Cross, run by the London Wildlife Trust, because what we were doing seemed to chime with its ethos. 'LWT is so concerned with the steady decline of the capital's natural pollinators that it has made this special group of insects one of its priorities over the next five years. And our nature reserve at Camley Street has become a focal point for modern urban beekeeping,' says Carlo Laurenzi, LWT's ebullient chief executive. 'People, in general, have an aversion to insects and small things that fly, yet life for people on this planet would come to a virtual standstill without these essential pollinators.'

We soon found our work was expanding in ways we could never have envisaged. Each summer the City of London hosts a programme of music, visual arts, film, walks and talks. 'For the International Year of Biodiversity in 2010 we wanted to give the festival a particular buzz by placing beehives at locations that reflected the diversity of activity in the City,' says festival director, Ian Ritchie. We were invited to act as consultants to determine where hives could best be located in the square mile and to train employees as volunteer beekeepers at each of the chosen sites. 'The idea was to create a network of City beekeepers so the bees flourished long after the festival was over,' says Ritchie. Drawing parallels between the global financial crisis and the collapse of bee colonies around the world, the festival aimed to highlight the complexity and fragility of both systems.

In June, eight hives were installed at some of the City's most iconic landmarks, including St Paul's Cathedral, the Lloyds building and Mansion House. Other sites were Middle Temple, the Museum of London, St Olave church, Sir John Cass primary school and

Swedish investment bank, SEB. In all, business, law, religion, politics, education and the arts were represented.

All these local initiatives have added up to a national wave of support for the humble honeybee. Several companies – from Saga and Burt's Bees to Jordans cereal and Rowse Honey – have seen the value of aligning their brand with saving bees. And politicians have not been slow to grasp the vote-winning potential of getting behind this cause. In December 2010, London's mayor, Boris Johnson, backed a competition to offer up to 50 community food-growing groups the chance to keep bees.

The nation's public broadcaster and its largest membership charity were also swept up in the craze. In May 2010 the BBC and the National Trust teamed up to ensure millions of local radio listeners and 3.6m NT members could join in the fun, with their 'Bee Part of It!' campaign. One of its aims was for each BBC local radio station to adopt its own hive based at a National Trust property.

More commercial sponsorship came from smoothie manufacturer, Innocent, which ran a cleverly titled 'Buy One, Get One Bee' promotion, donating money from the sales of a specially created lemon, honey and ginger smoothie to help fund the 45 hives at National Trust properties.

Online, there has also been an explosion in bee-related activity from beekeeping forums to Facebook pages set up to save the bees.

We mentioned at the beginning of this chapter that urban beekeeping was also in the ascendancy in other parts of the world. In New York, for example, since the authorities overturned a ban on keeping bees in the city in April 2010, the number of beekeepers has rocketed, and hives can be found tucked away in community parks, city farms and on the roofs of restaurants. The reasons for this growth sound all too familiar.

Vivian Wang became passionate about pollinators while working on a case at the Natural Resources Defense Council against pesticides potentially toxic to bees. She tends three hives on the roof of the NRDC's offices, high above mid-town Manhattan.

'It's a special way to connect with nature in a city,' says the 27-year-old lawyer. 'People think that urban environments are all about traffic jams, noise and dirt, and concrete and steel, but we're never outside of nature. Keeping bees is a transformative experience. It is also about the NRDC practising what it preaches and raising awareness about just how important our pollinators are.'

Wang believes she is the highest beekeeper in Manhattan (her hives are 12 storeys up), but not the youngest. 'There are lots of people in their mid to late twenties keeping bees in the city now,' she says. 'It ties in with the local food-growing movement.'

Likewise in Melbourne, Australia, hives are sprouting up at communal food schemes. Lyndon Fenlon has created a network of 30 hives across the city located at food co-ops, a Buddhist temple, Victoria University, and on individuals' roofs and backyards. 'I wanted to have an urban, nutritious local food source and to build a business model based on green, carbon-neutral practices,' says Fenlon, 42, who runs an enterprise called The Urban Honey Co. 'Low food miles, greener lifestyles and urban food production has fuelled interest in beekeeping among Melbourne residents,' he adds.

In fact there has been such a growth in interest that the local beekeepers' association is full to capacity with 160 members, and Fenlon says it has had to turn away potential new recruits.

Closer to home, prominent buildings in Berlin, including the House of Representatives, Berlin Cathedral and the Planetarium, now host hives as part of an initiative called Berlin is Buzzing, launched in March 2011 by the Environmental Forum for Action and Co-operation. It draws inspiration from Paris where more than 300 colonies now exist across the French capital following a programme to encourage city beekeeping. Indeed, Jean Paucton has kept bees on the roof of the Paris Opera House since 1982.

Back in the UK, we are going to introduce you to some of the people who are at the forefront of our urban beekeeping revolution. We start our journey with the guardians of the future generation of beekeepers: the school teachers.

The school beekeepers

Sheila Jaswon and Jennie Ingram are standing by four hives in a clearing in a wooded area. The hives are enclosed by a seven-foot, mesh-netted fence and are only accessed through a bolted door.

Here in the summer, six- and seven-year-old pupils stand on the other side of the fence behind the mesh netting while their teachers lift out the frames of bees from the hives and hold them up to the class.

'The children can identify the different castes of bee – workers, drones and the queen – and the eggs and larvae in all stages of development from grub to sealed brood [when the larvae pupates],' says Jaswon gleefully.

She and her colleague may seem unlikely revolutionaries. Both in their forties and teachers of young pupils at an independent, co-educational school for four- to 18-year-olds in north London, they are nevertheless leading the way in introducing bees into schools.

They have been keeping bees at King Alfred School for coming up to three years. The idea came from a parent who was a bee-keeper. 'I had a display on the wall in my second-year classroom about pollination and he suggested that he give us one of his hives and his time to train some teachers to become beekeepers,' recalls Jaswon. 'I loved the idea. It tied in so well with what I was teaching about pollinators.'

When she approached the head with the idea she was told to go away and carry out a risk assessment (see Appendix 1) and speak to the estate manager about where a hive could be safely located.

As the lower school's outdoor learning co-ordinator, she wanted the hive in full view of her Year 2 classroom, or on the school farm with the chickens and ducks. 'But both sites were ruled out as being too close in proximity to the pupils,' she sighs.

Instead we have to go out of the school, cross over the road, open a locked gate and walk across landscaped gardens to get to the apiary, which is in a secluded wooded area. It's a good three-minute walk; a lot more, we suspect, when you are escorting a group of young children.

The apiary expanded from the one parent-donated hive to four hives after Jaswon received £5,000 from the school's parent/staff fundraising committee.

'It allowed us to get the site cleared. It was thick with brambles and overhanging rotting trees that blocked any sunlight,' Jaswon explains. It also paid for the construction of the seven-foot fence and mesh netting, a large storage shed for beekeeping equipment, the extra hives – complete with glass observation panels on the side so pupils can see activity inside the hive – and more bees.

King Alfred is a member of the School Farms Network, which offers support and assistance to the 82 school farms across the UK. Some of these schools are thinking about keeping bees, but what often holds them back is the negative reaction of a few parents who are scared of their children being stung. So, how did King Alfred allay the concerns of a handful of anxious parents? 'They were informed at a Q&A session that all staff were first-aid trained, can recognise signs of anaphylactic shock, and know the GPS location of the apiary site, so an ambulance can come straight here rather than to the main school gates,' Jaswon explains.

Other considerations for any beekeeping school are insurance and bee-sitting during the school holidays. Jaswon and Ingram both joined a beekeeping association which gives them public liability insurance cover of up to £10m should the bees cause harm to others, as well as providing training and access to an experienced bee mentor.

Jaswon bee-sits during the school holidays because she lives close by. It can be a busy time of the year in the beekeeping calendar. Bees are prone to swarm around Easter, and in August honey needs to be removed and harvested and the main varroa treatment has to be administered (see page 211). She can call on help from a handful of parents and other members of staff who attended a free training course at the school run by their mentor.

Both teachers believe it is important to be clear how school bees are going to be integrated into learning. King Alfred's independent status exempts it from having to follow the National Curriculum, but their bees have been used to bring maths and biology to life.

'Part of how you control the varroa mite as a beekeeper is to count the number of mites you find on the tray at the bottom of the hive and divide this total by the number of days since your last inspection to get the daily mite drop. So we take the varroa tray into the classroom and using a magnifying glass the children count them and then practise their division,' says Ingram, who is a maths co-ordinator for the lower school. 'Another maths lesson is making the bees a feed of sugar-syrup solution, which requires mixing equal measures of water and sugar so the children learn about volume.' Older Year 4 pupils (eight and nine-year-olds) will be making lip balms and candles from the beeswax and helping with the honey harvest when the school has one.

She adds: 'The feedback from parents is they can't stop talking about the bees when they get home.'

Jaswon and Ingram's top tip for any would-be teacher apiarists is to 'ensure there is more than one school beekeeper to share the workload and responsibility'.

'Some weeks we'd almost forget to inspect them or to make up their feed,' says Ingram. 'You should also find an experienced beekeeper who is prepared to give their expertise generously to mentor novices. If it wasn't for our mentor this wouldn't have happened.'

A few other schools across the country have hives maintained by either staff, parents and governors, or even local residents.

Andy McClean is a parent and governor at his children's state primary school in west London. He wanted Oriel Primary to keep bees, he says, because 'it seemed to tick all the educational boxes'.

Beekeeping would enhance the children's experience in several areas: 'biology (understanding the environment); maths (collecting and handling data especially when correlated with weather data); project work and independent learning – all combined with the stimulus that wild, fascinating creatures would bring to the learning experience.'

Before the school agreed to have a hive, however, they had to consult parents and staff about the proposal via a newsletter and check school records to see if anyone had declared a reaction to bee stings on their medical forms. They hadn't.

However, McClean recalls that 'several parents did express concerns and were invited in to be briefed and reassured of the safety of children on site'.

McClean took advice from the Twickenham and Thames Valley Beekeeping Association about where to put the hive. 'Initially we considered keeping the one hive on a large second-storey flat roof, but having considered access issues and taken advice from the local beekeepers' association who did a site inspection, we now keep the hive in a fenced-off and secured area on the edge of a wood used for nature studies, which has controlled access where children are supervised at all times,' he says. 'The bees have space but they need to attain an altitude of 10 feet to leave the site, thus putting them well above the children.'

McClean has a key and 24-hour access to the site. He currently inspects the hive outside of the school day but hopes pupils will soon carry out the inspections as part of their studies.

'The plan has always been to keep the bees for the 2010 season to gain experience before introducing the Years 5 and 6 children to them in 2011,' says McClean, who is only a fledgling beekeeper himself and attends the weekly Co-op course at Camley Street. 'The teaching staff have shown a lively interest and we wish to introduce the Years 5 and 6 teachers to the hive before introducing the children,' he adds.

Based on his own limited experience, McClean suggests that anyone thinking of keeping bees in a school should 'take a course, join a local beekeepers' association, get an experienced assistant if possible, and build up confidence around the hive before introducing children into the mix'.

Richard Groves is another parent who has moved bees into his child's primary, Hollick Wood in north London, where he is a school governor. 'The plan is for all ages from three up to 11 to become involved in the bees – from watching them from the safety of the canteen, to doing hive inspections,' he says.

Groves is also new to beekeeping and has roped in young teacher Stephanie Turner to learn alongside him. The only dissenters when the idea was mooted were another governor who is allergic to bee stings, and a teaching assistant. They have been placated by the hive's out-of-the way location behind the school canteen and a five-foot fence surrounding it, which has removable panels for people to view the bees.

'We've had no child-related mishaps thus far – partly down to having lovely bees and also due to being extra careful to ensure no one places themselves in danger,' says Groves.

'One problem that did happen early on was when a group of Sunday school kids who use our school at the weekend decided it would be fun to go into the enclosure and try to push the hive over. They got as far as pushing the hive apart a bit, but luckily it didn't topple.' Part of the problem, he admits, was that they hadn't yet informed the Sunday school (it was the first Sunday after the bees arrived), and hadn't had time to fit a catch to the door of the enclosure.

Museum curator Ann Eatwell, 57, has her hive in the grounds of a local school. 'We live in a terraced house with a small garden and I prefer to keep bees separate from my husband and my neighbours,' she explains.

She wrote to all the institutions she could think of that owned land locally, including schools, the NHS trust and a museum, to ask if they would be willing to host her hive. 'The only response I received was from the bursar of this school,' she says when we meet at James Allen's Girls' School in Dulwich, south London.

In fact the school has form in this area: it pioneered botany teaching in the 19th century by creating its own gardens and ecological habitats, and during the Second World War the grounds were made over to vegetable growing, rabbit rearing and beekeeping to supplement rationing. So it is only fitting that it should host Eatwell's hive.

In return for the use of its land, the school has asked for a jar of honey each year and for its resident beekeeper to give talks to pupils about honeybees' important role as pollinators, which Eatwell is delighted to do.

The JAGS hive is at the back of the school and enclosed with high mesh netting and warning signs that read: 'Caution: bees at work'. But not all school hives are sealed off or hidden away. On the roof of Sir John Cass's primary in the City of London stands an unfettered hive among an array of flowers, vegetables and fruit trees that make up the school's thriving allotment. With the 180-metre (591-foot) Gherkin building looming above the Victorian schoolhouse, it is as incongruous and dramatic a setting for a school hive as you are ever likely to see.

With the hive entrance pointing away from the garden, pupils can file past in the summer to get to their outdoor rooftop classroom without crossing the bees' flight path.

Here, the volunteer beekeeper is the appropriately named John Mead, the school caretaker, who is learning the craft as part of the City of London Festival 2010. Once he has completed his training he hopes to share his fascination with Year 6 pupils. A mild-mannered retired policeman, he is so calm around the bees that he doesn't feel the need to wear protective gloves.

'I've wanted bees for a long time but my partner refuses to let me keep them on the small balcony of our flat,' he admits.

Mead often finishes his day with a mug of tea next to the hive. 'I'm intrigued by the pollen the bees are bringing back and how they behave. I think they go to the gardens of the Tower of London,' he says, pointing south, where they are situated less than a mile away.

While most schools keeping bees have embraced the activity as a novel way to enhance pupils' understanding of nature, one head teacher has successfully employed a beehive to dramatically improve the behaviour of his most unruly pupils.

When we go to meet Tim Baker, the inspirational head of Charlton Manor primary in south-east London, we know we are in for something special. We had heard Baker speak about the tremendous impact the bees have had on his school. It demonstrated the potential benefits of beekeeping far beyond helping the environment and the bees themselves.

We drive past leafy Greenwich and affluent Blackheath to the shabbier suburb of Charlton. Surrounded by streets of modest houses, Charlton Manor seems a million miles away from the wealth and privilege enjoyed by some of the other beekeeping schools we have visited.

'It all started in July 2008 when a swarm collected on a brick wall by the entrance of the school,' Baker recalls. 'What struck me was the different reaction by staff and pupils. Some of the children were fascinated by the bees and wanted to see what they were doing, while staff were panicking and some even called for the school to be closed.

'When a local swarm collector arrived, he told me that far from being dangerous, a swarm is probably the time when bees are at their safest. It made me realise we didn't know enough about them.

'I decided there and then that the school needed bees. I want our pupils to grow up understanding and respecting bees rather than fearing them,' he says.

Yet neither Baker nor Jo Sparkes, the school's young gardener, knew the first thing about beekeeping. Undeterred, Baker enrolled them both onto a 10-week beginners' course run by their local Ruxley Beekeepers' Association.

'I couldn't believe my eyes when we turned up the first Friday evening. I expected two old blokes and a dog; instead there were about 50 people, women as well as men, of all different ages,' admits Sparkes.

Baker had a different expectation. 'To be honest I had gone along thinking how difficult can this be? Why do you need 10 lessons?' he laughs.

As the course progressed it dawned on them that beekeeping was more of an undertaking than they had anticipated. 'But we owed it to the kids to fulfil their aspirations,' says Sparkes.

Support from the association proved invaluable. They advised on the location of the hive at the far end of the school's newly landscaped garden, by a bramble hedge and in front of a pond, so the bees are forced to fly up away from the garden and are near to a supply of drinking water. They also dissuaded Barker from keeping bees in a glass observation hive, which lets in too much light to make a suitable permanent home for bees. He was adamant, however, that pupils be able to see what is happening inside the hive even if they didn't want to do the inspections. The compromise is a customised wooden hive built with panels on each side that can be unbolted to reveal small glass windows.

The adapted hive, painted by pupils with flying bees, the words 'Home Sweet Home' and a yellow and black striped roof, has unique security features. It is not fenced off nor stands behind mesh netting as in most schools. Instead it sits on the shelf of what looks like a bus shelter with an imposing iron bar gate.

'The level of security may seem over the top,' admits Baker, 'but the challenging behaviour that some of my pupils are capable of meant we had to err on the side of caution. Otherwise there was a real danger that an unruly pupil would pick up the hive and throw it across the garden.'

From the start, Baker wanted to try and engage all the pupils from Year 3 (seven- and eight-year-olds) upwards, including those with severe behavioural problems. This is where the story of the Charlton Manor bees gets really interesting.

'You should meet Wayne,' says Baker, his eyes lighting up. 'Before he started getting involved with the bees he'd be in the school behaviour support house every single day,' he says, referring to the unit where disruptive pupils are sent. 'He'd be kicking off before class, after class, throwing chairs around, wrecking classrooms, kicking and punching. The teachers couldn't deal with him. He had no friends, because pupils were scared of him.'

But Wayne (not his real name) turned out to be a whizz at assembling the frames of foundation that go in the hive, onto which the bees build their hexagonal wax comb.

'While some of the more academic pupils were having trouble banging in a nail straight, he rattled off the frames,' recalls Sparkes.

'It must have been the first time he could do something better than anyone else and he was able to help his fellow pupils. It has earned him respect among his peers and boosted his self-esteem no end.'

Wayne has also shone at the weekly hive inspections. 'We think it is the scale of the responsibility and the trust that he has been given by the school that he is responding positively to. He can't kick off around the hive because we and the bees need to trust him.

'It's not just him, the other unruly ones have also risen to the challenge,' she adds. 'And they have finally found something they like to do at school and they are good at.'

Wayne enters the room. A chubby 10-year-old, he sits down and waits to be asked a question.

Are the bees his favourite thing at school? 'Yes. It's a brilliant idea having them here,' he replies.

Asked about the frame-making, he says: 'I find it very easy to make frames.'

Does he find anything else at school easy?

He doesn't reply.

Baker asks Wayne if beekeeping has changed his behaviour. He nods his head. 'Yes, it's made me better in class. I concentrate more.'

Why?

'The bees make me peaceful and calm.'

As a result, the pupil who was once at the behavioural support unit every single day has not set foot in there for more than four months. And the previously solitary boy now has four pupils he can call friends who are the founding members of the Charlton Manor School bee club. They meet every Tuesday with Sparkes to talk about and research bees. They are currently designing a leaflet to encourage more pupils to join. 'I'm going to be handing them out,' says Wayne.

The head has also asked Wayne to give an annual bee progress report to Ruxley Beekeepers' Association in a few weeks. 'I'm going to write a speech with my new friends in the bee club,' he tells us. 'I'm excited.'

Baker says that he can't stress to us enough just how much the bees have 'incredibly' improved pupils' behaviour. 'I had a hunch that they might help, but I had no idea that it would have such a dramatic impact,' he says.

Wayne's restlessness in class, his trouble paying attention, focusing and following directions and his aggressive, antisocial behaviour, along with academic failure, are all classic symptoms of what is medically termed Attention Deficit Hyperactivity Disorder (ADHD).

Research done by Andrea Faber Taylor and Francs Kuo at the Human-Environment Research Laboratory at the University of Illinois has found that contact with nature can relieve the symptoms of attention-deficit disorders in young people by boosting their attention span. Wayne is a textbook example of how children's connection with the natural world is essential for healthy emotional development.

The Charlton Manor apiary didn't come cheap: the bee shelter cost more than £2,000; the suits, £400; even a sign thanking Ruxley Beekeepers' Association was more than £500. But Baker points to the potential savings to society if keeping bees at school helps to tackle pupils' bad behaviour. 'There could be fewer exclusions and these are the kids that can easily end up unemployed and in jail. So just look at the long-term savings to be made there.'

The allotment beekeepers

Until 2009, Moorside allotment in Newcastle, like many of the 300,000 allotments that hug the fringes of towns and cities across Britain, prohibited the keeping of bees. Despite the obvious link between pollinators and vegetables, bees were banned because allotment holders were scared of being stung.

This attitude is slowly changing as awareness rises about the crucial role honeybees play in the environment and how urban areas can provide a reprieve from the risks they face in the countryside.

The driving force behind this shift in thinking are more environmentally- conscious allotment holders such as Peter Whewell. With his knapsack and walking boots, Whewell, a retired doctor, looks every inch the quiet revolutionary.

'When I took over as chairman of Moorside I wanted to bring our constitution and rules into this century,' he explains. 'They were around 40 years old and needed a complete overhaul. I was keen to introduce the concepts of biodiversity and valuing wildlife. The working group I set up to help me in this task was in agreement with this and it was then only a short step to the removal of the ban on honeybees.'

Moorside's 2.5 hectare (6 acre) site, which has 109 plots, was created around 1941 when many councils established allotments to help families find ways to supplement their meagre wartime food rations. The original rulebook read: 'The keeping of animals, bees, pigeons or any birds is prohibited.' In January 2009, a new constitution was ratified at the Moorside annual general meeting that omitted the word bees.

Whewell says he was unaware that any plot holders actually wanted to keep bees when the ban was lifted. But by the time we visit Moorside, 18 months later, two members have bees and a third is about to install a hive.

Hameed Haykal shows us his two beehives, one a standard National wooden hive, the other a green plastic Beehaus. They are at either ends of his adjoining plots surrounded by fruit trees, vegetables beds and brightly coloured flowers.

Despite the onset of autumn, there are bees buzzing around as they go in search of late forage. It is a serene scene just a mile west of Newcastle city centre on the Town Moor – 400 hectares (988 acres) of former pasture land preserved as open space by the council and the city freeman.

Haykal kept bees in Iraq before he came to England 20 years ago. 'Since I was a child I loved nature. I lived on a farm in a beautiful part of the country, surrounded by many rivers and canals,' he tells us.

One of the first things he did when he arrived in England was to put his name down for an allotment in the city that was to be his new home. But it was only when Moorside lifted its bee ban that Haykal was able to renew his lifelong interest in beekeeping.

The other allotment beekeeper is a fiftysomething Geordie, Tony Whittle, who lives just over the road in a small, one-bedroom flat. 'I've been wanting to keep bees for 25 years,' he tells us, 'but the rules had always made it very clear that you couldn't have bees on here. I never thought to challenge them but I was overjoyed when they were changed.'

Whewell is keen to show us that Moorside's bee friendliness extends beyond honeybees. It has created a bee garden that is a blast of colour even when we visit, with purple Michaelmas daisies, orange nasturtiums and bright yellow rudbeckias to attract all bees, including bumblebees and solitary bees. And it awards an annual prize for the most bee-friendly allotment plot. When we ask to see the inaugural winner, Whewell leads us through a painted wooden gate into a wonderful higgledy-piggledy mass of flowers and vegetables. This laissez-faire approach to allotment gardening is in sharp contrast to the bare regimented rows of seeds that we witness on other plots.

Whewell is now turning his attention to promoting beekeeping on all 63 allotments across Newcastle. He is the allotment representative on the city council's bee steering group and a member of the Newcastle Allotment Working Group, which now has a specific target in its five-year strategy to 'encourage beekeeping on its allotment sites'. To achieve this he has set up a sub-group dedicated to bees. Around 10 beekeepers attend its meetings.

'We have busied ourselves by successfully obtaining grants for low-cost beekeeping training and drawing up our own set of rules, recommendations and advice,' says Whewell.

The document aims to promote a responsible approach to beekeeping on allotments and to provide information that will avoid conflicts of interest with neighbours. As such, it could prove useful for any allotment holders thinking of introducing beehives (see Appendix 2).

For Whewell, the key to successful beekeeping on allotments is to have the committee solidly backing the project, so as to pre-empt any future difficulties and smoothing problems that will inevitably occur. At Moorside, for example, there have been complaints from two half-plot tenants who are located between Whittle and Haykal's plots. 'One complained he had been stung, the other that he felt hemmed in by hives on either side,' explains Whewell. 'We have recently held our own Moorside Bee Group meeting to decide how to proceed. If we can't reach a compromise with the tenants the committee will suggest they move, rather than the bees.' This, he says, is a 'vivid illustration of the importance of having the committee solidly on side'.

Helen Simmons, also from Newcastle, wishes she had had a more supportive committee when she took up beekeeping two years ago. She was told she was unable to keep bees on her own veggie plot when one of her neighbours objected because her granddaughter was afraid of bees. The committee then suggested she put her hive on a spare piece of land on the allotments under some trees. 'Unfortunately, despite the hive being at least 200 feet from the nearest plot, someone objected (I don't know the reason why) and I was asked to remove my hive immediately,' she recalls. 'But I had nowhere to put them. Living in a terraced Victorian house with no outside space to speak of meant keeping bees at home was impossible,' says the 36-year-old contracts manager.

Luckily she received a more positive response from another local allotment, Highbury North, where her bees now reside on Bee Hill, and she was invited to write about them in the allotment newsletter.

Simmons, who is a member of the Newcastle Allotments Bee Group, says of her experiences that she is sure the same thing would not happen today. 'People are now keener to support beekeepers and are more informed about the importance of bees to the world and to their very local vegetable allotments.'

The National Society of Allotments and Leisure Gardens (NSALG) says it has no objection, in principle, to bees being kept on an allotment site. But it emphasises that nobody has the absolute *right* to keep bees on an allotment – the only creatures that can be housed on an allotment plot as of right are domestic chickens and rabbits.

It does not know how many allotments have beehives. But the numbers are increasing daily as more grow-your-own enthusiasts understand the link between pollinators and food and have the courage to challenge existing bee bans.

Angela Richardson is one of them. The determined 66-year-old has an allotment in Ealing, west London, and wanted to keep her bees there because she is 'interested in them as pollinators'.

Ealing Council, however, had a ruling that you couldn't keep bees on a council allotment unless you had passed the Basic Beekeeping Assessment. Yet this test can only be taken after a year of beekeeping and Richardson was getting her bees halfway through her training. Fortunately she learned that another allotment holder on her site had just been given permission for his hive on the condition that he eventually took the exam, so she wrote to the allotment manager at the council to ask if this exception could be made for her too.

'The response,' she says, 'was to change the ruling for everyone so that now any new beekeeper can keep a colony without the certificate but only if they are attending bona fide training with the intention of taking the test.'

The NSALG suggests a code of good practice. This includes: keeping bees of a docile strain; protecting bees from the public; being meticulous about swarm prevention and having public liability insurance, such as that provided through membership of the BBKA; and erecting a barrier of at least six feet in height around the apiary to force the bees to fly up and outwards. But the NSALG stresses that above all there needs to be agreement about bees between allotment holders.

Allotment beekeepers, however, report a mixed reception. Esther Coles in north London recalls one allotment neighbour who was terrified of her suggestion of having a hive. 'She said her son was allergic to bee stings, but he never came to the allotment!' she laughs.

Coles got bees anyway after consulting the allotment secretary. 'She told me to keep the hive away from the pathway so the bees' flight path would not cross it.'

Her hive is at the back of her plot, south facing but shaded by a very tall bramble hedge. It is next to a buddleia, which Coles has chopped back so its branches don't overhang the hive. It is about a metre and a half from the pond that the bees drink out of and is standing on a concrete builder's slab as her plot is on a slope.

Despite the ambivalence of some of her neighbours, Coles threw a welcoming party when her bees arrived. 'The ceremony was a way to mark the start of me becoming a beekeeper and to welcome the bees without humanising them,' says the 42-year-old actress. 'This acknowledgement made us all think about what we were embarking on – a "marriage" of bees and beekeeper, perhaps – and also to remember how and when we started.

'The children particularly took it seriously whilst also having lots of fun. It was important for me to acknowledge those who'd made it possible for me to do this and to increase awareness of the fragility of the bee world. I had been quite anxious about becoming a beekeeper because of the responsibility, so it was a time to have fun!

We made bunting; Tom [her partner] made some elderflower champagne; and I invited people who lived nearby. People came along with poems. My mate dressed up as a bee.'

Although Angela Richardson, a charity fundraiser, did not mark the arrival of her bees in such fashion, they were well received by all her allotment neighbours in west London. 'Gardeners were asking what kind of plants the bees would like,' she recalls. 'When I got the bees an older Irish gardener told me he had visited the hive early in the morning and sung an Irish song to the bees. Since I've had the hive I've invited my allotment neighbours to come and watch the bees going in and out the hive. Everyone has been completely fascinated and they ask me more questions than I can answer.'

Richardson and allotment chairmen such as Whewell are at the vanguard of the urban beekeeping revolution, but is there a danger that with this newfound interest in keeping bees, allotments could become overrun with hives? What is the maximum number of hives that can be kept in one place?

The BBKA says there is no upper limit 'provided the bees can find forage over a distance of up to 5 km (3 miles) and the beekeeper has the time to attend to them'.

However, the Newcastle Beekeepers' Allotment Group (NBAG) recommends a maximum of three hives per acre. 'Most of the evidence appears to be based equally on concerns over available forage and risk of nuisance,' say Ian Campbell, who researched the Newcastle allotment bee governance document. 'My concern was over a new fad sweeping through a site with high uptake and little experience leading to conflict on and around sites followed by a clampdown on beekeeping on allotments in an area.'

Coles was shocked to discover that there were already 16 hives on the 2.5 hectare (six acre) allotment in north London where she keeps her hive.

'I didn't realise there were that many until I started to get to know all the others,' she says. 'We have decided as a group that we should have no more beekeepers.' Coles is concerned not so much about the potential lack of forage, as the allotment is on the leafy fringes of the capital, but about the possible spread of disease.

Certainly, one of the downsides of beekeeping in close proximity to other people's hives is that if they don't take effective measures to control the varroa mite their bees could spread potentially lethal diseases to other hives.

'I know at least three colonies have died out with disease, maybe more. I've discovered one woman has four colonies. She follows a beekeepers' biodynamic calendar and feels the vibrations from the bees. I saw her at the weekend with a basket of essential oils. She was treating varroa [with unproven methods] – a bit late,' says Cole.

Campbell says the Newcastle rules make it clear that a beekeeper could be asked to remove their bees from a site if they did not treat for disease in line with guidance on current best practice from a bee inspector. 'I would suggest any site facing such a problem contact their local bee inspector and discuss the issue,' he says.

As well as embracing beekeeping, Newcastle's allotment strategy states that it wants to 'promote education about the importance of bees and their decline, and how plots may be improved as a source of year-round forage for bees'.

If allotments across Britain followed Moorside's lead and introduced bee-friendly gardens, championed bee-friendly plots, and introduced habitats for bumblebees and solitary bees on their sites then they could potentially transform more than 8,000 hectares (20,000 acres) of urban land into urgently needed forage for bees.

The office beekeepers

The honeybees' industriousness is legendary and it has been embraced as a symbol of hard work and good business practice down the ages. The Roman poet Virgil vividly describes the division of labour in the hive from the forager bees 'employed in getting food and by fixed agreement, work on the fields', to the house bees, whose job is 'laying their foundation of the honeycomb'.

More recently the waggle dance, which allows foragers to tell their nestmates where to fly to find the best source of food, was held up by IBM as the communication system *par excellence* for all retail businesses to emulate.

Even the bee professor, Francis Ratnieks, has compared a beehive to an efficient supermarket, with the forager bees representing shoppers and the nectar-receiving bees as the cashiers. If there are too few receivers, other workers will switch to this role straight away.

Yes despite the numerous lessons that bees can teach the workplace, up until now few companies have actually kept a hive. But that is starting to change as workplaces begin to embrace rooftop beekeeping in some of the most unlikely places and to encourage their employees to become lunchtime beekeepers.

It is 1pm on a warm June day and Jonathan Hogg and three of his colleagues are clustered around a hive on the 10th floor of the famous Lloyds building.

Up on the windswept roof terrace, wearing protecting clothing over their suits and boots, these office workers are a new breed of urban beekeeper pursuing their newfound hobby in their work lunch hour.

Hogg says he was looking for a new interest when his employer, the insurance underwriter Canopius, offered him the chance to become a lunchtime beekeeper.

'Now that we had a baby at home, I couldn't go out after work for a few drinks any more, and an injury had ended my rugby playing,' says the 38-year-old IT trainer. 'I'd been thinking about keeping bees for a couple of years. I must have read an article about them. Friends had bought me books but they'd stayed on the shelves, so nothing had happened. Now I had the chance to be paid to learn beekeeping at work and to make mistakes with other people around to support me.'

More than a dozen of his colleagues responded positively to an email sent round the office to gauge interest about the project. Split into four groups they take it in turns to get hands-on experience of the workings of a beehive at the weekly training sessions.

The 10th-floor location for the hive is blustery and barren. The only vegetation in sight is the lavender, laurel and rosemary in the planters that act as a windbreak around the hive. At the weekly hive inspection, the office beekeepers peer at the frames of foundation that the bees make their wax comb on, and watch as the trainer gives them a few puffs of cold smoke from the strange contraption called a smoker, which helps to calm the bees.

When their hour is up, Hogg and the others head back into the office. 'We had a good reminder to check suits for stowaways after a bee decided to check out the office by clinging to my suit as we went back inside,' writes Hogg on his bee blog. 'Luckily we discovered her before she got too far and escorted her outside after she failed to produce a security pass.'

It was Sally Coryn, head of business development at Canopius, who had the idea of keeping bees at the office.

'I wanted to refurbish our roof terrace as it is quite visible from our executive floor and didn't reflect the Canopius brand,' says the

49-year-old city professional, neatly dressed in a smart suit with a blonde bob. 'A friend has a compost bin in the shape of a beehive for aesthetic reasons, and that led me onto the thought of bees on the roof. Canopius is known for a being a bit different and we are doing more and more in the environmental space so I thought it was a good fit for our brand values and reputation.

'I googled "bees, urban, roof" and came across the Urban Bees website. I rang up and said, "Can I keep bees on the 10th floor of a roof in the City?" – without having any idea that I'd chanced upon the consultant beekeeper to the City of London Festival.'

But despite the lucky encounter, it nearly didn't happen. Canopius rents office space in the Lloyds building and the freeholder initially turned down its request for a beehive.

How the company reversed that decision may have useful lessons for other workplaces who find themselves facing a similar predicament.

'Lloyds was nervous that staff, such as window cleaners, would get stung and take legal action,' Coryn recalls. 'The main issue was ignorance about bees' behaviour on the part of the freeholder management team. We pushed to put our case to a more senior member of the team. They then agreed to send their health and safety officer to see us and learn more. He admitted he knew little about bees but was at least willing to listen to a professional and experienced beekeeper explain about the limited risks. This was critical in convincing this person that the risks were manageable and acceptable,' says Coryn.

Under the licence that was finally granted to cover additional rental for the beehive, payment was set as one pot of honey per annum. But the freeholder wasn't the only one who had to be informed about Canopius's intention to keep bees. It also had to inform its insurance broker, as bees could affect its employers' liability or public liability insurance, and Coryn had to prepare a detailed document outlining the company's proposed safety measures.

Canopius also produced a disclaimer (see Appendix 3) for staff volunteer beekeepers to sign to indicate their understanding and acceptance of the risks.

Coryn's diligence paid off. Six months on, what does she think are the main challenges of keeping bees at work? 'Time commitments. Fourteen staff volunteered to be involved but some people simply found they were too busy to be able to fulfil their obligations,' she replies.

The logistics of training a large group and the practicalities of cleaning and storing equipment in an office environment were also tricky. 'And you shouldn't underestimate managing people's expectations that we would suddenly have plenty of honey to dispense to staff and clients!' she laughs.

On the upside, she rattles off a list of business benefits for the company:

'Publicity; supporting evidence for some of our brand values; creation of a new employee group with common interests stretching across different levels of the organisation, by department and seniority; interest from visitors – the terrace is visible from the chairman's office so it's a great icebreaker; enthusiastic support and involvement by our beekeeping group; and something positive and different for staff to chat about. I still frequently get asked by colleagues, "How are our bees doing?"' she says. 'I had not anticipated that it would be so enthusiastically embraced internally or would knit together a new group of staff. Companies are always talking about how they can break down silos between departments. Well, keeping bees does just that,' says Coryn.

For Hogg, it has given him a new lease of life. He has joined his local beekeepers' association and as one of the more knowledgeable volunteers in the company beekeeping group, he will be tasked with mentoring the less clued-up ones in year two.

Bank employees in the shadow of St Paul's also inspect their new hive in their lunch hour on the roof of seven-storey Scandinavian House. Paula Carvell and David Lockie are the volunteer beekeepers at the London office of Swedish merchant bank SEB.

Carvell, 42, who is head of catering and the facilities help desk, is using the work bees as a test run. 'I've got a three-year-old, so I thought I'd give it a go here before keeping bees in the small garden of my London flat,' she says.

Lockie, 49, the bank's head of legal, was keen to get trained at work by an experienced beekeeper provided by the City of London Festival because he had just started to keep bees at home.

The hive is fenced off and weighed down with a concrete slab and looks small and vulnerable amid the air conditioning pipes and vents. A space has been cleared in the air conditioning operating room to store beekeeping equipment and allow the lunchtime beekeepers to change into their protective gear.

'I suggested that we erect barriers along the roof and inform contractors where the hive is located and offer them bee suits to do their work,' explains Carvell, who was tasked with producing a risk assessment for the hive.

It was Roger Gifford, head of the bank in the UK and a City of London alderman, who decided to keep bees at SEB as part of the City's summer festival in 2010.

'I've always loved honey. My nickname is Bear and I have a collection of about 30 small jars of honey at home. So I wanted to keep bees for their honey and to prove how clean the City was,' Gifford tells us.

Carvell says office beekeeping takes more time than you may think. 'You can't nip up to the roof 15 minutes before a meeting. Give yourself a full hour to inspect the hive. And visitors from other offices are often popping in to look at the hive. We have three a week in the summer. Now they have to book a slot and there's a waiting list. Other tenants in the building are also interested.'

Lockie says at least three or four staff need to be responsible for the hives. 'If people are on holiday, or sick or on a business trip, you need to know that someone in the office is in charge of the hive,' he says.

But it is not just City slickers who are embracing office bee-keeping as a quick fix for workplace stress. At international brand consultants Wolff Olins, nine employees are keen to take up beekeeping on the roof of the company's canal-side office in London's King's Cross.

'I think what helped a lot was that last August a swarm of bees occupied a car in our car park. Every one was outside looking at the bees and no one was stung,' says building manager Stuart Robertson.

The company roof is already home to an employee-run vegetable garden. For Robertson, who was instrumental in getting the garden set up, having beehives seemed the next logical step. 'While tending the garden I have become aware of just how much nature there is in the big city: the bird life, insect life, bat life,' he says. 'I think it has been a natural progression for Wolff Olins to move from having the garden to having the beehives.'

Staff will learn about beekeeping alongside a group of young people as part of the company's ongoing relationship with charity Global Generation, which works with local young people.

'We have worked closely with the charity to make the garden an integral part of our culture and in doing so the young people have become part of the family here at Wolff Olins,' says 31-year-old design director Bethany Koby, who describes the collaboration and the roof garden as her 'babies'. 'I believe that businesses and brands have a responsibility to shift and become more collaborative, more open, more sustainable – and can do this through action and experience. The problem is most business do not have the space, physically and spiritually, to really do this kind of work. Global Generation and the roof garden helped us to create that space. Our roof is a space where new conversation can emerge, action and collaborations come together and food can grow that was not possible before,' says Californian-born Koby.

For Global Generation founder and executive director Jane Riddiford, the bee project represents a natural extension of Global Generation's work around King's Cross, which is all about finding creative ways of engaging young people in the natural environment and then building on this experience for these same young people to become green ambassadors amongst local business in the area.

'Our youth enterprise groups sell herbs and vegetables to local restaurants and of course honey will be an exciting new product,' says Riddiford. 'Of most interest to us, however, is the opportunity beekeeping will provide our young people to try something new, to see themselves and the world around them with new eyes; to become enterprising in the best sense of the word.'

And continuing our centuries-old tradition of drawing lessons from the beehive, Riddiford says: 'Our food-growing gardens on top of office buildings and in skips on developers' land are the work of many hands. Learning about the workings of a hive seems like the perfect metaphor for the kind of collaborative values we aim to encourage.'

The community beekeeper

Visiting Alessia Bolis's bees is like going on a secret tour of north London. Hidden behind hoardings, tucked away down alleyways and camouflaged among gravestones are her six hives, all within five minutes' walking distance from her tiny flat off busy City Road. It is a neighbourhood densely populated by concrete tower blocks and low-rise council housing with no parks close by. Not an area, then, that seems to lend itself to beekeeping.

'I have never had a garden in London so I had to look for local sites,' explains Bolis. 'I knew someone who was working in local regeneration projects and she asked around for me.'

Our first stop is St Luke's community centre, round the corner from Bolis's home. Peering through the chained gates you would never think that down the driveway, at the back of the old Victorian buildings, are three hives on a temporary mini-allotment site. Bolis unlocks the gates and lets us in. We walk past rooms used for a variety of groups including a day centre for over-55-year-olds, a Somalian women's group and an after-school club. At the end of the tarmac a car park has been replaced by a couple of dozen raised beds where local people grow their own vegetables. Behind the wooden planters is an area separated by a seven-foot fence and green mesh. Three wooden hives are clearly visible through the mesh. This is where, in the summer, local residents and their children safely congregate once a week to watch her inspecting the hives.

'I give the community centre the dates when I'm going to be here and people can come along and watch what's going on,' says Bolis. 'At our annual hive open day some of them get into suits and come the other side of the mesh with me. I've also taught a short course for six people who want to learn about beekeeping. When the bees first arrived [in 2008], I gave a talk about what bees do and then organised events for the community such as honey tasting, candle making and how to make cosmetics from beeswax,' says Bolis.

She proudly shows us a logo of a bee with crow-like legs clutching a suitcase full of pollen that was designed by a young local boy. 'We had a competition to design the logo for St Luke's honey. The prize was a jar of honey. This young person walks in and asks if this is the place where he can get a free jar of honey. We tell him what he has to do to win and in a matter of minutes he came up with this.'

For Bolis, 40, organising bee-related community events is the best part of keeping bees in a communal space. Despite having a full-time job as a project manager for a small business advisory service, she likes having a full diary, packed with evening and weekend community activities come the summer. 'I love organising classes and events that can teach people about bees,' she says. 'I'd rather have bees in a public space than a back garden. That for me would be boring. It depends on your motivation for keeping bees. Mine is to educate people about them.'

Bolis learned beekeeping a few years ago on an EC-funded course in her native northern Italy. 'I walked into the local co-operative in the countryside to buy a flagon of cheap wine and there was a notice about 60 hours of training to become a beekeeper, and I thought, "Why not?"' she recalls.

Yet the beekeeping she practises in central London is prohibited in Italy because the law stipulates that you are not allowed to keep bees within 50 metres (55 yards) of a house, Bolis explains. The irony is not lost on her that the country with the most docile honeybees, which are kept by urban beekeepers all over the world from New York to Sydney, cannot live side by side with humans in Rome, Milan or Naples.

At St Luke's she says: 'The people here see the bees as very much part of their community. They notice their behaviour and are interested in what they are pollinating. They are always telling me they saw the bees on this or that plant.'

But some communities are more receptive than others. At the second site we visit, Bolis has had a less-than-enthusiastic reception.

'I was invited to address the residents' organisation about the benefits of keeping bees and they initially seemed really excited about having them here,' she says as we arrive at a pocket of green space on the edge of a housing estate. But since then she says her public events have failed to engage the community. 'There was a bee brunch to taste the honey, but out of 100 residents only about 10 turned up and that included their children,' she recalls.

The Redbrick Estate is a salutary lesson that not all public spaces will work as a community apiary. In theory the wildlife garden should have been a dream location. It is a secure and safe sight for both bees and people, with an active residents' association who said they wanted the bees, an experienced beekeeper willing to run community events, and money from a regeneration agency to buy the hives and equipment.

'I think the problem is that it is a sprawling estate and unless you live on that particular part backing onto the garden you won't know the bees are there. So people don't feel they are *their* bees,' says Bolis. 'Some residents are now complaining that the garden has been given over to wildlife and their kids should be able to use it. And one resident whose flat is just above a small ceanothus tree that the bees cover in the summer has told us that the bees go into his flat, so we will have to move the hives.'

Her final publicly-sited hive is hidden among the gravestones of Bunhill Fields, a former Dissenters' burial ground where three of Britain's most eminent non-conformists – William Blake, John Bunyan and Daniel Defoe – were laid to rest. The four hectare (10 acre) site has been managed as an oasis of calm and greenery by the City of London since 1867 and today is a popular lunchtime spot for office workers in the summer wishing to escape the hustle and bustle of the surrounding City. It is also used as a shortcut by busy commuters.

'I tend to do my beekeeping at weekends or evenings when there are fewer people around,' Bolis says. But it is easy to miss the hive tucked behind Bunyan's tomb in an area closed to the public by a locked gate. Strangely, its wooden box does not look dissimilar to the weathered, moss-covered tombs that surround it. It brings to mind Sylvia Plath's 1962 poem, 'The Arrival of the Bee Box', in which she compares a new beehive to a coffin of a midget or a baby.

In the spring, the cemetery is blanketed in bluebells and in the summer it is shaded by a rich variety of mature trees including the very bee-friendly lime. Potential hive locations are everywhere, even in the heart of the city. On the five-minute walk back to Bolis's flat we pass a couple of other public sites she has identified as possibilities. One is on a flat roof, the other within the railed gardens of a historic house. But it could be as long as a year before she can put her hives there.

'Be prepared to have to wait a year from an initial meeting to moving in your hives,' warns Bolis. 'There are often lots of different people involved and lots of different committees who have to make a decision. You have to have a risk assessment at each site. It is not a quick process.'

Delays aside, Bolis is adamant about the benefits of community bee-keeping. 'Even if you just manage to raise awareness about bees to one or two more people it is worth it,' she says.

The commercial beekeepers

A few years ago, freelance arts consultant Camilla Goddard began to create honeybee sanctuaries in her neighbourhood of south-east London. Her first was in the grounds of a church. Another soon followed by the edge of a deer park and a third on her allotment. Last year she was contacted by a local university asking if she could keep bees on its land.

A bee sanctuary looks the same as an apiary. It is a site where beehives are located. Behind St Peter's Church, eight standard National hives sitting on plastic bread baskets are tightly packed together; in Greenwich Park there are six similar-looking stacked wooden boxes fenced off to the deer where Henry VIII used to hunt; at Exford Road allotment a pretty WBC hive sits among the four beehives on the edge of the 1.6 hectare (four acre) site; and at Greenwich University a mixture of hive styles are home to five honeybee colonies.

What sets a bee sanctuary apart from traditional apiaries is its purpose. The reason Goddard has 20 or so hives is not to produce local honey (although her honey is stocked by the wholefood shop on the corner of her street and other local delis and was named one of the top London honeys by *Time Out* magazine), nor is it to train aspiring apiarists, although she does run some beginners' courses at the church. Her motivation for keeping honeybees, she says, is to help conserve the species.

'My aim initially was to create a gene pool of bee colonies in London until the problems with bees have been resolved – hopefully

– and also because they seem to do better in the city than the country at the moment. The plan was to create a kind of "safe haven" like they do with endangered species, until they recover. You'd do the same thing with tigers in India; you'd keep a genetic pool.'

Six years on and it seems to be working. 'I'm not having any colony losses,' she tells us.

We meet up with Goddard on what turns out to be the first day of spring and her bees do appear to be thriving, emerging after a long, cold winter looking strong and healthy.

Goddard, 38, in many ways epitomises the new urban beekeeper. 'I'm interested in the relationship between plants and bees,' says the former *Country Living* Organic Gardener of the Year. Moreover, she is young, female, eco-conscious, and sees keeping bees as her small contribution to improving the planet.

'I had my first bees in 2002 in a wood in Kent that I bought with a friend. I started then because I heard the story about the guy who retired in France and quietly set about planting a tree every day until people started to notice a forest on Google Earth. I am not sure if it's a myth – it doesn't really matter – I just like the idea of doing something step by step as an unfettered individual when most of the time we can't seem to affect climate change, or any of the sad things that are happening to the Earth.'

She moved her hobby to London a couple of years later. 'By keeping bees in a city you're immediately putting 50,000 pollinators into an urban area and that can have such a huge impact on the environment.'

Goddard also describes urban beekeeping as a 'fantastic antidote' to city living.

'Nobody tells you that the best thing about bees is they show you so many wonderful insights and connect you entirely to the seasons in a cut-off place like London … I could go on about them forever; don't get me started!,' she says, laughing. 'I'm constantly amazed by them – their selflessness, the way they work together.'

Her small flat is crammed with beekeeping artefacts, from what looks like an Edwardian bee veil complete with a straw boater to straw skeps (wicker beehives), enamel honey extractors and antiquated bee books. 'It's interesting to see how beekeepers of the past coped with problems such as burning a dry puff ball to temporarily anaesthetise a colony!' says Goddard.

Not surprisingly, local organisations such as Transition Town Brockley and Greenshoots, an environmental charity, were soon knocking on her door, asking for her to share her passion by giving talks and selling them bees. Before she knew it, she was running a small business, Capital Bee (not to be confused with the Mayor of London's Capital Bee competition).

'It's not a major thing,' she says modestly. 'I really enjoyed looking after my bees and then people wanted to buy honey, asked me to do bits of training and give talks and they'd pay me for it.'

She sells nucleuses of bees (small colonies of 10,000 bees) to beginners. She makes them from splitting the hives located behind the church and selecting queens from her best-behaved colonies. Her bees are the 'peaceably natured' Carniolan race that originated from the Balkans crossed with native hybrids.

Goddard makes around 20 'nucs'; half in the spring and half in the summer. They sell for £150. Her spring orders are full and the summer ones are going quickly. It was the same last year. 'I could have sold them twice over,' she says. But she doesn't like parting with her bees.

'I do worry what will happen to them. However, I think it's important to encourage others to take responsibility and do something positive if they can. My bees are calm to handle and are used to local conditions, so if local beekeepers keep progeny from my colonies the theory is that perhaps the male drones in the area will perpetuate this tendency.'

Goddard is equally reluctant to sell her honey. 'In my flat I make a huge pyramid with all the honey jars. It grows as I harvest the honey throughout the summer. But as I sell the honey, I hate it that the pyramid gradually gets smaller and smaller. By Christmas it's all gone.'

Goddard learned her basic beekeeping from a friend and then read and taught herself. Being brought up on a farm in Worcestershire surrounded by livestock gave her the confidence to go it alone. Indeed she describes urban beekeeping as 'a way to farm in a city'.

'Checking on my hives is like my father going round the cows at home in the morning and the evening,' she says wistfully.

She has never belonged to a beekeeping association because she feels her bee sanctuary approach clashes with old-school beekeeping. 'There's a "beardo" thing going on,' she says, referring to the stereotypical bearded male beekeeper. 'I don't want to be patronised by them because I have a different outlook.'

She singles out the national honey show as an example of this orthodoxy. 'My honey show experience was interesting as I attended a class on how to win. Apparently the taste of the honey was only a minor part of the score, and sometimes if there was a fault in the glass of the jar or two jars of honey didn't match in colour the judges wouldn't bother taking the lid off. It seems to miss the wood for the trees!'

Goddard seems to articulate many of the reservations a burgeoning group of newcomers to apiculture have with the old guard. Instead, they are forming their own groups such as the Brockley Beekeepers' Group, which meets informally in a local pub every two months or so.

'It's mostly beginners wanting to share information. It's useful to compare notes. Most of the people are quite young and interested in bees chiefly for environmental reasons,' she explains.

Goddard says she has witnessed a huge change in people's attitudes towards bees since she started out. Whereas she had to find the first sites for her hives and pay St Peter's Church and Greenwich Park an annual rent, institutions and companies are now calling her with offers of free land and in some cases even wanting to pay her to maintain a hive.

'It's half the problem it used to be to get sites. Before it was all about health and safety,' she says. 'Just today a French honey-based beauty products manufacturer called up wanting a hive on the roof of their Covent Garden office.'

Capital Bee also provides an emergency swarm collection service. This part of the business could benefit from all those new urban beekeepers who forget to rein in their bees' swarming instincts. But Goddard insists that she is not simply cashing in on the recent craze in beekeeping.

'The current interest in urban beekeeping may come and go, maybe in another five or six years, but people do seem to have a real yearning towards anything that connects them with nature. I would like to carry on with the bees in my life, fad or not, as they have brought a lot of joy and fascination into my life, and all sorts of interesting people want to know about them.'

Goddard is not alone in turning her beekeeping hobby into a livelihood. The interest in bees, as well as creating thousands more amateur apiarists in towns and cities, has spawned a new breed of commercial beekeeper. Until recently, someone who made a living from bees was generally a rural bee farmer, who had often taken over a family-run business with a few hundreds hives making vast quantities of honey and pollinating orchards. Willy Robson, with 1,800 colonies in Northumberland and the Scottish Borders, is probably the largest bee farmer in the UK, running Chain Bridge Honey Farm. For years, the only commercial beekeeper in London was John Chapple, chair of the London Beekeepers' Association, whose 60 hives scattered around the capital's parks and green spaces made enough honey to augment his company pension.

But now a handful of beekeepers are making a living from either teaching aspiring urban apiarists, maintaining rooftop beehives for a range of corporate clients, or producing premium-priced honey from bees located on iconic city-centre buildings.

'Ten years ago I decided I wanted to keep bees in central London but there was a problem: we lived on the sixth storey of an ex-council block near Tower Bridge, with no garden. The only viable outside space – well, viable to me – was the flat roof, accessed via a fire escape. It worked like a dream. I located my first hive behind the lift shaft complete with a live bee webcam and the bees started producing incredible honey. It was the start of a thriving urban business,' writes Steve Benbow, founder of the London Honey Company, on his website.

A photographer by trade with a flare for publicity, Benbow, 42, was the first commercial beekeeper to keep beehives on the roofs of some of London's most famous buildings. In 2008, there was extensive coverage when his hand-crafted, eau-de-nil-painted, six-foot hives were installed on the top of Fortnum & Mason in Piccadilly. Customers have flocked to buy the store's honey. Benbow followed his Fortnum bees by putting hives on the Tate and Tate Modern, where the honey is equally sought-after in the art galleries' shops.

His honey production has now branched out beyond the capital, but Benbow also uses his experiences of rooftop beekeeping to teach fellow city dwellers how to keep bees on a flat roof with only a fire escape for access.

Beekeeping associations used to have a monopoly on training. But their failure to embrace the increased demand for courses has opened the door to commercial trainers such as Urban Bees, Capital Bee and the London Honey Company, who share a different approach and motivation for keeping bees that is perhaps more suited to a young, eco-conscious audience.

Toby Mason runs courses in the delightful surroundings of Regent's Park, where his 40 hives make the premium-priced Regent's Park Honey. Mason's wife is the main breadwinner in the family and he fits his beekeeping business around his childcare responsibilities.

Oxford-educated, Mason, 38, dabbled with many things before taking a course in beekeeping. He then began helping out the previous Regent's Park beekeeper and when he retired took over his operation and expanded it.

'I am fascinated by bees,' he says. 'But the major appeal of the job is that it is on my doorstop as I live near the park. I can cycle between the four apiary sites [in his specially-designed beemobile]; it is working outdoors in good weather; and I can be flexible with my time and work around my son.'

In Newcastle, too, Ian Wallace, former director of operational risk for Northern Rock, has turned his hobby of 15 years into a part-time business. In 2008, Pure Honeycomb began selling honey and running beekeeping courses in the north-east of England. Wallace, 58, now divides his time between chartered accountancy and his hives. He has a number of bee clients including Fenwick Department Store, where he maintains five hives on its city-centre roof.

'I'd heard about similar rooftop schemes in London and Paris, and I decided if it's good enough for them, it's good enough for Newcastle!' he says.

He is also an integral part of Newcastle Council's drive to become the first bee-friendly city in the UK (see page 89), running urban beekeeping courses at city farms and nature parks and maintaining council-sponsored hives in city locations.

'What I enjoy most is the outreach work,' says Wallace. 'I already have three bookings this summer to speak at a school and community events in deprived areas of the city.'

In Sheffield, Jez Daughtry, 42, started keeping bees when he lost his job as an IT consultant in 2009. A little over a year later he had 100 beehives on the surrounding moors and valleys and the roof of a Sheffield museum, and he had set up The Sheffield Honey Company.

'We didn't just want to do honey production; I had transferable skills that allowed me to do education and training,' says Daughtry. 'Commercially it only works for us if we are doing all these things with the bees. And I enjoy it.'

Back in London, Ian Bailey, 52, took redundancy three years ago from the Royal Veterinary College, where he was an animal attendant for 27 years. He now has a number of hives on city farms, an environmental education centre and a community garden, all in east London, where he runs beekeeping courses and sells Haggerston Honey. 'I became hooked on bees at the age of 10 when my parents took me to visit a stately home and I saw an observation hive,' says Bailey.

What these commercial beekeepers all share is a job they love doing and eschewing a nine-to-five lifestyle. But that is probably where any similarity ends.

Bailey, for example, advises against any of his students taking up beekeeping in order to save the honeybee. 'If your motivation is to save bees, I tell them you don't need to keep bees to do that. You can improve the environment instead by growing native flowers, keeping your garden untidy and getting rid of weedkillers and pesticides.'

In contrast, Goddard's rationale for setting up Capital Bee was to save the honeybee from possible extinction.

'In London I see a connection with nature that for me is essential. I get on well with bees and they seem to have a strangely calming and joyful effect on my life, so I think it's my odd fate to protect their interests,' she says. 'I always looked around for alternative ways of living beyond what everybody is being encouraged to buy into, literally. I had no plan for this, but I think it's great in life to look out for new paths that can become visible if you stop and see what arises naturally and have enough flexibility to respond, to fail, and to investigate.'

The inner-city youth beekeepers

Not everyone has embraced beekeeping for environmental reasons or to save the honeybee.

'For a long time I'd been looking for a way to engage young people in practical action,' says Zoe Palmer. 'Bees are fascinating and a little bit dangerous. This would be about giving young people skills and confidence.'

In 2008, while Palmer was trekking around the world filming a TV series for National Geographic, she had the idea of bringing young people and bees together. 'It was during filming in Albania with bees that the project started in my head,' say Palmer.

She was impressed with the relaxed and calm attitude of the local beekeepers, who casually blew cigarette smoke at their hives before lifting out the honey, all without any form of protection. And the local kids were fascinated. 'I thought bees, of course: bees and kids.'

It may not seem an obvious connection but for Palmer it was like a bolt of lightning. When she returned to London a few months later, she set about creating a social enterprise called the Golden Company. 'The idea was to teach business skills to inner-city young people by developing a business producing, marketing and selling urban honey and related products,' she explains. 'All the profits are invested in training the young people.'

We meet Palmer, 31, on a hot June day at St Mary's Secret Garden project – a 0.4 hectare (one acre) garden that is indeed secret, tucked away off a busy thoroughfare in east London – where she shows us around a small training apiary where young people learn beekeeping skills.

At the entrance of a leafy woodland area are signs proclaiming: 'Warning! Bee swarming season! … Please keep kids under control and keep to the path … Alert staff if any problems.' A few feet further into the woodland more positive information about honeybees is pinned on a notice board telling visitors about the health properties of local honey, the waggle dance, and details about the Golden Company, which owns the four hives that stand just behind.

'I knew nothing about beekeeping, or running a business, nor was I a trained youth worker,' Palmer admits, although she had worked part-time at an NSPCC refuge for runaway kids for three years. 'I had the vision. I bring people together, I know the products and services I want to deliver and the partnerships and the strategy.'

To run the organisation with her, she brought in Aisha Forbes, a friend of a friend who is an experienced youth outreach worker, and they paid commercial beekeepers to teach at the apiary. Forbes put the business elements together including recruiting a board of trustees and setting the company's protocols for working with vulnerable young people.

A £2,500 grant from UnLtd, a charity supporting social entrepreneurs, bought the hives and equipment. And funding from charitable trusts, foundations and City livery companies allowed the first 20 young people to start their four-month training in September 2009. The trainees, aged from 15 to 21, are referred from the Connexions youth service, youth offending teams and youth inclusion projects, or by word of mouth, and are what's known in social-policy speak as NEETs – not in education, employment or training. On the Golden Company course they learn about bees and how to turn honey and wax, scented with garden herbs, into scrubs and creams, and how to market and sell these products at Borough Market.

Palmer studied for a Masters in human ecology at Strathclyde University under Alastair McIntosh. She had been heavily influenced by his book, *Soil and Soul*, which is about how modern society undermines communities' sense of mutual responsibility, and how we can get it back. Growing up in inner-city Hackney, she was all too aware of the discord on the housing estates and the streets around her. 'I wanted to learn how to get community-level engagement to change things,' she explains.

The Golden Company is not without precedence. Sweet Beginnings is a Chicago-based social enterprise that offers transitional jobs for former prisoners in the production and sale of skincare products made with honey from its own urban apiary in the blighted North Lawndale community. Set up in 1999, it is now a multi-million dollar industry with impressive social as well as financial results. The recidivism rate for former Sweet Beginnings employees is below 4 per cent, compared to the US national average of 65 per cent and the Illinois average of 55 per cent.

Palmer wanted to do something similar here, but to help divert young people from the criminal justice system in the first place. Learning transferable business skills is key to the project: when we meet some of the young people at a honey harvest at the end of the summer it is evident that most of them are more excited by business than bees.

'I like being in a group and learning about the honey business,' says King, 15, whose favourite subject at school was maths.

'I'm a people person and I've got to meet lots of different people,' says Helen, 17. 'I'm learning interpersonal skills, written skills, and business mindedness – I enjoy exchanging cash for items like bath bombs, salt scrubs and honey. And I've learned about profit margins.'

King and Helen are among 20 young people who have just completed an *Apprentice*-style course.

'We handed the company over to them and told them to develop a new lip balm product and to sell it. The winning team will see their lip balm go into production,' explains Palmer.

The young people were split into three teams and every Saturday morning, in an art room in the basement of the nearby Geffrye Museum, they worked on developing their own product with a team of professional advisers.

'We had to decide who our target customer was, then work on the brand, the packaging, the smell and the price,' explains Helen, whose team, Home Sweet Home, won 'Best Design' and 'Best Teamwork' for their rose-flavoured lip balm.

King's Team Go won 'Best Financial Performance' for its unisex-style lip balm, called Citrus Mint. While they didn't sell as many as the others, the higher price they charged meant they made a larger profit.

The teams included a dozen young people who had been on the first Golden Company course and returned to act as mentors for the new recruits. Among them is Lakshmi, a shy 17-year-old. 'It's something to do on a Saturday, otherwise I'd just sit at home being bored,' she admits. Once a directionless teenager who dropped out of sixth form, she adds: 'I have become more organised, hardworking and creative. I hope it will look good on my CV as I'm now going to apply to study costume design at art college.'

The course also taught Lakshmi that she could overcome her fears. 'When I first got in that bee suit I was so, so scared … I could feel myself shaking inside. But every week when I went back to the bees it got easier. The fact I've managed to conquer one of my biggest fears is an achievement in itself,' she says.

Fear is something many of these young people live with every day. St Mary's Secret Garden is a stone's throw from where 16-year-old Agnes Sina-Inakoju was shot dead in April 2010 and the shadow of gang warfare hangs over the project.

'Gangs are a live issue. Kids are scared to come here because it's not their patch. Lots of young people said they couldn't join this project. It's got worse over the year,' says Palmer. 'We had to move off the housing estate, where we used to meet at a community centre on a Saturday morning to do the business training, 10 minutes' walk away from here. Local residents were worried there would be trouble between rival gangs with kids coming in from another area.

'It's a parallel universe that most people aren't aware of. But when you're out with the kids you see them physically tense up,' says Palmer.

They did think about doing the beekeeping in a completely different area away from rival gangs. 'But we are working with kids that have never left the neighbourhood. They won't travel. When we took them to Pestival [a festival about insects] on the South Bank it was the first time one of them had seen the Houses of Parliament!'

The Golden Company has two further apiaries, one at a nearby recording studio and another at the Waterhouse restaurant on the Regent's Canal where we meet the young people.

After lunch, a commercial beekeeper shows the young people how to harvest honey. Devente, 16, is the first to have a go, running the uncapping fork just under the white cappings that cover the honey. Once the cappings are removed, he puts four uncapped frames of honey in an extractor and turns the handle.

He is one of three young people who have really taken to the beekeeping and passed the junior level BBKA basic assessment. 'Have you seen how difficult it is?' Palmer asks us. 'That's quite an achievement in itself.'

Devente holds a small jar under the tap on the bottom of the extractor and slowly turns it. His face lights up with delight as he sees a light-coloured honey ooze out.

'I feel happy when I look after bees,' he tells us as he sells the tiny jars of honey for £1.50 to Golden Company supporters and parents.

The company has no shortage of corporate benefactors and well-wishers, including law firm Linklaters, accountants Grant Thornton, and bank UBS. And some 300 individuals support its Golden Adopt scheme, paying from £3 a year to adopt a Golden Company bee, and up to £50 for a beekeeper.

But despite all this goodwill, Palmer admits that the Golden Company is far from being a long-term sustainable business. It pays its young people, whom it calls Bee Guardians, a small income for being part of the business, but profits from the sale of honey and other products only just cover these wages and other costs.

In its short existence the Golden Company has won many friends and plaudits for its novel approach to helping at-risk young people. But how can it demonstrate it has, for example, raised levels of personal aspiration, and what impact has that had on getting its young participants jobs or into further education or training?

'It's too early to evaluate the long-term impact. We have carried out self-esteem testing which is positive but it is very difficult to quantify this type of benefit,' Palmer responds. 'But 10 of our young people have achieved ASDAN accreditations [credits for life skills, learning skills and job skills training] in sustainable enterprise.'

For Palmer, the best thing about the Golden Company is 'empowering communities to do things for themselves and with each other'. She also tells us it is about providing a space where the young people can relax and be themselves. 'You see that they start to let themselves be, when they realise they have nothing to defend. They can allow themselves to be a kid. They can get away from the estate, school and family, and all that history and baggage. Some have said they can leave it at the front door, but for others it's a life's work to help them.'

The rehabilitation beekeepers

In November 2010, the *Evening Standard* asked amateur apiarist and BBC journalist Martha Kearney to judge the best of the capital's honey by taste alone. The surprise winner was a honey from a little-known charity in south London that helps people suffering from drug and alcohol addiction. Kearney described the Kairos Community Trust honey as having 'a wonderful creamy flavour, almost like Scottish tablet/toffee, with subtle underlying scents of different flowers'.

We had come across Kairos almost a year earlier when it sent two residents and a member of staff on an Urban Bees taster course. We remembered that they were very keen and their presence was a breath of fresh air among our predominantly white, middle-class audience.

But it was not until we read the article in the *Standard* that we knew they had actually gone ahead and got bees. We called administrator Dorothy Woodward, who tells us they have three hives at three of their houses in south London. We ask if we can visit to find out more about how a rehabilitation charity has become part of the beekeeping revolution.

The Streatham HQ of the Kairos Community Trust is such an unassuming semi-detached house in a road full of unassuming semis that we think we must have the wrong address. But we are ushered into an office where Woodward sits at a desk in front of a computer. She greets us warmly and informs us we are going to meet Kenny and Mario, two of the trainees who came on our course, and Simon, who has recently taken up beekeeping.

'They are so excited,' she says, as through sliding french doors in the kitchen we see two National wooden hives near the back of the 60-foot lawn. There are fruit trees and shrubs but no out-of-the-ordinary vegetation that might explain why the honey tastes so good. Neither Kenny, Mario nor Simon know why their honey should be voted the best in London, but they are all clearly thrilled about winning the competition.

'It's brought such positive attention to the charity, instead of the usual negative headlines about junkies,' says Kenny. 'We're immensely proud.'

Kenny is the most talkative of the three. A former bank robber, he has spent much of his 45 years in and out of prison. He has been clean now for six years thanks to the Kairos programme: a community-based detox followed by a 12-week residential course of therapy; a period of time living in a move-on house, where residents are supported to continue their recovery and prepared for living independently; and finally aftercare.

Kenny is also one of a number of former Kairos service users who now works for the charity as a support worker. He manages three of its 30 move-on houses and has a hive at one of them.

When Kairos director Mossie Lyons told staff about his idea to keep bees, Kenny was the first to volunteer. 'I'd not got any hobbies. Other people have golf or fishing. So I thought, why not bees? But I was also keen to use it as a way to bring the community together. When I was living in move-on, we'd organise community meals and evening socials but now that I manage three houses I'm aware that the community spirit has waned. I had this vision of the bees creating a social utopia at the bottom of the garden,' he explains.

Kenny also admits he had an eye on the moneymaking potential of local honey. 'Initially I thought there was a few quid to be made out of it,' he says with a grin. 'I checked out local delis, to see how much they were selling local honey for, and earmarked the local Waitrose and independent cafes.' But in the end, the bees didn't make enough to sell in their first year – just 4.5 kg (10 lbs).

Kenny certainly has the makings of a salesman. Once he gets on the subject of bees it is difficult to stop him, and he talks in terms of a Damascene conversion. 'It has opened my eyes to nature, to the world around me,' he says. 'My life was just about going from A to B, to get this or that. I never looked at what was going on around me. I was a selfish person. It was all about Kenny. But this has changed everything. I've gone from a bank robber to a beekeeper,' he laughs.

Asked how popular the bees have been with residents of the house, Kenny admits that despite his best efforts there has not been as much interest as he would have liked.

'I've taken them round the hive and showed them I can stand right next to it and as long as I'm not in the flight path they won't bother me,' he says. 'But many of them are still scared.'

Nevertheless, the bees serve another useful purpose. 'When people in my houses are not getting on, I talk to them about the bees working together for the common good in their colony and how as 11 recovering addicts they should take a leaf out of their book,' says Kenny.

This sentiment is shared across the organisation. The Kairos 2010 annual report even has a photograph of a swarm of their bees on its cover accompanied by a quote from US pastor H. E. Luccock: 'No one can whistle a symphony. It takes a whole orchestra to play it.'

The swarm pictured are hanging from a branch of a tree in the garden where Mario manages a hive. 'When they swarmed and we lost the old queen, I spent a nervous, nail-biting two weeks waiting to see if the new queen was all right, and had mated and was laying eggs,' he says. 'It was like a partner having a baby,' adds the father of two.

'Beekeeping is a form of therapy for me. I am a person who buries emotions and this has helped me to unlock feelings. It has brought out – what d'you call it? – my nurturing side,' he says.

Mario has been in treatment for four years and for one of those has lived in a Kairos move-on house. He has a sensitive, almost childlike nature that belies his 48 years.

'I needed to have a bit of responsibility. I wanted to be responsible for them. You have to give them respect.'

The bees have also given him some newfound confidence. 'I feel it is one of the few things I have stuck at,' he says. 'I've stuck to recovery, I've stuck to education [he is studying for an NVQ in social care] and now this. It's a new start.'

Mossie Lyons introduced Mario to bees when he was looking for a topic to speak about at college. 'I didn't have anything I felt I knew about or was that passionate about. Then Mossie told me Kairos were going to get bees and suggested I read up on bees and talk about them.'

He did, and then Kairos sent him on the Urban Bees course. 'It was the first time I felt I knew about anything,' says Mario.

Simon, the quietest of the three beekeepers, has spent just 18 months in treatment. He lives in the only Kairos move-on house in north London and travels to Streatham once a week in the summer to help inspect the hives.

'I get really excited when I'm coming to see them,' he tells us. 'It gives you a purpose. When you're in treatment you're in a bubble and six months feels like a hell of a long time. It's good to have an outlet.' With his dreadlocks and baggy jumper, Simon looks every inch the eco warrior, so it is little surprise when he says: 'I've always liked bugs. I'm at my happiest sitting in a park watching nature.'

Moreover, beekeeping gives the 35-year-old something to focus on other than the drugs that have dominated his life. 'My main objective was to go out and get off my head with people – this is doing something positive with other people. And it gives you something else to talk about.'

It was a conversation Simon had with his support worker that led him to participate in the Kairos beekeeping project at the end of the summer. 'I was talking to him about bees one day and he told me they were going to start keeping them here. I couldn't believe my luck. I kept pestering him until he said I was ready to take part.'

We ask if it would have helped his recovery if he could have started beekeeping earlier, when he was in detox or residential therapy perhaps?

'It's too early,' jumps in Woodward, who has been listening to our conversation. 'They [the former addicts] are just about alive and able to have a conversation at this stage. They are not ready to be responsible for something else. And even when they first go to move-on accommodation they need to settle in, get benefits sorted, think about college etc. It is only when their support worker thinks it is the right time that beekeeping would come up in conversation and it might be suggested that it is something they could do voluntarily,' she explains.

Simon agrees: 'When you get out of rehab your head is all over the place,' he says.

Simon is also doing a carpentry course as part of his recovery and hopes one day to build his own hive. Learning new skills helps to take the focus off the former addicts' problems. 'Beekeeping has taken them out of themselves and given them a sense of perspective about their own role in life,' Lyons tells us when we meet him a few weeks later.

'Where I grew up [in Kerry, Ireland], bees were part of summer,' he says. 'I knew about their importance to pollination and had been reading abut their demise. Kairos had a three-year business plan that included addressing environmental issues. We had put solar panelling on one of our houses, have composters at the back of our gardens, water butts and greenhouses. I decided keeping bees would fit in with this objective.'

The idea actually took shape during a staff weekend away at Buckfast Abbey in Devon, a monastery and conference centre. It was here, almost a century earlier, that Brother Adam created the famous Buckfast bee. Lyons met a beekeeper during their stay who by chance lived not far from the charity's south London headquarters and agreed to become a mentor for its beekeeping project.

But the proposal to keep bees was not universally supported by staff. 'They thought it was just another of Mossie's harebrained ideas,' Lyons recalls.

Woodward was one of the detractors, but she has to admit her boss was right. 'It has been amazing seeing the marked difference,' she says. 'When they came back from the Urban Bees course they were buzzing and couldn't stop talking about it.'

Speaking with the three recovering addicts around the kitchen table, it is evident that what started as a project to boost the charity's green credentials has had a palpable effect on the participants' self-confidence. This could hold lessons for other charities and organisations working with vulnerable people.

Both Kenny and Mario say they would like to get more training and pass their beekeeping knowledge on to other residents. 'When you put the suit on you feel really professional,' says Kenny. 'I want to have the confidence to teach others.'

The academic beekeeper

Francis Ratnieks is the only professor of apiculture in the UK. He heads up the Laboratory of Apiculture & Social Insects (LASI) at Sussex University, where he is in the middle of a five-year plan to investigate the decline of the honeybee and potential ways to save it.

He has spent 30 years studying 'social insects that live in colonies with a queen and workers' (such as bees, ants, wasps and termites) all over the world, and has taught honeybee biology at five universities including Cornell, Berkeley and Sao Paulo. In 2008, he was lured away from Sheffield University by the offer of a 'proper research laboratory' for himself and a team of researchers on a campus on the edge of the South Downs.

Ratnieks also knows what it's like to keep bees outside of a laboratory. He worked for the New York State apiary inspection service and was a commercial beekeeper with 180 hives on an almond farm in California. In the Peak District he helped with attempts to breed pure-strain black bees that are native to the British Isles.

It is this marriage of academic excellence and practical know-how that sets Ratnieks apart from his peers and makes him one of those rare academics who talks in layman's terms and seeks to make their research as accessible and applied as possible.

'We want to provide information on what plants to grow at which times of year for honeybees, for everyone from gardeners to park and estate managers,' Ratnieks says simply about one of the four projects in his Sussex Plan for honeybee health and wellbeing.

We visit LASI in April 2010 as part of a one-day meeting about bees, land use and the community. It is intended to help mobilise people working in disciplines as diverse as education, conservation and urban planning to make Britain a more bee-friendly place. Ratnieks believes that everyone can play a part in helping the honeybee if they are equipped with better information. And the lecture hall is packed with representatives from the worlds of business, farming and local communities.

LASI comprises four offices, a tropical ant room, and a large open-plan laboratory, near to the entrance of the red-brick campus. Immediately outside the laboratory is a garden and apiary, a workshop for making beehives and research equipment, and a storage shed. Within easy walking distance on the campus is another apiary and there are two more off-site. In total there are more than 50 hives, including six observation hives.

Ratnieks heads up a team of 16 scientists and students, including Norman Carreck, the senior technician. Carreck is a well-respected figure in the beekeeping world for his work as a research scientist at agricultural research centre Rothamsted Research and as the scientific director of the International Bee Research Association.

Three of the team are working on the urban land management project. They have enlisted the help of four undergraduate students to help decode the honeybees' waggle dance – the unique and sophisticated language honeybees use to communicate to their nestmates where to fly to find a rich source of food.

Using glass-fronted observation hives and video cameras in three hives connected to large computer screens, they have analysed more than 2,000 dances made by forager bees to find out exactly where they are going for food. The speed and angle of the figure-of-eight-style dance on the wax comb conveys how far the flowers are from the hive and where they are in relation to the sun. If a bee makes a waggle vertically up the comb this means the flowers are in the direction of the sun. For every degree the sun moves across the sky, the bee will have to alter her dance direction on the comb by the same degree. The slower the dance, the greater the distance to the patch of flowers being advertised by the dance.

During our visit we are able to see how the researchers go about this painstaking and time-consuming data collection, with each hour of videotape taking several weeks to decode. Dr Margaret Couvillon shows us how they use a protractor to measure the angle of the dance. Plumb lines on the observation hive give vertical lines that are easily seen on the video.

The waggle dances reveal whether these campus-based bees, 5 km (3 miles) north-east of Brighton and at the foot of a national park, are visiting urban, rural or suburban locations for forage.

The initial findings Ratnieks presents that day clearly show that honeybees visit different areas at different times of the year and they will travel much further for food in certain months when forage is less abundant nearby. 'In March, the average foraging distance was 1 km [0.6 miles] when spring flowers were in plentiful supply in the grounds of the university and surrounding gardens, while in August the bees had to do a 4 km [2.5 mile] trip to the countryside,' he points out. 'These results indicate that here flowers are in shorter supply in summer than in spring so in terms of helping bees, the conclusion we draw is that it is more useful to plant stuff for bees that blooms in the summer.

'Our research also shows that bees forage in both urban and rural areas,' he adds. 'We know there is more diversity of flowers in cities, with gardens, parks, railway sidings and bits of wasteland all planted with different species. But it is not necessarily greater diversity that is important; they also need an abundance of flowering plants,' he points out.

This is an important observation that is often overlooked by advocates of urban beekeeping who forget that as well as providing a variety of year-round bee-friendly forage, cities need to proffer large quantities.

Building on the waggle dance research, the Sussex Plan's latest project aims to scientifically assess the value of different species of garden plants to honeybees and other pollinators.

'We are told that lavender is a good late-summer flower to plant for bees, but this project is testing 14 popular varieties of lavender along with other popular plants including geranium, nasturtium, dahlia and borage to find out which are the most attractive to honey-bees,' Ratnieks explains. 'It's a popular misconception that bees only like blue flowers. They like flowers with nectar. They don't give a damn what colour it is.'

LASI's flower constancy project, undertaken by third year under-graduates using drinking straws, different coloured laminated paper and Plasticine to make flowers, demonstrated how a bee returns to the flower that rewards its visit with nectar, regardless of colour.

Preliminary LASI analysis of the most popular bee flowers shows that bees prefer some lavender to others. Lavandula x intermedia attracts a wide range of insects including honeybees, butterflies and hoverflies, Ratnieks says.

'Borage is extremely attractive to honeybees. As an annual plant, it very quickly grows and blooms and is probably the quickest and cheapest way to get a large patch of bee-friendly flowers into your garden. It self-seeds and the seedlings are easily recognised the next year, so a patch can be kept going with little effort.'

The Sussex Plan is designed to provide practical solutions for the beekeeping community, farmers, growers and landowners. Ratnieks has already put his research on bee-friendly forage to practical use by drawing up a list of year-round bee-friendly trees and plants for Brighton and Hove Council's park managers.

Other Sussex Plan projects include breeding disease-resistant 'hygienic' bees – he hopes to be able to offer beekeepers hygienic queens to trial – and testing which methods work best against the varroa mite.

It is apparent that Ratnieks cares deeply about the future of an insect he finds truly remarkable. As the UK's only bee professor, he sees one of his roles as being an advocate for the honeybee. His appointment at Sussex caused much interest and column inches. And he hopes he will be able to use his profile to help people to appreciate the natural world around them and realise we are dependent on it for survival.

'The world's most interesting animal lives in your backyard,' he told one interviewer. 'What I want to get across, to schoolchildren in particular, is that while watching Sir David Attenborough in the Amazon Basin or Borneo, it's easy to forget that the creature with the most complicated communication system of all is on your doorstep.'

PART II

Making our urban environment more bee-friendly

Have our bees got enough to eat?

In December 2010 the London mayor, Boris Johnson, announced a competition that offered 50 community food growing groups the chance to keep honeybees.

'The humble bee is vital for food production, helping green spaces to thrive and acting as a reliable ecological barometer for the health of our natural environment,' he said. 'As a logical next step to our initiative to create 2012 new community food gardens and beautify neglected parts of London, we are taking practical steps to create a "buzz" around urban bees.'

The £43,000 Capital Bee scheme, funded by the Greater London Authority and the National Lottery, was designed to provide the successful groups with long-term training, a hive, bees and basic equipment. Training was scheduled to start in spring 2011 with hives expected to be operational by the following spring.

The competition followed a scheme funded by the Co-operative Group to introduce 20 new beekeepers into the capital and another to locate eight hives in the City of London.

But the mayor's bid to encourage more urban beekeeping didn't meet with universal approval. John Chapple, chair of the London Beekeepers' Association, accused Johnson of 'jumping on the beekeeping bandwagon' and raised concerns that there wouldn't be enough food to go round for all these new honeybee colonies.

'Before introducing more than two million more honeybees he should make London more bee-friendly,' said Chapple. 'He should stop parks from planting double-headed flowers that provide no nectar or pollen, cutting back trees and shrubs that provide vital nectar and pollen for bees, excessive mowing of dandelion-strewn lawns and spraying with chemicals.'

Chapple is the Queen's beekeeper. For the last three years he has looked after four hives in Buckingham Palace's 18 hectare (45 acre) garden. We arrange to meet him in the grounds of Lambeth Palace where he has kept six hives for the past decade. We want to hear more about the concerns of this 68-year-old beekeeper who was one of the first to have bees in central London.

'When I first started keeping hives in the centre of London 20 years ago, in Hyde Park, St James's Park and Regent's Park, I'd get maximum honey yields from my hives,' says Chapple. 'I made well over 2,500 lbs [1,100 kg] of honey from my 60 hives that were scattered across the capital and I was the only commercial beekeeper in London.

'Standard rent for the hives was one jar of honey that I'd present on Michaelmas Day [29 September], which is traditionally the last day of harvest. The rest I sold at farmers' markets and festivals. The Archbishop buys all my Lambeth Palace honey to sell at fetes and open days.'

Now he says honey yields are at a minimum. 'I'm lucky to get 1,000 lbs [450 kg]. That's why I'm worried that London can't sustain more honeybees.'

Yet when we tot up a list of where he now keeps bees, including four at Westminster University and an observation hive in a tree trunk at the Natural History Museum, it only adds up to about 30 – half the number of hives he once had – so you would expect the amount of honey to have fallen accordingly.

Chapple, however, points to specific hives such as the two at Regent's Park that have dramatically suffered since another beekeeper installed 40 hives nearby.

There is certainly no shortage of bee forage in the Archbishop of Canterbury's London garden. These four hectares (10 acres) of tranquility, the second-largest private garden in the capital after Buckingham Palace, are home to a herb garden, an avenue of lime trees, a pond and informal lawns that are dotted with daffodils and crocuses when we visit. As we walk towards the hives, Chapple points to an evergreen tree we don't recognise and says: 'That's the best bee forage in the capital. It's covered in bees in June and July.'

So what is it? 'A privet,' he replies. We have only ever seen privets trimmed into neat green hedges. That's the problem, says Chapple. 'It's great bee forage when it flowers but very few gardeners ever leave it to flower.'

Despite Chapple's pessimism there is no overall agreement among beekeepers on whether our cities will be able to feed the influx of new honeybee colonies as urban beekeeping continues to expand.

The other Regent's Park beekeeper, Toby Mason, insists that the 200 hectare (490 acre) park provides ample forage for his bees. And Chapple's counterpart at the North London Beekeepers' Association, John Hauxwell, tells us that his two hives in an inner-city builders' yard produce twice as much honey as the ones located in a more suburban location. In Liverpool, Doug Jones who keeps hives on the roof of one of the museums in the city centre, says it does better than his hives at home in the suburbs. But the reason he gives is not an abundance of inner-city forage. 'Where I live there are so many beekeepers that competition is fierce and we don't get much honey,' says Jones, echoing Chapple's gripes about London.

Research from other countries suggests bees reared in cities are more productive than their country cousins. A study by French beekeepers' association Unaf, for example, found bees in Paris had higher honey yields and lower mortality rates than bees in the countryside. But that could say more about the poor state of intensively farmed and pesticide-ridden rural France.

Here, with two thirds of London given over to green spaces, many believe that it is unlikely we have reached bee saturation point just yet. But Chapple is right to raise concerns about the influx of bees in our cities putting a potential strain on food resources. Bees provide a valuable pollination service for many crops and plants. In return for visiting the flowers, they obtain food in the form of nectar and pollen. But many highly cultivated flowers that add a splash of colour to our urban environment have been selected for increasingly showy blooms that produce little or no pollen and nectar, or make it very difficult for pollinators to get to it.

If we are serious about halting the decline of honeybees we can't just blithely introduce thousands more colonies into urban areas without being aware of the potential consequences if there is scant forage to sustain them.

Pamela Brunton from the food charity Sustain, which is managing the mayor's Capital Bee competition, points out that there has been no research into how much forage different pollinators need, so it is impossible to say how many hives London can support. 'In fact, urban environments have been shown to be very good for bees because of the year-round, diverse forage available to them in our parks and gardens,' she says.

It is true that there is a dearth of research or even guidance on the maximum number of hives that, say, an acre of urban land could support. In the countryside we have heard beekeepers quote seven hives per acre as a standard. In the US, where 1.2m hives are trucked thousands of miles to the central valley of California each February to pollinate 240 hectares (600,000 acres) of almond trees, the almond growers' insurance companies insist on two hives per acre for maximum pollination.

'I don't think that any specific recommendation can be made about the number of hives per unit area as this depends very much on the amount of flowers, and will also vary month by month,' says Sussex University's Professor Ratnieks. 'Honeybees have large colonies so the density might appear to be low, but it is not when you work it out per bee.'

His own research, while at Cornell University, showed that the colony density of Africanised honeybees in rural Chiapas, Mexico, was around six colonies per square kilometre – higher than the density of man-kept hives.

Here in the UK, a decline in bee forage in the countryside is thought to be a contributory factor in the honeybees' demise. Since 1947, industrialised farming methods have wiped out 97 per cent of our flower-rich grasslands, from 3 million hectares (7.4m acres) to just 100,000 (250,000 acres), leaving sheep to graze on clover-free pasture, and massively reducing the amount of wildflowers on arable land. A fifth of heather-rich moorland in England and Wales has also been converted into agricultural fields; all of which has robbed bees of vital sources of food.

Although the countryside can still provide a bee feast when the oilseed rape is in full bloom, turning the landscape a garish electric yellow, after the feeding frenzy comes the famine. Bees need to be able to forage throughout the year. A three-week sugar rush is no substitute for a constant and diverse diet with plenty of pollen in early spring to feed the larvae, and nectar in the summer to create honey stores for winter.

So do towns and cities now provide richer food sources for honeybees as some anecdotal evidence suggests? And, if so, how do we better manage this urban environment for them?

This question has prompted a flurry of academic research from Sussex University (see page 68) to the National Pollen and Aerobiology Research Unit at the University of Worcester. Here, Professor John Newbury, head of the Institute of Science and the Environment, has been commissioned by the BBC/National Trust's Bee Part of It! project to analyse samples of pollen in urban and rural hives.

At Kensington Palace in central London, where the Duke of Gloucester keeps bees, samples of pollen carried back to the hives in the summer of 2010 were found to contain large amounts of pollen from rock rose, eucalyptus and elderberry. By contrast, pollen samples taken from hives near farmland at the National Trust's Nostell Priory in Yorkshire and Barrington Court in Somerset were heavily dominated by just one crop: oilseed rape.

Matthew Oates, nature conservation adviser at the National Trust, says the preliminary findings back what has long been suspected: 'Bees today often fare better in urban environments than in contemporary farmland. Apart from crops such as oilseed rape and field beans, there are precious few pollen sources around for bees and other insects in modern arable farmland and surprisingly little in areas specialising in dairy, beef or sheep production.'

In 2009, five major founders of scientific research launched a £10m Insect Pollinators Initiative (IPI) to examine the decline in bees and other pollinators. Of the nine research grants awarded, two are investigating bees' nutritional needs and whether the current rural and urban landscape can meet them.

'We're divvying the cities up not just into gardens – we'll also look at bits of wasteland, industrial estates, shopping malls – to ask where there are the little oases for plant pollinators. We'll ask what we can do in cities to make them more pollinator-friendly,' explains Professor Jane Memmott at the University of Bristol, who was awarded a £1.2m grant to identify the hotspots of insect biodiversity in Bristol, Reading, Leeds and Edinburgh.

The project will also plant large swathes of wildflowers on council land, similar to field margins grown on farms under the environmental stewardship programme, to see what impact this has on biodiversity. 'There is plenty of anecdotal evidence about cities being havens of biodiversity but no statistics, no proper science to back this up,' says Memmott.

Her findings will be presented at a conference in 2014 and she hopes will provide a blueprint for towns and cities all over the UK. 'The trick is to show councils that these flowers can look beautiful rather than like weeds. And if we can demonstrate that it is cheaper and better to plant longer-lasting native perennials and wildflowers than expensive short-term bedding plants then we will be able to improve biodiversity in our cities,' she says.

In Newcastle, the city council says making its horticultural services and ground maintenance bee-friendly has been cost neutral (see page 89). Newcastle University's Dr Geraldine Wright, who is advising the council on its bee-friendly planting, also won a coveted IPI grant.

'My project will examine both the nutritional needs of honeybees and bumblebees and the nutritional quality of pollen and nectar. This will allow us to estimate both whether the amount of forage in a given habitat is sufficient and also whether it is nutritionally "complete",' explains Wright.

'I agree that having more folks keeping bees in urban environments could actually lead to trouble if there isn't enough food for the bees being kept.

We plan to build an online database of the nutritional quality of nectar and pollen where the information will be freely available to the public so they can improve the foraging habitat for bee species in their gardens.'

How to help city bees without becoming a beekeeper

So what can we do more immediately to help bees flourish in our backyards?

As we have seen, John Chapple from the London Beekeepers' Association says that the obvious answer isn't necessarily the best one. He advises people to 'plant bee-friendly trees and flowers in their garden rather than becoming a beekeeper'.

Gardens are certainly a huge resource. They now contain more flowers than most agricultural land, and in Britain they cover more than one million hectares, which far exceeds the combined area of our nature reserves. However, a lot of gardens are not especially friendly to any wildlife. Many are covered with paving or decking or are planted with exotic or highly cultivated garden flowers such as pansies, petunias, busy Lizzies and begonias that produce little or no nectar or pollen, and keep it hidden away from the bees.

But if people started to think of their backyards as mini nature reserves, the future of bees and other pollinators would be a little more secure. Nowhere is this better illustrated than in Leicester, where garden ecologist Jennifer Owen has recorded more than 2,500 species in her suburban backyard since 1972. Her findings are published in *Wildlife of a Garden: A Thirty-year Study*. Over the whole period, Owen, who has an academic training in zoology, recorded 474 plants, 1,997 insects, 138 other invertebrates (such as spiders, woodlice and slugs) and 64 vertebrates, 54 of them birds. In some groups, including bees, this small garden in Leicester was visited by a quarter or more of the total numbers known from the whole of Britain. 'Gardens are extraordinarily rich habitats,' Owen writes. 'I didn't attempt to create an artificial countryside – it was a typical suburban garden growing flowers and vegetables. I enjoyed it and I was not an overly tidy gardener. I used to love working in my garden, sowing seeds and taking cuttings. I didn't use pesticide or poison on any creature because I was interested in what shared the garden with me.'

There is a plethora of information from wildlife trusts, the British Beekeepers' Association and the Bumblebee Conservation Trust about which plants and flowers will attract different bees and other pollinators to your garden, window boxes or hanging baskets (see also Appendix 4 for a list of bee-friendly plants). The Bumblebee Conservation Trust has produced a table of bumblebee-friendly plants that flower at different times of the year. 'If everyone provided just one plant from each of the seasons shown in the table, the future of surviving bumblebee species would be a little more secure,' it says.

Other organisations are out there planting wildflowers on derelict pieces of wasteland in our cities, some of them illicitly, under cover of darkness, such as the guerrilla gardening movement.

'Let's fight the filth with forks and flowers,' says Richard Reynolds, who pioneered guerrilla gardening in the UK in the noughties. The clandestine cultivation of neglected pockets of urban land with flowers and crops began in New York's lower east side 30 years earlier and is now a worldwide crusade. These green-fingered insurgents beautify concrete sprawl with splashes of floral colour in empty verges and barren wasteland. Unfortunately, because it is an illegal activity, many of the flowers are often destroyed by councils and contractors.

River of Flowers is a more legitimate and permanent response to a lack of urban forage for pollinators.

'It seemed to me that all the pollinators were in trouble not only because their territory, and therefore food sources, had been taken over by urban development, but also because their pollination systems had been disrupted,' says Kathryn Lwin Brooks, who in

2008 founded an organisation dedicated to growing corridors of wildflowers in urban areas.

'The "river" in River of Flowers is an evocative way of describing the strategic planting of urban meadows in "pollination streams" in order to help our vanishing pollinators, including bees, find forage in the city. It describes the flight path of the pollinators as much as it does the flow of wildflowers,' she explains.

'River of Flowers operates under the concept that the wildflower and the pollinator form a single unit, so when we damage wildflowers, we also damage the organisms that depend on them.'

The river started in north London, where she was director of the Archway Herbal Clinic, and is spreading across the capital in schools, allotments, city farms, parks, woods, gardens, public spaces and on roofs; in fact many of the same places where there has been an explosion in urban beekeeping.

One of the reasons Lwin Brooks is championing all pollinators is because research suggests that honeybees can have negative impacts on other pollinators. In Scotland, David Goulson, professor of biological sciences at the University of Stirling and a world expert on bumblebees, has found there is competition for food sources between honeybees and bumblebees, with bumblebees losing out when forage is limited.

'Our data clearly demonstrate that workers of four common bumblebee species [studied] tend to be smaller in areas where they co-occur with honeybees,' says Goulson.

'For conservation purposes, some restrictions should be considered with regard to placing honeybee hives in or near areas where populations of rare bumblebee species persist,' his research concludes.

Britain had 24 different types of bumblebee. Three species have vanished in recent years and six are on the government's endangered species list. Lwin Brooks's solution is not to restrict urban beekeeping but to mitigate its potentially adverse effects by increasing wildflower forage in urban areas. 'This research makes the planting of wildflowers for all pollinators even more urgent,' she says.

Invertebrates conservation trust Buglife has its own campaign to create 300-metre-wide forage-rich corridors across England called B-lines. Matt Shardlow, chief executive of Buglife, explains: 'The project would depend on a new "conservation credits" scheme that would require developers and others whose sector degrades wildlife to purchase credits that would secure wildflower habitats.'

In a similar vein, River of Flowers is starting to campaign for every new urban building to replace the space it has taken from wildflowers by installing a wildflower roof.

Up until now sedums have proved the most popular flowers for planting on roofs in the UK to green them, but a study in Switzerland has shown that roofs planted with a mix of both wildflowers and sedums were visited by pollinators for a much longer period. Whereas sedum roofs had visitors during June and July when sedum species are in bloom, roofs planted with both were attractive to pollinators, including bees, from April through to September.

In London, bees were observed on several green roofs during summer 2009 to find out which species visited and which plants they foraged on. The long-flowering viper's bugloss (Echium vulgare), with its bell-like purple or white flowers on large spikes, and the pale toadflax (Linaria repens), with flowers shaped like small snapdragons, attracted honeybees all summer on one green roof. On another, clovers, poppies and sedum provided forage for honeybees from May onwards, while on the third roof in Canary Wharf honeybees were only spotted in May when the field sow thistle (Sonchus arvensis) and pea-like flowers of the kidney vetch (Anthyllis vulneraria) were in bloom.

Leading UK green roof experts Gyongyver Kadas and Dusty Gedge say that these studies show that 'it is imperative that a mix of both sedums and wildflowers need to be used to ensure that the roofs provide benefit throughout the foraging season'.

We ask Tony Leach, director of the London Parks and Green Spaces Forum at the Greater London Authority (GLA), if the mayor could make it a condition of planning approval in the capital that all new buildings have a green roof. 'Unfortunately not; he can only promote the concept and has been doing so as a climate change adaptor,' explains Leach.

What about making sure the city's parks and green spaces are bee-friendly? 'Parks aren't part of the mayor's remit,' he replies. 'It's up to the individual boroughs and the Royal Parks to increase their biodiversity.'

In fact the London Biodiversity Action Plan has 26 targets to improve habitats and increase species that are important for the capital. But none include bees. It does however aim to 'encourage wildlife-friendly gardening across London'.

'The trend over the last 20 years is for councils to employ biodiversity officers and for the municipal parks to be looking at how they can cater for both people and wildlife,' says Leach. Nowadays, plants are not just chosen because they are low-maintenance shrubs or are annual bedding plants that make a colourful civic floral display, he argues.

In Ealing, west London, for example, formal parks have been 'reducing chemical application and in some places replacing annuals with perennial flowering beds,' says project manager Nicola Masters. In the City of London, Don Lawson, superintendent of West Ham Park and City Gardens, says: 'Our open spaces do not use chemicals for pest or weed control these days and efforts in varying the biodiversity of sites have been outstanding, such as varying grass heights and creating conservation areas.' Similarly, Andrew Bedford, principal parks manager at Islington council, north London, says: 'We have done some work around increasing meadow areas in parks and creating significant areas of wildlife-friendly herbaceous planting.'

Outside of London, Brighton & Hove is planting roadside verges with colourful wildflowers to increase nectar availability between May and November, and city parks ecologist Matthew Thomas – with the help of Professor Ratnieks at Sussex University – has put together a guidance note for all city parks area managers on bee-friendly plants appropriate for planting in parks and open spaces. Thomas also points to a new greenway that has been created as part of the city-centre Brighton station development, which is planted with a range of cultivated and wild nectar-producing plants.

Leach singles out the biggest development in London, the Olympic site, as evidence of the capital's increasing bee-friendliness. A 10 hectare (25 acre) golden meadow of nectar- and pollen-rich long-flowering wildflowers will be a centrepiece of the Olympic park. Leading horticultural and planting design consultants Professor James Hitchmough and Dr Nigel Dunnett from the University of Sheffield's department of landscape have been trialling the meadow two years ahead of the Games.

'The Olympic Park meadows have been carefully formulated to flower at their peak during the Games, producing exciting, vibrant sheets of uplifting colour with high biodiversity value,' says Dunnett. The meadow is a combination of various wildflowers that will change from yellow and blue in July to gold in August. Shorter and taller perennial meadows are also being sown across the park.

The meadows will no doubt look spectacular and provide a feast for any honeybees within a 5 km (3 mile) radius – thought to be the maximum distance bees forage in normal circumstances – of the Olympic Park in late summer. And it has inspired a scheme led by London in Bloom and the London Organising Committee of the Olympic Games, together with the London Wildlife Trust (LWT), to get residents to create as many urban, small-scale meadows across the capital as possible. Even planting wildflowers in a window box can help.

More vital to honeybees, however, will be the 4,000 semi-mature trees that will be planted in the Olympic Park, including bee-friendly cherry, hazel, alder and lime.

According to the BBKA, four or five large trees can provide as much forage for bees as a whole acre of wildflowers. It produces guidance on its website on the best trees to plant for bees. Hazel is particularly important early in the year when few other sources of pollen are available. The LWT recommends apple, cherry and plum trees along with raspberry and flowering currant bushes.

In Manchester, the city council is planting 20,000 bee-friendly soft fruit bushes, strawberries and fruit and nut trees in all of its 135 parks. The scheme is targeted at educating children and allowing local residents to pick fresh, locally produced fruits from the orchards and soft fruit canes.

'We have been amazed by how many children don't know where fruit and nuts come from so we see this as a useful educational tool and a wonderful community resource where people can literally help themselves,' said councillor Mike Amesbury, executive member for culture and leisure when the scheme was launched in 2009.

Although he made no mention about the fantastic forage the trees and bushes would providing for bees, the scheme coincided with 60 hives being set up in parks across the city and staff being trained as beekeepers as part of the Co-op's Plan Bee campaign.

Until 2006, only one Manchester park had any fruit trees. So how did the council get the idea to introduce them citywide?

'A local environmentalist approached us with the idea and we were immediately interested,' Amesbury says.

There is a lesson here for anyone who wants to save bees. Lobby your council to plant more bee-friendly trees as an educational tool. How many children know how honey is made, or that honeybees pollinate fruit and vegetables?

'If you are serious about saving bees, having your own hive pales into insignificance compared to what you could achieve by lobbying your council to create a more bee-friendly town or city,' says Chapple.

Some councils are starting to encourage beekeeping on allotments and city farms and even planting more wildflowers, but have yet to change some of their most biodiversity-unfriendly policies. Excess mowing is a particular problem. Dandelions, for example, may look like weeds but they are important wildflowers that are out early in the year when there are not many other options for bees.

Despite taking steps in the right direction, one of the limitations of these new bee-friendly policies is that no one is monitoring their implementation. So in most cases it is left up to the discretion of the local park manager.

'No compulsion, no monitoring,' says Matthews about the guidance he has drawn up in Brighton with Professor Ratnieks. And with council budgets being slashed there is little chance that this will change.

This is where the Bee Guardian Foundation comes in. A social enterprise set up to help landowners, communities and individuals to protect all their local bee species, it is developing an assessment tool to judge how bee-friendly a town or city really is and whether it achieves bee guardian status.

It also shows how individuals, institutions and businesses can help city bees without taking up urban beekeeping themselves. Instead of donning a bee suit it suggests following six simple steps to become a bee guardian:

1. Undertake to use no insecticides in the management of land under your stewardship.
2. Promote bee diversity by providing nesting sites for bees of all species, through leaving suitable wild areas and providing artificial nesting boxes or 'bee houses'.
3. Undertake to plant bee-friendly plants on land under your stewardship to provide food for bees throughout the 'bee season' (February through until late October).
4. Take every opportunity to educate others as to the diversity and importance of bees, and how we can help them.
5. Become a part of Bee Guardian Network.
6. Become a member of the Bee Guardian Foundation.

The Foundation is currently working with Gloucester City Council to develop its Bee Guardian kitemark (see page 95). But it could already learn much from one city in the north-east which is leading the way among local authorities in its determination and drive to make its urban environment more bee-friendly.

The UK's most bee-friendly city

We are standing on the rooftop of Fenwick department store in Newcastle. The 360-degree view is magnificent. We can see St James's Park, home to the local Premier League football club, Grey's Monument, the River Tyne and the city of Gateshead, and even the coast and up towards Northumberland. It also reveals no shortage of parks and green spaces. Within a 5 km (3 mile) radius lies the Botanical Garden, Exhibition Park and closer to home the city-centre trees and flowerbeds, which is just as well as on the roof are five hives with 250,000 hungry mouths to feed at the height of the summer.

The first hive arrived in a blaze of publicity in May 2009, installed and managed by commercial beekeeper Ian Wallace.

'It was quite an experience carrying the hives up in the tradesman's lift,' recalls Fenwick general manager, Keith Hutton, as he takes us on to the roof. 'We are committed to local food. We stocked cheeses and other local products. So when Wallace approached us to stock urban honey produced on our very own roof we liked the idea.'

And Fenwick honey has proved so popular that when we visit the food department, where the highly prized jars sells at £7 for 227 g (8 oz), the shelf is bare.

Now Wallace's honeybees are set to get a further boost as Newcastle transforms itself into the first bee-friendly city in the UK. Its ambitious plans include giving all of its 16 parks and other council-owned green spaces a bee-friendly makeover, raising awareness across the city about the plight of bees, encouraging urban beekeeping and increasing habitats for other bees.

'As I'm interested in wildlife and was greatly concerned about [bee] colony collapse, I had started to ask questions about the council's policies to prevent this and discovered that we had nothing specific,' says Liberal Democrat councillor Doreen Huddart, who has spearheaded the city's drive to boost bees.

In January 2010, she tabled a motion at the council calling on the city to address the issue of the decline in bees. It was passed and a group was set up to look at the problems and find ways to prevent further damage.

We are met at the town hall by twentysomething council employees Russell Nelson and Jo Timothy, who jumped at the chance to develop their careers by turning Huddart's motion into a council-led bee strategy.

'The first thing we did was bring together experts from across the city to form a bee steering group,' says Nelson, the more energetic of the duo. Representatives include the Northumberland Wildlife Trust (NWT), Natural England, Newcastle University and members from local beekeeping and allotment associations, plus a range of council officers from across horticulture, educational and leisure departments, with leadership provided by the director of neighbourhood services and Huddart.

To give us a flavour of what they have achieved in the first year they are taking us on a whistle-stop tour of the city. After Fenwick's roof it's off to Gosforth Park primary school where eight-year-old pupils show us their bee-friendly garden planted with lavender, buddleia, sedum and cotoneaster. Upstairs, we interrupt a German lesson to look at the bee displays pinned on the back of the classroom wall that include photos and bee facts as well as a number of 'Love our Bees!' leaflets. The council has produced more than 1,000 of these information leaflets and distributed them in schools, libraries and at events throughout the city.

A thick lever arch file labelled 'Bees in the Curriculum Key Stage 1 and 2' sits on a table below the Gosforth Park display. Alistair

Wilson, a member of the council's enviro-school team, explains that the NWT has funded 20 Newcastle schools to have a copy.

'Kids go home and tell their parents to turn off the lights,' he says about the council's long-running environmental education project. 'Now they may start telling them not to use pesticides in the garden and to grow more wildflowers.'

In adjoining school Broadway East, the head teacher is keen to redevelop an area of the playground as bee-friendly. 'Three planters are in place and the council's nursery is giving us advice about which flowers to plant,' says Helen McKenna.

The local high school, meanwhile, is getting advice from the park's ecology officer on wildflower mixes to plant on an acre of land it is turning into a wildlife centre for its science and biology students.

The Jesmond Dene plant nursery on the outskirts of the city is central to making Newcastle's citywide initiative to boost bees a reality. It is here where up to 500,000 plants are grown each year for the council's parks, floral displays and hanging baskets.

But Nigel Hails, director of neighbourhood services, tells us it was apparent at the first bee steering group meeting that the nursery would have to change its practices. 'Within an hour our staff were saying, "Crikey, we're growing the wrong flowers,"' he admits.

At the nursery we meet horticulture manager Mark Lamb, whose job it was to put this right. He shows us around the large site. In the greenhouses, he points to the rows upon rows of lavender, rosemary, Californian lilac and a small variety of buddleia as evidence that the council is now choosing plants that attract bees throughout the summer.

'Our strategy has changed to include bee-attracting shrubs, trees and bulbs,' says Lamb, reeling off the names of a host of other plants including hydrangeas, forsythias, and honeysuckles. 'In addition to the annual bedding, the city has now introduced permanent planting within the floral displays,' he adds.

Councils have been criticised by environmentalists for their bedding displays, which have traditionally been ripped out and replaced with new flowers each year. Newcastle may not be ready to completely ditch this short-lived colourful flora just yet but at least it has started to put in more long-term flowers and to replace sterile multi-headed varieties, which don't provide any nectar and pollen, with single-headed flowers, such as white daisy-like marguerites and yellow bidens aurea.

In 2011, a wildflower meadow is planned in a city-centre park along with the nectar-rich beds, and more fruit trees, such as pear, plum and apple, will be planted. 'All of this will be provided by the nursery at no extra cost,' says Lamb, who is keen to stress that going bee-friendly is cost neutral.

The council is also in the process of planting 67 lime trees over a one-mile stretch of the Great North Road, which will provide ample bee forage in late summer.

But it's not just about what trees and flowers are planted. Cities that are serious about saving bees need to reduce their use of weed-killers and pesticides. 'We have some trial areas in place, where we aim not to use pesticides within 200 metres of bee colonies,' says Lamb. Where weedkillers are used it is a non-bee-toxic Glyphosate-based product applied with precision by a purpose-built vehicle with sensors and nozzles to prevent any spray drift.

Jesmond Dene nursery is the location for one of two beehives purchased by the council. The other is at Ouseburn City Farm. At both sites staff will be trained by Fenwick beekeeper Ian Wallace.

We drop in on the city farm, which is dramatically located under Byker Bridge in the east end of the city. Ouseburn Farm manager Mandy Oliver says she can't wait to be taught beekeeping: 'I'm so excited,' she enthuses. Children who visit the farm will be able to get close to the bees in suits purchased by the council.

A care home will host the third council-sponsored hive. 'Adult and culture services have a massive portfolio in the city which includes vast amounts of council land for care homes and other residential accommodation, all of which have gardens,' says Nelson. It is hoped that some of this land will eventually be loaned out to individual beekeepers.

In the west end of the city, charity Scotswood Natural Community Garden has just received European funding to install six hives on a roof on its 0.8 hectare (two acre) site and offer free beekeeping courses. The council hopes it will become a central training apiary in the city.

As a result of the council's actions to boost bee courses, Helen Simmons, 36 – a beekeeper on the bee steering group and a member of the Newcastle & District Beekeepers' Association – says that the association can now link up beginner beekeepers with organisations running taster days and short courses. 'In contrast, when I wanted to start beekeeping in 2006, the nearest beginners' course I could find was in Leeds!' she exclaims.

The council is also making and installing an observation hive in a local museum and working with the new citywide allotment bee working group to encourage beekeeping on its 63 allotment sites.

But as we discover on our tour of the city, becoming a bee-friendly city is more than improving the environment in which just honeybees can flourish.

'A lot of the work we have done to raise the issue of declining bees, to encourage residents to plant bee-friendly flowers, for example, are of benefit to all types of bees,' Nelson points out. Its dedicated website has a host of information provided by Buglife and the Bumblebee Conservation Trust about gardening for bumblebees and building them a home.

One of the last stops on our tour is to see a bumblebee box being installed in Pets' Corner, a petting zoo run by city rangers and volunteers, set in a beautiful narrow wooded valley. Here we meet city ranger Sarah Capes putting in one of the council's 20 bumblebee boxes. 'We have thinned out trees up the slope and hope to grow more foxgloves and bluebells in an attempt to attract the bumblebees,' she explains.

The small wooden boxes with two chambers and a rubber tube to provide an entry tunnel, rather like the spout of a teapot, are being placed in various locations across the city by rangers, university students and community groups in an attempt to boost bumblebee numbers in the city.

'Next year a priority for the bee steering group will be to increase efforts for solitary bees,' says Nelson.

On our final visit, to Tyne Riverside Country Park, a 24 hectare (60 acre) green space on the western edge of Newcastle on the site of a former coal mine, we see the south-facing wall of a sensory garden where holes are being drilled for solitary mining bees to make their nests. There are also air bricks with chambers at the back for other solitary bees. A short walk from the garden a meadow has been created for the benefit of all pollinators.

What singles out Newcastle from other towns and cities that are raising awareness about bees in schools or changing allotment rules is the sheer scale of the operation, the number of partners involved, and how they are being supported by the city council. Above all, the political will and leadership has made it happen, says Timothy. He points out that after the bee steering group was created, Cllr Huddart continued to contribute ideas and chair meetings.

Working in partnership has kept down the costs of the bee strategy. The council has drawn on partners' expert knowledge, such as the design of bumblebee boxes, to make things in-house, and partners have been able to access extra funds not available to the council. The council's financial contribution of around £10k has paid towards publicity material, equipment, training, bumblebee boxes and helping to make allotments more bee-friendly.

'I met with real support when I knocked on the right doors for a bit of finance for the project,' says Hails, who chairs the bee steering group. 'In a short space of time we have been able to rethink practices, bring in new initiatives and plan for more, and at a very minimal cost,' adds Huddart.

All of which has put Newcastle on course to become the first major city in the UK to achieve Bee Guardian status – the new kitemark being developed by the Bee Guardian Foundation.

And the city council is hoping to host a bee conference with the university to bring local authorities and academics from across the UK together to discuss future work.

'I'm sure that what we have started in our small way could easily be reproduced in any other urban local authority,' says Huddart.

The bee guardians making cities safe havens for bees

Jessie Jowers is on a mission to make cities across the UK safe havens for all bee species. She is one half of the Bee Guardian Foundation, an organisation set up by herself and Carlo Montesanti, to help landowners, communities and individuals to protect their local bees.

'There has been so much publicity about the threats faced by one type of bee, that bumblebees and solitary bees have been over-looked, and there are a lot more of them,' says Jowers. 'Honeybees have lots of people looking out for them but we wanted to be the public representative of other bees, of which there are around 250 species in the UK.'

The foundation is based in the Cotswolds town of Stroud where it began its crusade. In 2009, it rented an empty shop in the town centre and set up a bee emporium where customers could buy a bee house – in which solitary bees can lay their eggs – or commission a wooden sculpture to provide a solitary bee habitat, and take part in educational and artistic bee-related workshops.

Jowers, 32, put her set design training to good use enticing people in through the front door with eye-catching window displays of bees and flowers. There was just one problem.

'People generally came in asking to buy honey, but we didn't sell any. So they were a bit confused that here was something calling itself a bee shop that didn't sell any honey or beeswax candles,' Jowers laughs. 'But when we explained to them that there were hundreds of other bees in this country that didn't make honey or beeswax but were important pollinators and also under threat most of them wanted to know how they could help.'

As well as the usual advice to grow bee-friendly plants and to avoid pesticides and weedkillers, they were also told to set up nest boxes and leave areas of the garden undisturbed for ground-nesting bees. 'By taking these small steps we told them they would become bee guardians,' says Jowers.

Schoolchildren and volunteers also constructed 350 solitary bee houses that local residents are now monitoring for use in gardens across Stroud. Stroud High School also ran a Royal Society-funded project investigating the nesting behaviour of solitary bees. The data from both gardens and the school will be collated and analysed by Gloucester University to produce guidance on the best way to help solitary bees.

'With bees very much at the forefront of people's minds, but with everyone focused on honeybees, this work could not be more timely,' says Adam Hart, social entomologist at the university and the foundation's scientific director.

At the university's Cheltenham campus, Hart and Jowers show us the wildflower meadows that have been planted, and the biggest bee house we have ever seen, with hundreds of hollow chambers where different bees can lay their eggs. An information board with photos explains to visitors that red mason bees, tawny mining bees and leafcutter bees are the species of solitary bee they are most likely to see.

'Andrena fulva's a beauty,' says Hart, using the Latin name for the small, bright orange tawny mining bee that nests in lawns and emerges in early spring through a little volcano-shaped mound.

Hart's and Jowers's enthusiasm and passion for these bees is palpable. They want to share this with the public, to communicate their crucial role as pollinators and to alert people to their dramatic decline and the simple things we can all do to help.

'Wild bees can be more effective on certain crops than honey-bees. In apple orchards, 600 solitary bees can perform as much pollination as 30,000 honeybees,' explains one of its leaflets. 'Wild bee populations are declining dramatically corresponding to the decline in wildflowers. Agricultural intensification has reduced the availability of forage and nesting sites for wild bees and other pollinators. As populations of bees become isolated they are more prone to extinction.'

People in Stroud have responded positively. Some 8,000 people have become Bee Guardians and, after being contacted by the foundation, local MP Neil Carmichael raised the profile of solitary bees in the local newspaper.

'Hives are not the only place where bees can be found, some live underground – know as mining bees – and others in cavities,' he wrote. 'A proper understanding of the facts about bees will ultimately protect them and aid conservation.'

Now the foundation is taking its message to Gloucester. In November 2010, ITV viewers in the south-west of England voted for the foundation to win £46,000 of lottery funding to make Gloucester the world's first Bee Guardian city.

Arriving on a bright spring morning, we have come to see what this bee-friendly city will look like. As we drive into the centre, Jowers points to a roundabout covered in colourful pansies – the type of civic floral display that can be seen the length and breadth of Britain at this time of year.

'This is the last time you'll ever see those in Gloucester,' she says triumphantly. 'In May they will be taken up and replaced this summer by bee-friendly flowers. In the autumn bee-friendly herbaceous perennials will be planted that will take the place of annual bedding plants forever.'

At the council offices, Phil Matthews, who is in charge of grounds maintenance for Gloucester City Council, confirms that Victorian bedding schemes have had their day, not just for the city's 15 main roundabouts, but in council parks and open spaces.

The Bee Guardian Foundation can't claim all the credit for this change of heart. 'We have to manage our grounds and neighbourhoods better and differently in these austere times,' says Matthews. But he adds: 'It was fortuitous that the Bee Guardian Foundation approached us at the same time the council was re-examining its practices.'

Herbaceous and longer-lasting plants as well as wildflowers require less watering, less weeding and less fertiliser compared with more traditional floral displays. The council will also cut the grass less often and allow clovers and dandelions to flower. 'Grassland management currently costs hundreds of thousands of pounds a year and we have cropped the grass so short that it is a desert for wildlife,' says Matthews.

This summer, the foundation plans to involve and educate local residents in this new approach and to bring in grants and sponsorship. It will work with a dozen community groups and primary schools and four secondary schools across the city to get adults and children designing and building bee habitats and engaging in bee-related arts projects. Each school will receive a Bee Guardian package of wildflower seeds and fruit trees for planting in their grounds to provide long-term blossom for bees and, in some cases, fruit for pupils.

The Stroud High School project demonstrated that if there is not enough forage in the vicinity not even the most elaborate bee house will attract visitors. Its project to monitor solitary bee nesting habitats was initially unsuccessful because of a lack of forage.

When we visit, the foundation had just applied to the Forestry Commission's Big Tree Plant funding scheme for 1,600 additional bee-friendly trees in Gloucester. The species were carefully chosen by the council's tree officer to flower from early spring to late autumn and to flourish in the city's heavy clay soil.

'We'll ask local people where they would like the trees to go and get them to help plant them,' says Jowers. 'My dad used to plant trees in the villages around where we lived in the Forest of Dean and I remember helping him when I was a child,' she recalls. 'Now when I go back they are mature trees and I think, "Wow, I planted that." It gives you a real sense of connection with the place.'

Gloucester will be a test bed for the Bee Guardian Foundation's ambitious plan to create bee-friendly cities across the UK and beyond. It is developing the Bee Guardian kitemark based on the principles of the fairtrade movement. 'Just as hundreds of towns have achieved Fairtrade status by adhering to strict criteria about supporting and using products with a fairtrade mark, cities will be able to achieve Bee Guardian status if they can demonstrate a commitment to things like eliminating pesticide use, setting up bee-friendly habitats and following planting schemes beneficial to all pollinating bees,' Jowers explains.

Stumbling blocks that have emerged in Gloucester, and could prove hurdles for other cities applying for Bee Guardian status in the future, include the relationship between the city and county council, and issues with the planning process for new builds. In Gloucester, the county council is responsible for highways maintenance and is still planting grasses rather than wildflowers, and the planning process fails to make the provision of bee-friendly landscaped gardens a condition of planning consent.

The foundation started its project here without the support of elected members, so it had no councillor championing its cause. As we have seen, this is in sharp contrast to Newcastle where Cllr Doreen Huddart spearheaded its bee strategy. The foundation has since visited Newcastle to learn from its bee-friendly model and is now trying to win the support of both city and council councillors.

It hopes in the future to raise funds to become an independent assessor of Bee Guardian status and to run awards for Bee Guardian schools, businesses and families. Eventually, the foundation wants to turn itself into a grant-giving organisation to support communities and schools to help bees.

With their ambition, drive and vision, it is no surprise to learn that Jowers and Montesanti were recognised as among the top ten young social entrepreneurs in 2010.

Not content with the foundation's busy summer schedule, Jowers will spend next winter studying solitary bees in Mexico, Ecuador and the US on a Churchill Fellowship to examine the cultural significance of indigenous bees in the United States and South America before the honeybees' introduction by white settlers.

'The ancient Mayan civilisation worshipped the meliponine bees in the forests and their priests harvested this stingless bees' honey as part of a religious ceremony twice a year. I want to come back with more stories like this,' she says. 'There is a cultural understanding of the honeybee, but maybe if we had the same for other bees people may feel more concerned about saving them.'

PART III

How you can become an urban beekeeper

The basics

So, you've read about the new explosion in beekeeping and you think you might like to take it up yourself. Great. But be aware that honeybee colonies are complex social structures and there is a great deal to learn if you decide to take up beekeeping.

To give a brief overview: at the most basic level a colony contains one queen bee (the egg-laying female), and in the summer a few hundred drones (fertile males) and up to 50,000 sterile, female worker bees.

After the virgin queen's nuptial flight, in which she mates with several drones away from her home colony, her job is to lay eggs in the single hexagonal cells of the wax honeycomb, which is produced by the worker bees. Workers live for about six weeks in the summer – three weeks in the hive attending to the brood (the larvae), receiving and storing nectar (their energy drink) and pollen (their protein) from the forager bees for food, and guarding the hive from intruders, and three weeks outside foraging, using a pattern of dancing to communicate to fellow bees where the best sources of food lie, and pollinating flowers as they visit them for food.

Inside the hive there will be separate areas of honeycomb where nectar is transformed into honey and stored to feed the colony during winter. As beekeepers, we can harvest the bees' honey in the summer, but we need to leave enough for them to survive the winter.

We will examine all this in detail later in the chapter, but first let's look at how you get started as an urban beekeeper.

Planning and preparation

Anyone can take up this urban pastime, given the right location, a small amount of time, a few hundred pounds and some know-how. You have read about how school teachers, office workers and allotment holders are among the people doing it. So how do *you* do it?

You need to be prepared to read some books and invest in some training before getting your bees. You'll also need to give up an hour a week during the summer to look through the hive to make sure all is well and, when necessary, to give your bees an extension to their home where they can store their honey. The great news for fair-weather outdoor types is that during the cold months the bees are not active, so there is little hands-on beekeeping and you are not exposed to the elements. In fact, you must not open a hive from October to February when the bees are keeping their home warm and snug. Instead, you'll probably find yourself using this time to read up on what you need to do for the following season, buy extra equipment and make new frames of beeswax foundation that go in the hive.

What you can't do as a beekeeper is simply put a hive at the bottom of the garden with your bees in and just leave it. Although honeybees have survived for millions of years in dark cavities, such as the hollow of tree trunks, we as beekeepers have a responsibility to care for our bees. Nowadays, the species of honeybee kept and bred throughout Europe, the western honeybee, comes with a parasitic mite, called varroa destructor. While we can't completely eliminate this bloodsucker that spreads viruses and weakens our bees, we can help to reduce its numbers by careful animal husbandry. Methods vary, so one very good reason for joining a local beekeeping association and registering with the government's online information resource, BeeBase, is to keep abreast of the latest scientific thinking and products for mite control.

In a built-up urban environment, where there may be many beekeepers in close proximity, it is especially important for beekeepers to be vigilant against viruses and disease. If a colony of bees a few streets away from yours has disease, chances are they could spread the problem to your bees and vice versa.

Another major concern in a densely populated area is that bees and humans are going to come into conflict. You don't need permission to keep bees in your city backyard. There are no by-laws that we know of, although if you want to keep bees on allotments, office rooftops, school grounds or other land that isn't yours, permission will need to be granted.

At home, it is up to you to decide whether it is appropriate to tell your neighbours that you are planning to keep bees. You may want to come to a mutually beneficial arrangement about when to do the weekly hive inspection, well before the new arrivals move in. Maybe Saturday lunchtime when they are out doing their weekly shopping, or a Sunday morning before they are out of bed? Our neighbours have always responded positively to having bees next door. They have even asked if their children can take a look.

In fact, young children are commonly fascinated by bugs, and beekeeping is a great way to introduce them to nature. Friends with bees and children tell us that eight or nine is a good age to get them helping with hands-on weekly inspections and honey harvests later in the summer (see page 209).

We often get asked if pets and bees go together. If our cat is typical, then the answer is yes. She lay sprawled across our flat-roof hive, empty of bees, sunning herself every day for weeks while we waited for a call to collect our first swarm. When they finally arrived and had been transferred to their new home we were concerned she might get a nasty shock. But we needn't have worried, because she never set foot near the buzzing hive again. Dogs can be more boisterous, so it is worth shutting them indoors when you are doing a hive inspection.

As for other urban animals, such as the foxes that frequent city gardens in search of food, we have not heard of anyone whose hives have been vandalised by vulpine visitors. Reports of badgers intruding on urban areas are potentially more worrisome. These well-known honey and worm-lovers dig up bumblebee nests in the countryside and are strong enough to knock over a hive and root out the honey and grub-like brood with their sharp claws and long snouts. So you may have to erect a fence to protect your hives if these nocturnal raiders come calling.

Woodpeckers can also prove a nuisance on the edge of towns and cities. They feed on bee larvae and are adapt at pecking through wooden hives to get to the brood. Putting chicken wire around the hive should see them off.

The potential for disputes with neighbours means that it is crucial in an urban environment to find a location for your bees where they will have minimal contact with people, and of course you should also practise some form of swarm management. A black swirling cloud of bees, while fairly harmless, will alarm most people who witness it. One of the objectives of weekly hive inspections throughout the spring and summer is to check for signs that your bees plan to swarm and to manage this natural process. You can learn about swarm control on a second-year beekeeping course, from books or an experienced beekeeper. But like anything to do with beekeeping, you will find there is no right or wrong way. 'Get two beekeepers in a room and there will be three opinions' is a typical adage about beekeeping.

What you don't want to do is to become so bewildered by all the different, and often conflicting, bits of advice you receive from well-meaning old-timers that you give up beekeeping in the first year. The key is to find a way that is good for you, your bees and your local community. We believe that you can make beekeeping as complicated or as simple as you want. You don't need a biology degree, a woodwork diploma or a horticultural certificate. Just a little time, patience and a willingness to learn will suffice. Beekeeping is both an art and a science so there is always room for creativity and invention.

But beekeeping isn't right for everyone. The sight of a nucleus of 10,000 bees when you open the box they arrive in, ideally in spring or early summer, can be overwhelming. People often ask us if they could have just a mini-colony of bees. It's a nice idea, especially for a small urban space, but unfortunately nature is not so accommodating. To survive, honeybees need to live in colonies of around 10,000 in the winter and grow to five times that size in the summer. You would never know, however, that such a huge population was packed into your hive from the few you seem to see coming and going. It is only when you open the hive that the magnitude becomes apparent. And even then if you look during the middle of the day many of the foraging bees will be out.

If you are intimidated by the thought of so many insects in close proximity, or the commitment or knowledge required to become a beekeeper, you could think about sharing the responsibility and building your confidence by buddying up with a friend, work colleagues or someone you have met on a beekeeping course who lives locally. You could either get one hive between you or buy two and maintain them separately but carry out the inspections and the honey harvesting together. We know of two women who recently met on a course in London and live down the road from one another. Each got their own hive and bees, and then decided to put both hives in the largest garden and do all of their beekeeping together. It's a great way to spread the workload and learn together. And you'll find you will have different strengths; while one of you might like knocking up frames, the other might be better at making meticulous notes about what was seen in the beehive after each inspection. Four eyes are better than two for spotting the queen bee and where she is laying her eggs. It also makes beekeeping a more social event where friends can get together on a sunny afternoon or summer's evening to chat and check on their bees. And of course when one person is on holiday, the other can bee-sit. If you are really lucky, or persistent, you may be able to encourage an experienced beekeeper to mentor you and your buddies.

Buddying is also an excellent way to share costs. Who needs their own £200 extractor for spinning honey off the comb? And where do you put the cumbersome contraption in a small terraced house?

With the cost of beekeeping spiraling over the last few years due to a decline in the bee population coupled with an explosion in the number of people wanting to take up the hobby, money could hold you back. Let's face it: beekeeping will never save you money. Honey will always be cheaper to buy in the shops than producing it yourself, but it won't be local and it is not nearly so exciting taking a jar from the supermarket shelf as removing a frame of honeycomb from your hive.

If you are handy with a hammer and enjoy DIY, beekeeping will cost a little less because much of what you need can come through the post flat-packed. But don't worry if you can't put together the simplest Ikea furniture. You can get the hive already assembled for a slightly higher price. The frames of beeswax foundation will also need piecing together. But this is a much easier job that even someone who finds it hard to hit a nail straight should be able to master with a little guidance and practice.

In general, don't expect change from £800 in your first year. Although costs are considerably less thereafter, you still need to have an annual contingency fund of, say, £200. And it is not advisable to try to do beekeeping on the cheap. Second-hand equipment can harbour disease and hives made from less durable material than cedar wood or good pine will not last as long.

Keeping bees at work

If you are planning to keep bees at work, your employer may well insist that a group of you takes responsibility for the hive to cover holidays or business trips. For us, beekeeping was a pursuit away from the office that we could enjoy together. But if you don't have outside space at home, or a partner who shares your passion for bees, or you just don't want your *pied-à-terre* cluttered with beekeeping paraphernalia, then a roof at work could be the solution. And it may be a hobby you'd rather do in your lunch hour than after work or at the weekends. Some employers may be particularly receptive to having their own company beehive because it ties in with their biodiversity strategy or they like the idea of having their own honey in the staff canteen, so you may be lucky and find that they agree to cover the costs of the bees and equipment and pay for a group of you to be trained.

The beekeeping community

We have met lots of interesting, like-minded people on our apian travels, but just like any community beekeepers are a mixed bag. There are people who get very involved in their local association, those who just come along to meetings and others who pay their subs but hardly ever turn up. We found that the times some of the meetings were held, for example 6 p.m. on a Friday, made it impossible for busy professionals who work long hours in the City to attend, or they were not conducive to younger people with an active social life. But it is impossible to please everyone, so it's up to you to find your own place within the beekeeping community and to decide how involved you want, or are able, to be. Don't be put off by the old guard of retired men who are probably running the show. After all, they have been keeping bees and running the assocations for years when no one else was much interested. Now with the flood of new members, many will be delighted if you are willing to write a newsletter or collect the subs. But there may well be some friction between the old hands and the new blood.

The last organisations we each belonged to were the girl guides and scouts. We're just not the committee types. So joining a beekeeping association was anathema, but we were keen to learn and wanted the support of experienced beekeepers. We also wanted to feel part of a community. We joined two different associations but as a couple we could accompany each other to their association meetings, so we were able to take what we liked from each. One association met at a convenient time in a nearby venue and had some like-minded younger members; the other was further away and met at an awkward time for one of us, but it was renowned for its training apiary and the standard of its teaching.

It can be quite intimidating when you meet apiarists who have been keeping bees for 20 years or more (and many have). There is a tendency to think that you need to have been doing it for this length of time before you have anything to say on the matter. But don't be afraid to ask questions. After the initial silence, most people will be only too pleased to share their wisdom. And you'll soon find out that the longer you keep bees the more perplexing their behaviour becomes. There is an old adage in beekeeping circles that bees don't read books. So no matter how knowledgeable an apiarist you are, your bees can always surprise you.

If you are thinking of keeping bees on an allotment, many insist that you pass the BBKA basic beekeeping assessment after your first year of beekeeping to demonstrate that you know what you're doing. Most associations will teach this or you can do the BBKA correspondence course, with a practical exam taken at your association apiary. There are more advanced modules in every aspect of beekeeping. In fact, if you're the type of person who likes taking courses and exams then you can always find something to master. If, however, your last exam was at school, and you have no intention of ever doing one again, you can still keep abreast of the latest thinking on disease prevention by attending the occasional talk or workshop, often given by a government bee inspector.

Many urban-based associations are a branch of a countywide beekeepers' group, so, for example, North London Beekeepers' Association is part of Middlesex beekeepers, Liverpool is part of Lancashire, and Birmingham is part of Warwickshire. Most local associations are affiliated to the BBKA, which has more than 65 association members. BBKA membership entitles each beekeeper to third-party liability in the unlikely event that your bees cause any harm and to product insurance if your hives have to be destroyed because of disease. Your association will send delegates to the BBKA's annual delegate meeting (ADM) to elect the BBKA's executive committee and vote on matters arising.

If urban beekeeping is in its infancy where you live you may not have a local beekeeping association. Try to find other aspiring apiarists in your area to form one. In east London, where hives are shooting up on rooftops, housing estates and city farms, a number of beekeepers have got together on an informal basis to share advice.

You may decide that you don't want your new association to be affiliated to the BBKA. For the past few years it has been endorsing certain pesticides in exchange for cash. With some pesticides implicated in the death of honeybees worldwide, this cash-for-endorsement policy has led to heated debates among members over the ethical issue raised. Although the BBKA finally ceased its endorsements in 2011 after a concerted campaign by a few members, it has not ruled out taking money in the future from pesticide manufacturers, and is proposing to develop new relationships with them as different products come onto the market.

BBKA president Martin Smith says it has a 'policy of actively engaging with the plant protection industry in an attempt to provide stewardship of pesticides and agricultural practice to minimise damage to honeybees and to ensure that the views of the beekeeper are taken into account in the development of pesticides and their application in the field.' As a result, it has allowed its logo to be used on four synthetic pyrethroid-based pesticides. 'These products ... appear to offer reduced risks for harm to honeybees when used correctly,' he says. 'The BBKA has received modest payments for these endorsements ... The four products are today of declining commercial importance [which] means that the relationship with the plant protection industry should be reviewed. The trustees do not preclude accepting funds in the future from the crop protection industry.'

Yet Graham White, a beekeeper who resigned over the endorsement policy, speaks for many apiarists when he says: 'The BBKA is not fit for purpose and will never recover its moral integrity until it is ... willing to campaign against all uses of systemic pesticides on British farms.' It is, of course, up to you to decide where you stand on the matter.

Natural beekeeping

We describe ourselves as bee-friendly beekeepers because our motivation for keeping bees was to reconnect with nature and to provide them with a safe haven. Unlike most old-school beekeepers we aren't in it for the honey, so our beekeeping practices are focused on the bee rather than maximising honey production. As a result we don't, for example, rob most of our bees' honey at the end of summer and replace it with an inferior sugar-syrup solution. And we don't try to stop our bees from swarming because it will slow down honey production. But we are not part of the so-called 'natural beekeeping movement' which promotes a hands-off style of keeping bees.

If you are planning to keep bees in an urban environment, densely populated by both humans and bees, you owe it to your bees and other beekeepers to practice both varroa control and swarm management, otherwise your bees could spread disease and come into conflict with people. How long before complaints about swarming bees lead to a council passing by-laws prohibiting beekeeping in urban areas? This would be a sad day not only for the bees, which seem to be thriving in towns and cities, but also for urban apiarists who are nurturing their love of living things and for the urban environment which greatly benefits from their presence.

Stings

You will inevitably be stung, even through your new bee suit. How often partly depends on you and partly on the temperament of your bees. Bees are not sting-happy creatures because the action kills them, but if they feel under threat they will respond. And as a beekeeper opening the hives either to check the health of the bee colony or to take some honey, you are a potential target.

Bees can't see slow movements, so the more calm and relaxed you are around the hive the less likely you are to disturb them. If, however, you are tense and your movements are jerky, clumsy and hurried, chances are they will become agitated and sting.

Taking care to zip up your bee suit, sticking down the Velcro bits and tucking your trousers into socks or boots will reduce your sting count. Bees can get into the smallest gaps and they seem to be attracted to dark places, such as inside sleeves or trousers legs. We found wellies are the best safeguard against getting stung on the ankle, which is a memorable experience. Marigold rubber gloves seem to protect hands pretty well, but replace them regularly as they can get holey.

When a honeybee stings, she leaves her venom sac and pump in the skin after she pulls away. Most of the venom will be injected in the first 20 seconds but the pump can continue for up to two minutes. You can mitigate the impact of a bee sting by scraping out the sting with a fingernail or hive tool quickly. But the bee also leaves a pheromone in her sting that tells her sisters to also attack you. You can prevent this happening by moving slowly away from the hive and smoking the area that has been stung to mask the smell of this alarm pheromone.

A normal reaction to a sting is pain and a localised swelling followed by a couple of days of itchiness. Some beekeepers build up an immunity to bee venom to the point where there is hardly any swelling or itchiness. Others can develop an allergic reaction that in the most serious cases can lead to a potentially fatal anaphylactic shock. It is impossible to tell how your body may react over time. We had no idea when we started out that one of us would end up hardly reacting and the other would have to attend an allergy clinic.

Alternatives to beekeeping

If you decide that you aren't ready for the commitment, costs and possible pain involved in urban beekeeping, there are other ways to participate in the growing movement without owning a hive.

As we discussed in Part II, you can help to save honeybees more effectively by planting a variety of trees and plants that are rich in nectar and pollen throughout the year. And instead of having a hive in your garden you could create suitable habitats for bumblebees and solitary bees in small urban green spaces.

There are more than 20,000 species of bee worldwide. The majority are wild solitary bees that as their name suggests do not live in colonies but alone. In the UK there are some 250 different types of solitary bee. The most common of these are mining bees, leafcutter bees (which cut circles out of leaves and petals to build nests), and mason bees. You can help these wild bees by providing nests in your garden called bee houses or hotels. These simple structures are made from attaching a collection of hollow tubes, often made from bamboo canes, to a sunny wall where the female bee will hopefully check in for a short stay to lay her eggs. Drilling holes in a south-facing wall will do just as well for mining bees to make their nest. You can now also buy solitary bee houses in most garden centres or from organisations such as the Bee Guardian Foundation or the Golden Company.

There are 250 different types of bumblebee globally. Of these, 24 are found in Britain, including the red-tailed bumblebee, the common carder and the early bumblebee, which is increasingly found in cities. Three species have already become extinct in the UK and six more are at high risk as intensive farming robs them of food and shelter. Bumblebees live in colonies like honeybees, but they are much smaller, consisting of up to 1,000 bees. Unlike honeybees, they die out each year leaving only the queen to hibernate through the winter. She will make a new colony in the spring. Some bumblebees make their home underground in nests vacated by mice, others in long grass. By having a few upturned flowerpots placed on the ground with a small gap, you may provide a queen with a nest for the winter. Leaving a section of your garden untidy all year round with piles of leaves and small twigs may also encourage bumblebee colonies to nest there, as well as many other creatures. An old teapot buried in the ground with the spout providing an entry tunnel makes a good secure nest site if it can be kept free from damp. Some garden centres now sell bumble boxes, but the success rate of these artificial nest boxes is low. In a Canadian study, only 7 per cent of nest boxes were occupied. Closer to home, a study at Stirling University had just 3.1 per cent of nest boxes showing any kind of occupancy.

Courses

If you decide from what you have read so far that you do want to give beekeeping a go, you can't just buy the hive and the bees and start doing it. Careful planning and preparation are required. Is the sliver of urban space you have identified going to work for you and the bees? Have you sufficient time and enough money to take up this hobby? Above all you need to know how to manage bees in close proximity to people and to find out if you are comfortable handling a 50,000-strong colony.

There are plenty of beginners' books, but they can't answer all your queries, illustrate all the problems you may encounter on your beekeeping journey, or give you hands-on practical experience. You will need to go on a beekeeping course.

'Keeping bees without doing an introductory course is like driving a car without having any lessons. You're a menace to yourself and others,' says Chris Deaves, chairman of the BBKA education and husbandry committee.

There are a variety of beginners' courses and more advanced ones to help you progress. What they offer is partly determined by the time of year they are run, how long they last, and where they are held. Your choice of course may be limited by the availability of places, when you want to learn, and how far you are prepared to travel.

Learning about bees on a taster beekeeping course for just a few hours during the winter or early spring has its drawbacks, namely that it is too cold to open the hives and handle the bees, so the courses will be theory based. Instead they will provide an introduction to how a bee colony works, what you need in order to set up a hive, the workings of a hive, seasonal bee management and how to harvest your honey. They are designed with the intention of equipping aspiring apiarists with the knowledge they need to decide whether or not beekeeping is really for them, and if so what to do next, as well as introducing them to some like-minded people with whom they may be able to share their newfound passion.

One advantage, however, of going on a one-day course in the winter is that should you decide to give beekeeping a shot it gives

Urban Bees blog   7 October 2009

'Just wanted to say thanks again for Sunday's taster course. I've been reading my bee books again and it all makes much more sense now. I was interested in keeping bees before but am now definitely planning to make a start next spring.'

Cathy

you plenty of time to enrol for more hands-on training, buy the kit and order your bees for the coming spring.

Many beekeeping associations run courses for beginners on long summer evenings, others have introductory courses for about 12 weeks that start in the classroom in winter before moving out to the apiary in the spring.

Hands-on learning really gets you established as a beekeeper. It builds your confidence in being around bees and develops your knowledge and skills over time. Each week you will be inspecting hives with an experienced beekeeper, so you will become familiar with the workings of a colony, what a healthy brood looks like, when and how to add honey supers (see page 207) and how to harvest the honey. If you get your own bees while attending a course, you can immediately transfer what you have learned in the training apiary that night to your hive the next day.

In our first year of beekeeping, one of us regularly attended Friday nights at Twickenham and Thames Valley Beekeepers' Association in west London. Here, a few novice beekeepers are assigned a hive to inspect every week with a mentor. We found it invaluable to have a hive we could compare to ours, as well as having someone whose brain we could pick about what was going on in our hives.

When deciding which course to take, you may also need to make a choice between two fundamentally different approaches to beekeeping: the conventional school of frame-based beekeeping promoted by beekeeping associations, or the more hands-off top-bar, or 'Warré hive', beekeeping practised by the natural beekeeping movement (whose chief proponents Phil Chandler, the Barefoot Beekeeper, and the Natural Beekeeping Trust are based respectively in Devon and Plaw Hatch biodynamic farm in Sussex). This unorthodox style requires different training and equipment, neither of which is so readily available as the more established frame-based method.

Our advice to anyone thinking of taking up urban beekeeping is to first learn the basics from a conventional trainer. Once you understand how a colony works and what hive management is required in an urban environment, then you are ready to decide if you wish to pursue a different beekeeping technique in your backyard.

Until recently, the more orthodox training was only provided by local beekeeping associations. But the huge surge of interest in beekeeping has left many associations oversubscribed for beginners' courses, while others have closed their doors to new members because they do not have the capacity to mentor them.

This widening gap between demand and supply, particularly in towns and cities, is being filled by a new breed of beekeeper: the commercial trainers, who we have seen are at the vanguard of the urban beekeeping revolution.

Many of these trainers are being funded by charitable foundations, companies or councils to deliver urban beekeeping courses. What these sponsored training schemes share is a focus on long-term, free education. By doing so they address the limitations of traditional beginners' classes.

'Those 10-week summer courses run by associations only teach you half the story,' says third-year London beekeeper Rowena Young. 'Come the following spring, you've got no idea about cleaning the hive, or swarm management techniques.'

In contrast, at the Co-op-funded London training apiary at Camley Street Nature Park, trainees gather on a cold, bright morning at the beginning of January to continue classes started the previous May. They learn how to apply oxalic acid (see page 192), checking the hives to see if the bees had sufficient winter stores, and they discuss the extra equipment needed for the forthcoming spring clean and swarm management.

The BBKA states that many new beekeepers drop out in their first year as their bees die out over winter and they lose interest. The new courses intend to reverse this trend.

'It is not enough to cover the bare essentials,' says Anna Cooper, project manager of Groundwork Sheffield's Bee Buddies scheme. 'An in-depth knowledge of the logistics of bees and beekeeping equipment is needed to understand the workings of a hive and produce a sustainable honey stock. Courses that provide a few days' theory and free equipment do not work. Ongoing support is required as seasonal problems will be encountered.'

In addition to providing free training and a year-long mentor for each trainee, the scheme, like many of the sponsored training programmes, gives away bees and equipment to participants.

'We only let hives pass into the ownership of trainees if the head beekeeper feels they are competent,' says Cooper. 'This is often overlooked on some courses and trainees are given bees anyway at the end of the course.'

Once you have found the right course for you and secured a place, you will need to start thinking seriously about the exact location of your urban apiary. You may find that the place you have in mind turns out not to be appropriate for either you or your bees.

Location, location location

where to put your hive

So you've got a vague idea that you want to keep a hive in the backyard or on the allotment or at the terrace at work. But what do you need to consider when you choose the exact location for your bees?

Morning sun, for example, is nice to have as it encourages bees to forage early, which will bring in more food. So, in theory, they are likely to make more honey if they live in an east-facing hive. But are you only keeping bees for their honey-making prowess? Bees in our old west London garden got the sun all afternoon and seemed more than happy foraging until late on balmy summer evenings. Moreover, we got plenty of honey.

Bees don't like wind by the entrance of the hive; it makes it tougher to fly in and out. Think of yourself cycling home in a gale. So a sheltered spot protected from prevailing winds is best. This can be achieved by placing the entrance towards a hedge or a wall. But if a windy rooftop is your only option, you can minimise the blustery conditions by constructing a wind break or by strategically placing some hardy plants in close proximity. You should also weigh down the hive by placing something heavy, such as sand-bags or a paving stone, over the cross bars of the hive stand, and strap the hive to the stand to stop the roof blowing off.

Bees regulate the temperature inside the hive to keep the brood (the eggs and larvae at all stages of development) at a cosy 35°C (95°F). But don't put the hive in a dip where cold air can get trapped, as it will mean the colony has to work harder to keep the brood warm. That said, bees survive in much colder climes than the British Isles. A covering of snow in the winter will actually insulate the hive. So there is no need to wrap it up in a duvet if the weather turns freezing.

Damp is more of a problem. The inside of a hive is already humid because bees evaporate water from the nectar to turn it into honey. They get rid of excess moisture by rapidly fanning their wings at the entrance of the hive, but if it is in a damp location the bees may not be able to reduce the humidity and when you open up the hive after winter you will see frames of beeswax black with mould. Lifting the hive off the ground by placing it on a hive stand can help; a milk crate or pile of bricks will act as a hive stand just as well as the bought ones.

Bees leave the hive to collect four substances: protein-rich pollen to eat and feed their larvae; energy-boosting nectar, which they turn into honey; propolis, a tree resin they use like Polyfilla to seal any small holes and which also serves an antiseptic in the hive; and water to drink, to cool the hive and to dilute the honey they feed to their young.

Studies show that bees will fly anywhere from between a few hundred metres to up to 12 km (7.5 miles) in extreme circumstances to find a plentiful supply of food, although in cities where there is forage in parks, gardens and tree-lined roads they are unlikely to have to venture more than a mile or so. They will not forage, however, within a few feet of the hive. This is because it is the vicinity in which they will defecate. Bees go on shorter trips to find water, so if your neighbour has a good source they make a beeline for it and hang around their pond, which may not be appreciated. If that is a problem, you may have to create a source yourself nearer to home. Bees can't swim, so the best option is damp moss that they can walk on without drowning, rather than a pond, drinking fountain, or even a bowl of water. These will require you to add some floating sticks or stones for the bees to stand on while they quench their thirst.

When you come to site your hive it is worth remembering that bees only fly from dawn to dusk, so if you are tight for space in your

Co-Op Plan Bee blog   11 May 2010

'I am still undecided as to where to place my hive – Brian says that a spot that catches the early sun is good, but that would have to be very close to my vegetable patch. I might need to build a fence around the hives to make them fly above me when I attend to the veg. Don't want them getting in my hair.'

Kate Griffiths-Lambeth

garden it is reassuring to know you can walk around your hives unprotected at the end of the day to get to the compost bin, pick fruit or pull up weeds.

Wherever you choose to put your hive another question you will need to ask yourself is: 'Is there space to expand?' Bees have a natural tendency to swarm, and if you manage the process correctly (see page 156) one colony will rapidly become two. Many bee-keepers in fact recommend that you start with two colonies rather than one because given the rates of loss you could end up bee-less and demoralised after your first winter and give up the hobby. A second hive could be handy for providing a new queen should one stop laying or become aggressive, and it can act as a comparison if you decide to try out different management techniques in each of your hives.

You can put hives within a couple of feet of each other. The bees will know which one to come home to. It is worth thinking hard about the number of hives you may end up keeping before you get your first hive. There may be enough room in your small backyard for one, but if you'd prefer two or even three, you may have to spend some time finding a larger location.

Our first hive was at the back of our 9 m (30 ft) garden, facing a 2 m (7 ft) wall in west London. As you'd expect with a Victorian terrace, it was surrounded on all sides by other gardens, but one of the advantages of living in a city was that they were hardly ever used. The neighbours on one side were a succession of tenants who had let their garden go to rack and ruin and never attempted to navigate the jungle-like overgrowth, and on the other side were empty back-yards attached to a row of shops. The couple of gardens backing on to the wall occasionally had clothes drying on a washing line, but there were never any barbecues or parties. Yet even if the gardens had been teeming with people, by placing the entrance of the hive facing a high wall we forced the bees to fly above head height when they came out so they would not bother the neighbours.

When bees return home, laden with up to half their body weight in nectar and pollen, they approach a hive like an aeroplane coming in to land: on a flight path. Again, facing the hive entrance to a high wall forces them to fly above head height until they have cleared the wall and safely reached your garden. Only then will they start to make their descent.

The ex-council maisonette where we now live in south London in the shadow of tower blocks doesn't have a back garden, just a handkerchief-sized one leading to the front door. Unusually for a front garden, however, it is not exposed to the street. It backs onto garages and parking spaces, is accessed through a gate and has a wall around it. We have added a 1 m (3 ft) trellis to increase the height of the wall and planted a variety of fast-climbing vines, so that residents walking past to get to their cars don't notice the constant flow of bees flying far above their heads on warm sunny days.

The hive is in the corner of the garden, as far from the gate and front door as is possible in such a small area – about 1.2 m (4 ft) from the gate and 9 m (30 ft) from the door. Again, the hive entrance is facing the wall, so the bees are forced to head up and out. This allows the postman and other visitors to walk up the garden path untroubled by the bees and allows us to enjoy what little outdoor space we have without crossing the bees' flight path.

The one location we got wrong was in Alison's parents' 30 m (100 ft) suburban garden. Her father likes to mow the lawn, so we decided to put a couple of hives under the apple and pear trees at the bottom of the garden away from the lawn. It looked idyllic and some shade is useful in hot weather, but come the summer the hives were lost under a thick canopy of leaves and the easiest way for the bees to get out was not up through the branches but out into the open garden. It was fortunate that there was plenty of room. We also forgot that in suburbia, neighbours love to garden and make bonfires to dispose of their mountains of green waste; in the inner city, the few weeds we pull up end up in the recycling bin. For wild honey-bees living in their natural habitat, such as a hollow tree trunk in a forest, the sound of crackling flames and smell of smoke means it is time to vacate and find a new home. So putting a hive close to a bonfire is a no-no if you want to hold on to your bees. Fortunately for us, the smoke from the neighbour's fire must waft just the wrong side of our hives because they are still well and happy.

We couldn't imagine living without bees in London. Our experience demonstrates that with a little thought and some precautions it is possible even in rather cramped conditions. After all, the footprint of a standard National hive is only that of a paving stone. It grows in the summer, as you give the bees extra space to store their honey, but upwards rather than outwards.

The size of a hive makes it possible to even squeeze it onto a balcony. Indeed, balcony beekeepers swear that keeping bees a few floors up in a tower block or a mansion flat is a perfect location for a hive. 'Balconies are ideal: bees fly out and don't bother anyone and they are so accessible,' says one. But she does admit that the bees come indoors. It is one of the reasons why we would advise anyone thinking of keeping bees so close to their living space to seriously consider if it is really the correct spot. Questions you'll need to ask yourself are: will I ever be able to sit on my balcony again? Is the balcony really big enough to allow me to properly manage my bees by, for example, splitting one hive into two colonies to manage swarming (see page 158)? Where am I going to store all the equipment and hive parts? Despite the hive taking up little space, beekeeping paraphernalia soon mounts up, so you will need to earmark a cupboard or part of a shed, utility room or garage for equipment.

In our west London flat, the garden shed sufficed; in south London, a garage houses most of the equipment we now need for six hives, but it is not unknown for hive boxes and frames and foundations to creep indoors at busy times of the year.

Access

There are beehives tucked away in many corners of our cities, hidden from view behind high walls, on rooftops and in private gardens, oblivious to people going about their day-to-day business.

They are concealed or elevated not because they are outlawed or clandestine but to prevent them being vandalised or stolen, or to try to keep the bees from coming into conflict with local residents.

For many urban beekeepers, the saying 'out of sight, out of mind' features heavily in their choice of hive location. But if keeping your hive away from the prying eyes of neighbours dictates your decision you can easily overlook what you as a beekeeper need: easy access.

The hive may be all but invisible on the roof of the house, but if your only way up there is via rickety pull-down stairs and through a small hatch which is hard to open you need to consider whether you could negotiate the opening and the stairs with pieces of hive and equipment, or a box of bees, or even a full super of honey, which can easily weigh 9 kg (20 lbs).

Luckily, you don't have to carry all these things at once and if there are two of you it will make it possible, assuming you really have no choice but to locate the hive in a difficult-to-reach place. You can also reduce the weight of honey you remove from the hive by taking out one or two frames of honeycomb at a time, and replacing them with empty frames of foundation, rather than the conventional practice of waiting until a whole super of 11 heavy frames of honey is ready to be harvested and then carrying it in one go.

Kate Jenrick has mastered the art of unbolting a hatch door, pushing it up and clambering onto a roof in a matter of seconds. The lithe 42-year-old is standing on the top of Essex Court, part of Middle Temple, one of the four Inns of Court in London where barristers have their chambers. It overlooks an acre and a half of immaculate flowerbeds and pristine lawn sweeping down to the Victoria Embankment, tended by Jenrick and the Temple team of gardeners. When she volunteered to take charge of the temple's bees, Jenrick had to find a flat roof among the sloping parapets of the 17th century legal offices to put the hive. It was quite a challenge, she says. But wouldn't the bees have been happier at ground level, we ask, looking down at the lavender-lined walkway that she calls bee alley in August?

Unfortunately, that wasn't an option. The garden is a venue for weddings and parties in the summer and has a café open to the public, so children are often running around unsupervised. As a result it was decided to put the hive on the roof, out of harm's way.

Keeping bees in our small garden has never stopped us from hosting summer parties, but they are always at night when both bees and children are safely tucked up. Guests have been fascinated when they find out there is a hive at the bottom of the garden and the bees are not bothered by the night-time revellers.

Out-apiaries

If on careful consideration you feel that your outside space is insufficient for a beehive or you don't feel comfortable about keeping bees in close proximity to your neighbours, children or pets, you will need to find an out-apiary.

In the countryside, beekeepers often have an out-apiary in a corner of a farmer's field or in an orchard where they can keep more hives than in their garden and provide a pollination service.

In towns and cities out-apiaries, as we have seen, can be sited on allotments, the grounds of schools and universities, city farms, housing estates, cemeteries, office rooftops and even other people's gardens.

The same considerations about wind, sun and space are as relevant to an out-apiary as to putting a hive in your backyard, but in addition you will need to think about access, safety – for the bees and the public – and security.

Angela Richardson, whose allotment plot in Ealing, west London, hugs the Piccadilly tube line that runs out to Heathrow, says of her hive location: 'I have a wild embankment on the other side of the fence and I like this contrast of wild and urban, with the planes going overhead and the trains rumbling by, side by side with foxes, slowworms and frogs. And now honeybees.'

You should not underestimate how much time and effort it could take to find an appropriate site in a town or city. Health and safety fears can make even the most promising-looking location a no-no. Wherever you want to put your hive you will have to seriously consider how potential risks to the public could be mitigated.

A site inspection will have to be carried out to establish exactly where the hive should be located at the proposed site. It is worth getting an experienced beekeeper from your local association to take a look, as they will know what will work for you, the bees and the public. As the school teachers' experiences revealed, very few of their first choices for an apiary were given the go-ahead. Their ideas of having the hives in full view of their pupils or near to where they worked were deemed to be too dangerous.

A rooftop out-apiary at work will probably require the permission of nervous freeholders and insurers. Your risk assessment will have to allay their fears that contractors will be stung and make claims against them. You may want to think about whether there is anywhere on the roof you could change out of your bee suit after a hive inspection to avoid the risk of bringing bees into the office?

The mixed reception received by allotment beekeepers demonstrates that if you are planning to keep bees on your allotment plot you may first have to overturn an allotment-wide bee ban and then persuade neighbouring plot-holders of the value of providing a home for honeybees next door to them.

If the hives are going to come into close proximity to people or pupils, say on an allotment plot, a community garden or a school, you will need to think about fencing off the hives or putting them behind high netting which will encourage the bees to fly above head height.

If they are in public view, display some signage near the hives both to warn people about their presence and inform them who to call in an emergency, but as importantly to educate passers-by about the importance of honeybees.

As the beekeeper, you will ideally have 24-hour access to the apiary, and there will be car parking nearby or secure storage where you can keep your hive parts and equipment.

Commercial beekeeper Ian Wallace advises the use of National single-box hives in out-apiaries. He says in his experience it prevents vandalism because people don't think the stack of boxes is a hive so they leave it alone, whereas if you use a gabled-roof WBC hive, which is most people's common perception of a hive, they know it contains bees. He's had hives tipped over, kids trying to set fire to them by pushing a burning piece of paper through the entrance and even people trying to take the honey. When they open the roof and see all the bees they inevitably run off but the lid is off and the bees are in danger, he says.

His experiences reinforce the importance of having a site that is secure, behind a locked gate to which only you and your bee buddies have the key. But there is also another reason why security is paramount: bee rustling.

It may seem far-fetched but with reports of a nucleus of 10,000 bees changing hands for £220 and a hive full of bees containing five times that number at the height of summer, thieves can make a lot of money from stealing hives. There have been stories of bee rustling in the countryside with criminals using Google maps to hunt out apiaries from the air. In March 2011, five hives were stolen from an apiary just inside the M25 when thieves broke through the locked gates, and now urban beekeepers say they are concerned that they could be targeted in night-time raids. Hives can be tagged like bikes with anti-theft paint, but a secure location is preferable.

One reason it is so important to get the location of your hive right before your bees arrive is that once they are housed, you can't really move their home. Bees make a mental map of their immediate surroundings when they fly out to forage for the first time to stop them getting lost on their return. But they will only redraw this map if the hive is transported more than three miles away. So if you decide that you want to move the hive a few feet further from the back door, forager bees returning home would be unable to find it. They would simply fly back to the original location. Disorientated by the disappearance of their home they would buzz around, huddle together to try and keep warm, but would eventually die.

Melanie Lenz knew this. That is why she was so shocked one night to find that someone had moved her hive. Lenz, 29, keeps her hive on the roof of St Margaret's House Settlement in east London, a four-storey house that provides offices for 30 local charities. Lenz has a key to let herself into the offices and is known affectionately as 'the bee lady' by staff whom she greets on her way upstairs. It was on a visit after work one night just weeks after her bees had arrived that she discovered that the hive she had deliberately placed on one side of the roof had been moved some 3.5 m (12 ft) to the other side.

She knew that all she could do to save her bees was to lug the hive back across the roof that night.

The easiest way to carry a hive is for two people to bend down, put their hands either side of the stand, underneath the brood box, and lift it up as you would a large piece of furniture. Doing it alone is not recommended. Lenz says she was bruised and ached for days afterwards from putting both arms around the hive and slowly shuffling along that interminable roof.

She later found out that the secret hive movers were contractors who needed to get to a water tank fairly close to the hive. They had moved it either to protect themselves or the bees. Either way it wasn't helpful. A scrawled note Sellotaped to the roof of the hive is testimony to Lenz's ordeal. It reads: 'Under no circumstances must this hive be moved. Doing so, even a little, will kill my bees.'

It may seem a tad melodramatic, but hopefully it will prevent any further disturbances. However, her experience is a salutary tale for anyone thinking of placing a hive on a rooftop: keep it away from any tanks, pipes or air-conditioning systems that contractors may need to service or repair.

Hosting hives

Not everyone who is fortunate enough to enjoy an urban garden wants to keep bees. Some, however, may be willing to host hives. Alison's parents, for example, were more than happy for us to put a couple of our hives at the end of the lawn but had no inclination to don a bee suit or puff a smoker. And we know of other garden owners who like the idea of helping honeybees by providing a home for a hive as long as they don't have to become beekeepers. After we had been contacted by a number of these 'armchair apiarists', we decided to create a map at www.urbanbees.co.uk with the aim of helping to match potential hive hosts with would-be beekeepers. For such an arrangement to work, however, both host and beekeeper will need to establish some ground rules.

Hosts, you will need to:

- allow unlimited access for the beekeeper, through an unlocked back gate, for example, unless you can guarantee you will always be in when the beekeeper wants to call by
- provide a car parking space for the beekeeper
- buy a bee suit if you want to see what the beekeeper is doing
- come to some agreement upfront about training if you are expecting lessons from your beekeeper
- come to an agreement about how many jars of honey you get from the hive and if the messy honey harvest can take place in your kitchen.

Beekeepers, you will need to:

- ensure the location being offered is right for the bees and convenient to access
- agree storage for equipment if necessary
- agree on the level of involvement of the host
- provide contact details in the case of a swarm.

Now you have chosen a suitable location for your hives, it is time to decide which hive and equipment to buy.

Hives and equipment

On the windswept rooftop of Fortnum & Mason in Piccadilly stand four six-foot-high eye-catching objects that look like miniature temples or shrines. It is only the bees coming in and out of the unusual arches that betray their real purpose. These are specially commissioned, oak-wood hives, complete with copper-clad roofs and gilded finials, and painted Fortnum's signature colour, eau de nil.

Craftsman Kim Farely-Harper handmade each one to a design by Jonathan Miller, Fortnum's chief buyer for the sweet grocery and bakery department, who has a passion for classical architecture.

Farely-Harper describes his creations, which cost £1,500 apiece and took nine months to complete, as 'good cabinet-making'.

Their handsome features were on display at the Chelsea Flower Show in 2007 as part of Fortnum's show garden to celebrate its 300th anniversary, and fetching photos have graced the pages of colour supplements. Sadly, since they went onto Fortnum's roof in 2008, the only person who gets to admire them is beekeeper Steve Benbow from the London Honey Company, who maintains them.

The Fortnum hives illustrate how the exterior of a hive can come in all manner of shapes of sizes. One designed to stand on the roof of the Royal Festival Hall was made in the shape of the modernist concert hall on London's South Bank. In the town of Cottageville, South Carolina, in the United States, a model village is made out of beehives, featuring buildings such as the Glory Bee Church.

But behind the façade, the inside of these hive are all basically the same: a collection of wooden boxes filled with evenly spaced frames of beeswax foundation that provide a home for a colony of honeybees and a storehouse for their honey.

Most of us cannot afford to commission hand-crafted hives made to a design of our choice. We are limited to what is sold by bee-keeping suppliers. In the UK, there are two main types of wooden beehive: the WBC and National hive, both of which follow the frame-based principle of beekeeping and are widely used by hobby apiarists. In addition, there are top-bar hives much loved by the so-called natural beekeeping movement for encouraging bees to make their own wax comb. The newest hive is a funky, brightly coloured plastic beehive, cleverly called the Beehaus.

When it comes to a beehive beauty is in the eye of the beholder, but there is a consensus that the gabled roof and sloping sides of a wooden WBC hive make it the most alluring, especially when painted pretty pastel shades and stood in a cottage garden surrounded by flowers. This is how you will often find it in picture books. So it is little surprise that when we started beekeeping we had our hearts set on a WBC to perfect the rural idyll we were trying to create in our city space.

But as we quickly learned, looks aren't everything when it comes to urban beekeeping. Swarm management and controlling disease will always need to be at the forefront of your mind, so you need a hive that will help rather than hinder these priorities.

The WBC is a double-walled hive designed by a Mr William Broughton Carr in the 1890s primarily for extra insulation against harsh winters in the north of Britain. What this means is that those pretty sloping sides, known as lifts, are a casing that you have to remove before you can get to the inner brood and the super boxes that actually house the bees, their brood and their honey. Having two layers of boxes to negotiate can be time-consuming and cumbersome and the lifts will require extra storage space. So if you have neither a lot of time to inspect your hive, nor a lot of space in which to do it, and little storage for your beekeeping equipment, then you should think again before investing in a WBC. As you become more advanced as a beekeeper you will find that it limits the type of swarm management you can practise.

As beginner beekeepers in London with a small garden and shed, and little time for hive inspections, we put practicalities before aesthetics and plumped for a National hive instead of a WBC.

It certainly won't win any beauty contests, but this single-walled hive made up of a series of floorless and roofless boxes stacked one on top of another, in which you insert 11 frames of beeswax foundation, is easy to use and by far the most popular in the UK.

An American reverend named LL Langstroth is credited with inventing single-walled box hives in the 1850s, reportedly out of champagne crates. His eponymous hive is widely used in the US today. The National in the UK and the Dadant in France are variations of it.

The WBC and National follow the same principles. They both come with two depths of boxes, deep and shallow, usually known as brood boxes and supers. Brood boxes (deep) are where the brood – eggs, larvae, developing pupae – live, while the supers (shallow) are placed above the brood box in the summer for the bees to store their honey. Some 10 or 11 frames containing beeswax foundation are inserted into the boxes. The foundation, a pre-made sheet of beeswax moulded on both sides with impressions of hexagons, gives the bees a head start in creating the wax cells they use as birth chambers, resting rooms and the larder. They 'draw out' the foundation on both sides of the sheet by adding beeswax to the impressions secreted from their wax glands.

Each of the frames is about 9 mm (⅓ in) apart. This gives the bees just enough room to pass each other without getting squashed, but not so far apart that they lose the feel and contact of one another. This distance is called the bee space. The invention of moveable frames separated by a bee space revolutionised beekeeping. Before then bees were kept in upturned baskets called skeps where the honey couldn't easily be separated from the colony so when it was collected all the bees and their brood were destroyed.

More than 150 years after modern beekeeping begun, a new hive has been created to appeal to a new generation of apiarists. It still uses moveable frames inserted a bee space apart, but they and the hive are made out of a 20th-century synthetic material instead of wood.

Made by Omlet, the company behind the Eglu plastic chicken house, the Beehaus was launched in August 2009. For urban beekeepers, the one metre long (three ft) plastic box on legs has its attractions. It is twice as long as traditional hives because it is in fact two brood boxes side by side with separate entrances at both ends. The thinking behind this design is to ease swarm management. Most urban beekeepers will be preoccupied in spring and early summer by when their bees are going to swarm and how best to manage it, especially in densely populated areas. One method is by splitting the colony when the bees are ready to swarm (see page 158). The Beehaus aims to make the beekeeper's life easier by having the second brood box – into which you will move half the bees and the old queen (the swarm) – right next to the first box. In contrast, if you split a colony in a traditional box hive, you will need to buy a second hive and decide on a location for it in which to house your 'swarm'.

On top of the two Beehaus brood boxes are four supers with shallower frames and foundation for honey. They are half the size and weight of a traditional super box, so when they are full of honey they weigh less than 8 kg (18 lbs), making them much lighter to carry. The step ladder you have to climb down backwards from the roof suddenly becomes much easier to negotiate.

What beekeepers like most about the Beehaus is that the box is raised much higher off the ground than conventional hives, making it a more comfortable working height for hive inspections. It also eliminates the sometimes back-breaking bending and lifting of heavy boxes. It has won many plaudits and has probably helped to boost the profile of urban beekeeping among younger people.

Yet despite its obvious attractions we don't own a Beehaus. Why? Firstly, using plastic – even the 100 per cent recycled kind the Beehaus is made of – doesn't chime with the environmental reasons we took up beekeeping. Are people going to be digging them out of landfill in thousands of years' time? Plastic is also not as easy a material to clean as wood, which you can scorch with a blowtorch, so there is more risk of bacteria and disease festering.

Secondly, its sheer size is just too intrusive in a small, urban garden and its plastic features jar with the flora. It can work, however, on an urban rooftop where its bold colour brightens up otherwise drab surroundings. It should squeeze through the hatch that leads to the roof but you will only be able to get it up there if there are two of you to manoeuvre it. Luckily, Omlet as part of its service will come and install the Beehaus for you.

At the other end of the beekeeping spectrum are the top-bar hives. Instead of inserting frames with beeswax foundation, these hives encourage the bees to build their own wax comb as they do in the wild and are much vaunted by beekeepers who believe in a hands-off, minimalist approach to bee husbandry. The comb hangs down from the top-bar frames in the hive. There is no separation of comb for brood and for honey, although the honey is usually stored at the top of the comb, so the whole comb is removed when the honey is harvested. The simplicity of this style of hive, consisting of just one box and a few top bars, means it is a less expensive method of beekeeping. As a result, top-bar hives are popular in Africa and developing countries where they have become a profitable alternative to honey hunting and log-hive beekeeping.

However, it is worth remembering that while they may work in Tanzania, in Tottenham or Toxteth where swarm management and disease control are more of a priority, they are less practical.

Bees don't naturally make straight comb; it is often crooked, can cross over itself and can get very messy in the hive. The beekeeper will have to straighten it up otherwise it will be impossible to remove single combs of honey. This, however, can be difficult for a beginner and rather defeats the purpose of letting the bees go *au naturel*. And if you don't remove the unwieldy old comb, the bees will have no room to replace it with a new, clean version in the spring.

The other issue for beginners is that few beekeepers use top-bar hives. There are online forums and books, but you are unlikely to find hands-on help and advice at your local bee-keepers' association.

The Warré hive is a variation on the top-bar hive. Developed by French priest Abbé Emile Warré in the early 20th century as a way to help poor people maximise honey production, today it is promoted by natural beekeepers because it mimics how a wild colony lives in a tree cavity by allowing the bees to build their comb downwards. But it has exactly the same drawbacks as other top-bar hives. The honey can be difficult to harvest; it is not easy to manage swarming; and a hive designed for minimal inspection by the beekeeper is probably not best suited to today's urban beekeeper who lives with the ever-present threat of varroa killing their bees.

From our own experience, we would recommend that beginner beekeepers in an urban environment learn the basics of beekeeping with a National hive. They are easy to use and because nearly all beekeepers use them help and advice is always close at hand.

Owning a National doesn't mean that you can't practise a more sustainable form of beekeeping. As 'bee-friendly beekeepers' we leave our bees a super full of their own honey at the end of the summer; we don't put synthetic pesticides in the hive to control mites; and we let our bees swarm, but in a managed way to prevent them from frightening the neighbours.

If you have more than one colony of bees and decide to buy different hives to compare and contrast them, be warned that the hive parts are not interchangeable. A WBC brood and super box, for example, are slightly smaller than a National. If, like us, you don't have separate store rooms for the WBC hive parts and the National, they tend to get muddled up together in the garage, and we often pull out a super in the summer to add to our WBCs or Nationals only to find we have made a mistake and taken the wrong one. At least the frames and foundation fit both hives.

Where do you get them and what do they consist of?

Cost could be a determining factor in deciding which hive you buy, as they range in price from around £100 up to £500. The cheapest are the top-bar hives, followed by the single-walled National and the double-walled WBC. The two-hives-in-one plastic Beehaus is the most expensive. The different styles of wooden hives can be made from most wood materials. Pine is the budget option, but cedar, with its built-in oils and preservatives, makes it the most durable wood for outdoors and the one that we usually choose.

The Beehaus is only available direct from Omlet's website, but you can order wooden hives from most beekeeping suppliers (see page 237). They come flat-packed but if you are prepared to pay, up to £100 or more in some cases, they will be delivered ready-assembled.

If you would like to use your new hobby to help support local businesses, you may be able to find a local carpenter or artisan who makes hives or would be willing to make one for you. There are drawings and plans online with the dimensions for constructing different types of wooden hives. You could even build your own if you are a serious DIY enthusiast.

Frames and foundation also come flat-packed but are much more straightforward to assemble and many beginners' courses even teach you how to make one. There are lots of different frames to choose from in the suppliers' catalogues which can be very confusing. We generally use Hoffman National self-spacing frames because we have found they are the easiest to use.

A WBC or National hive, as we have said, is a collection of floor-less boxes (and lifts in the case of the WBC). But in addition to a brood box, a couple of shallower super boxes, and the frames and foundation to go in each, there are a number of other components that make up a hive.

Varroa screen and tray: A piece of mesh that sits underneath the brood box and lets the varroa mite fall through the screen and die. When you place a tray under the screen and pull it out a few days later you will be able to count the number of mites. This is an integral part of any integrated pest management programme (see page 186).
Entrance block: A moveable piece of wood that is used to change the size of the hive entrance at different times of the year.
Mouse guard: A piece of metal that is attached to the entrance of the hive during winter to prevent mice getting in.

Dummy board: This solid wooden frame can be inserted if there is a slight gap in the brood box at the end of the frames of foundation. It will stop the bees filling the gap with wild comb.

Queen excluder: A wire-mesh screen which sits between the brood box and the super box and allows worker bees access to both, but prevents the queen getting through and laying eggs in the super. This means a super box only contains honey.

Crown board: This cover fits on top of the brood and super boxes to keep the heat in the hive and has a hole through which you can feed the bees in the winter.

Eke: A 40 mm (1½ in) piece of wood that you put on top of the brood box when you give your bees their anti-varroa treatment. It enables you to put the crown board on without squashing the treatment, which sits in a shallow tray on top of the brood box.

Roof: A flat galvanised sheet of metal that protects the hive from the elements and has ventilation holes that allow it to breathe. A WBC roof is gabled. You can buy gabled ones for National hives to make them look more attractive.

Make sure your hive comes with all these parts. You may have to order the mouse guard, dummy board and eke separately but everything else should come as standard.

Many suppliers now offer starter kits that include all the basic beekeeping equipment as well as the hive for not much more than the price of a single hive. Omlet, for example, will supply all your essential beekeeping equipment with your new Beehaus for just an extra £30.

Some suppliers even have budget starter kits containing hives made of inferior cedar timber and second-rate quality frames. The drawback with these is that you don't get a chance to choose your own equipment, so you may end up with a hat and veil instead of an all-in-one bee suit and gloves that you don't get on with. We have become quite attached to some of our carefully selected and trusted tools and would recommend that it is worth paying the extra few pounds to get equipment you feel happy with. After all a bee suit, a smoker and a hive tool could last a beekeeping lifetime.

Co-op Plan Bee blog   4 May 2010

'Brian gave each of us a "going-home present" – a shiny metal smoker and a hive tool. I held my smoker with pride as I travelled home on the tube. Now, as Chantal, one of my fellow trainee beekeepers, said: "We will need to practise smoking behind the bee sheds, important to have the right gear on though …"'

Kate Griffiths-Lambeth

As well as the basic hive, these are the other essential beekeeping items and equipment you will need to buy:

Hive tool: This shaped piece of metal, sharpened flat at one end and hooked at the other, will become your beekeeping workhorse. The blunt, curved end can prise open propolis-closed hives and prise apart propolis-stuck frames, and the sharp end can trim frames that you are putting together. You should have it with you at all times around the hive in the pocket of your bee suit and you should use a different one for each of your hives to prevent the possible spread of disease. The red-coloured tools are the best because they are easier to spot if you put them down on the grass or on the roof. It may be worth having a spare so you can always lay your hands on one as you will soon feel bare without it.

Smoker: This strange-looking contraption is a shiny metal canister with bellows attached that you use to pacify your bees before you open up and inspect their home. You will need it smouldering by your side when you do your inspection in case you need to calm the bees down. The idea is to produce lots of cold smoke rather than flames and to gently give the entrance of the hive a few puffs a couple of minutes before going in. So you will need to fill the canister with material that will catch fire easily and not go out. Hay, grass cuttings and wood shavings all do a good job but you're more likely to have cardboard to hand. It works well when cut to the height of the canister, rolled up into a cylinder with the grain running vertically to create an airflow. If you roll it up with hessian sacking, which you may be able to find at your local greengrocer or on eBay, you can with a bit of practice have a smoker that will last 30 minutes. Alternatively, some beekeeping suppliers will wrap your order in shredded cardboard, which is efficient smoker fuel. Light the material, push it down into the smoker, pump the bellows a couple of times and Bob's your uncle. Bees will move out of the way of the smoke so you can use it to herd them off frames and puff it on yourself if you get stung to deter other bees from following you.

The reason why smoke helps the beekeeper is because bees are alerted to fire by the smoke so they get ready to vacate the hive and find a new safe place to live. But before they leave they dive into the comb and suck up three days' worth of honey to enable them to survive. With their bellies full they become a bit sleepy and are unable to bend their abdomen so easily to sting. Too much smoke, however, will make them angry. It is worth spending some time practising the art of using your smoker. We don't like tricking our bees, so use our smoker sparingly, but it depends to some extent on the temperament of your bees as to how much you need to puff.

Bee suit: You may look like a chemical weapons inspector with your full body suit, but if it makes you feel stress-free and relaxed around your bees it is a good investment. Traditional suits are made of heavy-duty white cotton, zipped at the front with a veiled hood attached. We wear a lightweight, olive-coloured, polyester version with a fencing-suit-style hood over our jeans and a long-sleeved top. We find these suits are cooler in the summer and quicker to dry, which is important if you have hives at different locations because you should wash your suit before wearing it to another apiary. A suit can cost from £50 to £100. A cheaper option is a hat and veil that covers your neck and shoulders and can be tucked into a shirt or jumper, or there are smocks and trousers you can buy separately. Ensure you do not leave ankles and cuffs exposed, as bees like to climb upwards into dark spaces. Woolly jumpers, fleeces and dark colours are also a no-no as you will remind bees of a big furry animal that steals their honey. Whichever protective gear you choose, make sure that it has a pocket for your hive tool and queen cage. Consider getting spare protective clothing, and in small sizes, because everyone, especially children, find bees fascinating and may want to see you open your hive when they visit.

Gloves: You can buy gauntlets made of thin leather that will offer complete protection from getting stung on the hand or wrists. But we have found them hard to clean and clumsy to use. Also the leather smell seems to agitate the bees. In contrast, normal household rubber washing-up gloves make excellent beekeeping gloves, protecting your hands, facilitating a delicate touch and cleaning easily. They can tear after a few uses, though, so always check for holes and have some spares handy.

Footwear: After being stung too many times on our ankles we now wear wellingtons. They are not to everyone's liking; too hot for some in the summer. But it is advisable to cover your feet and ankles.

Feeder: When your bees arrive you will need to give them a welcome meal of cane sugar dissolved in warm water. Pour this clear sugar-syrup solution (one part sugar to one part water) into a feeder. There are a variety of feeders you can buy. We find the easiest to use is the one that looks like a plastic bucket with a tight lid and a mesh-covered hole. They hold either 1.1, 2.2 or 4.5 litres (2, 4 or 8 pints) of liquid. A 2.2-litre feeder should be sufficient. You place the feeder upside-down over the hole in the crown board. A vacuum is created in the bucket so the liquid does not spill out.

Porter bee escape: An ingenious piece of plastic that fits in the crown board and contains a one-way valve. If it is placed below a super full of honey, 24 hours later the super will be free of bees and ready to remove and harvest.

Queen cage: Sometimes you will need to isolate the queen, either for her own protection or to mark her. The easiest way is to pop her into a cage the size of a matchbox and place it in the dark pocket of your bee suit.

Record book: You'll need to keep a record of what is happening in your hive, as it is surprisingly easy to forget from one visit to the next. One way is to have a notebook divided into ruled sections. We usually keep a record of the date of our visit, whether or not we

---

Urban Bees blog   26 April 2009

'The 21st March was one of those sunny, warm days that we had in the middle of all that wet and cold weather so I took the opportunity and had a peek into the Queen's Park hive. I was very disappointed to see that I had a weak colony. Not terminal but very weak. Only one-and-a-bit frames of bees. I could see a few eggs so I knew the queen was laying. I left them with a feed. Had a look yesterday and I am pleased to report that there are now five full frames of bees. This is good news. Looks like we will be getting some Queen's Park honey after all.'

---

saw the queen, how many frames had brood, what stage the brood was at, the level of food stores and the temper of the bees, as well as anything else we feel is worth noting such as varroa sightings or queen cells. It will help you to judge if all is going to plan in the hive and when you will need to add supers, carry out swarm management or treat for varroa. Even if you can't see your queen, you will know she is there if you recorded newly laid eggs.

Beekeeping box and bee sting kit: We like to keep our tools all together in a wicker basket along with matches to light the smoker and antihistamine tablets in case one of us gets stung. A box or bag will do just as well. If you are beekeeping alone in an isolated place, consider taking a mobile phone just in case you need to call for help in the event of an accident or a seriously allergic reaction to a bee sting. Scraping the sting quickly with your hive tool will get it out before the sting's pump has had time to inject all its venom.

Honey harvesting tools: An uncapping fork, a 30-litre (6½-gallon) bucket with a tap, sieves, jars and an extractor … Before you know it the process can get costly. We didn't buy an extractor in our first year, but instead scraped the honeycomb through a sieve. It was messy and time-consuming but possible with just one hive, especially if you decide to harvest one comb at a time rather than a super full of honey. You could club together with other local beekeepers and buy an extractor between you. They range in price from £200 for a plastic hand-turned extractor to more than £800 for a metal-motored one.

***BeeCraft* magazine:** When you join a beekeepers' association, they will usually offer a subscription to this practical monthly beekeepers' journal at a reduced rate. Take it. Its 'What to Do This Month for Beginners' section is invaluable even for the most experienced beekeeper. You always learn something new.

Treatments: These are not included in starter packs but at certain times of the year you will be encouraged to treat your bees for varroa and bacterial infections. Once you have decided which treatment to use – and be warned, there are a bewildering array to choose from and as many different opinions as to which are the most effective (see page 188) – make sure to order them for delivery at the correct date for application.

Food: Starvation is one of the most common causes of bee deaths over winter. Even if you leave your bees a super full of honey there is no guarantee it will be sufficient, especially if we have a long winter. Bees cannot turn sugar-syrup solution into honey in low temperatures so you are better feeding them an alternative called fondant. It is the soft white icing that bakers use on top of cakes, but bakers' fondant is often flavoured so to be on the safe side we buy ours in 2.5 kg (5½ lb) blocks from a bee supplier. If necessary we put a slab of it above the hole in the crown board when we think the honey stores may have run out (see page 204).

Second year supplies: Many beginners make the mistake of only budgeting for equipment they need in their first season, but in your second calendar year of beekeeping you'll need to give the hive a spring clean to rid it of old, possibly diseased, comb. To do this requires having a second brood box full of new frames and foundation and a blowtorch to scorch the original brood box when you have removed it from the hive. You will probably also need a third super with frames and foundation. So remember to put aside £150 for year two.

Beekeeping suppliers' websites and catalogues can be daunting for a beginner, a bit like a DIY-phobe trying to negotiate their way round B & Q, so it's worth checking your order list with a more seasoned beekeeper before you buy. We have always found the suppliers we use to be very helpful at the end of the phone. But next-day service isn't the norm in the beekeeping world, so make sure you order kit early. As one new beekeeper commented: 'The lassitude of summer beekeeping seems to form the customer service philosophy of most suppliers.' This can be particularly frustrating in the spring when there is a meltdown as everyone is ordering hives or realising they have run out of new frames and foundation. Buying an assembled hive adds to delivery times, so it is not unusual to have to wait six weeks at this time of year. Better to buy your hive and equipment in the winter when there is less demand and often sale discounts to be found. Even better, put you order on your Christmas list and get other people to buy it.

Second-hand equipment

There is something of the make-do-and-mend mentality about old-school beekeepers that can sometimes manifest itself in resentment against newcomers investing in trendy hives, designer bee suits and shiny new tools. But the truth is that in this age of varroa, and a whole host of bee diseases, it is safer to buy new equipment. Second-hand equipment can harbour pests and disease which could be transferred to your bees, so unless you can be 100 per cent sure that the used equipment you are buying has been thoroughly sterilised, err on the side of caution.

Tool maintenance

Always have a bucket of water and soda crystals at the ready after you've finished your hive inspection. Scrub the propolis off your tools and gloves after each inspection and you'll remove any infections. There's always a temptation to just clean your tools sporadically, but try to factor the clean into the time you allow yourself to do the hive inspection: that way you won't see it as a non-essential part of the routine. Equipment should not be swapped between apiaries without a thorough cleaning first because of the risk of spreading infections. Likewise, wash your bee suit regularly between inspections, especially if you have two apiaries. During the winter you can scorch spare wooden supers and brood boxes to get rid of pests and disease. For someone who has never used a blowtorch it takes a bit of practice.

Once your hive is fully assembled and in the correct location, your equipment is delivered and you have learned basic hands-on beekeeping on an introductory course, you will be ready to collect your honeybees.

All about bees

Where to get your bees

Most of the beekeeping books say the best way to get your own colony of bees is to contact your local beekeepers' association and put your name down on a swarm list. This is certainly the cheapest option as swarms will be captured and put in a box for you to collect for free. But with the huge surge in demand from aspiring apiarists you may be waiting a very long time.

You could face a similarly long delay for a split colony. This is a colony that a beekeeper has split in two. We recommend that city beekeepers split their colonies when there are clear signs their bees want to swarm (see page 157) rather than letting them do it themselves and alarming the neighbours. Many city beekeepers will have neither the space nor the inclination to keep a second colony, so you could ask around for a split.

However, if you want to guarantee that your bees arrive in the spring, which is the best time for you and your bees to become acquainted, the most reliable method by far is to order a nucleus of bees from a commercial beekeeper. Don't underestimate the competition you will be up against, so the earlier you can order them (say January or February), the better. By March or April everyone will be trying to get their hands on bees, including those beekeepers whose colony has not survived the winter, so you may be disappointed.

Many commercial beekeepers advertise in bee magazines and the internet, but buy from one who comes with a personal recommendation from an experienced beekeeper, or ask around all the beekeepers you know to see who they get their colonies from and whether they are satisfied with the bees. It's worth spending a bit of time researching the market, because the increased demand for bees and subsequent hike in prices has, unfortunately, attracted cowboys. Some new beekeepers were badly stung, pun intended, in summer 2010 by a few unscrupulous bee farmers who sold them small, weak colonies with little brood and a non-laying queen.

In 1947 a British Standard for a nucleus of bees was introduced. If a nuc box carried the famous quality BSI kitemark you were guaranteed a five-frame standard consisting of five brood-size frames with bees, food and brood in all stages of development, and a young queen that was mother to the colony. Unfortunately, the British Standard was withdrawn in 1984, probably because the BBKA did not have the funds at the time to pay for its annual renewal, or see the need to continue the standard as there was no particular problem with nucs back then.

In its place, the BBKA has produced an information leaflet that incorporates as much of the old standard as it thought seemed sensible and has added a lot more material on disease, medication and developing the nucleus.

According to these criteria, what you are looking for is a mini bee colony on three to five brood-sized frames, which is ready to expand as soon as you get it home. The brood should be on at least half the frames, not less than 30 per cent should be capped (in which the cells are covered with a porous 'cap' to isolate the brood during their non-feeding pupal stage) and no more than 15 per cent should be drone brood. The two outermost frames should have honey stores.

If your queen is marked with a coloured spot you will be able to tell her age because of an internationally recognised colour coding system. For years ending in a 0 or 5 she will have a blue dot; white for 1 or 6; yellow for 2 or 7; red for 3 or 8; and green for years ending in 4 or 9. When you order a nuc you can ask for a marked queen. It is worth the small extra cost, or else she can be difficult to see surrounded by her courtiers.

The BBKA doesn't specify the number of adult bees in a nuc. Around 10,000 is a rough rule of thumb, though it's impossible to count them. Instead it advises the frames should be well covered in both young and flying bees, they should be good-tempered, and both bees and the brood should show no sign of disease.

The BBKA believes its leaflet is sufficient to help buyers avoid rogue sellers. 'There would be little benefit to be gained from renewing the standard and a considerable amount of work and money to be expended in getting a BS written,' it told us.

It added that there is no legal imperative for a seller of bees to adhere to a BS, any more than they have to adhere to the BBKA advice leaflet. This may be true, but surely it misses the point. Not every meat producer has to rear their livestock organically, but we can choose to buy from ones that are Soil Association-approved. Similarly, if the standard was reintroduced, beekeepers could choose to buy from a seller that carried the BS kitemark.

Urban Bees blog

6 June 2006

'As I drive round Hyde Park Corner on my way back from Roots and Shoots in Kennington, I hear a thud. I look in my mirror only to see to my horror that there are bees buzzing around in the back of the car! I manage to somehow pull over, and get out the car to take a closer look at what's happened. The box has fallen on its side (why didn't I wedge it in?) and lots of bees are clinging to the box or flying around. What now? I call the Bee Man. "Oh dear," he says and then calmly tells me not to panic. That's easy for him to say. "The bees aren't interested in you, just drive home," is his advice.

'He is right. I get home unscathed. Most of the bees have managed to get back into the box, so I put on the Marigolds and carry the box through the flat into the garden and place it in front of the hive.'

From our own experience, you are so excited, grateful and not a little apprehensive when picking up your first nucleus that you will never remember to check if it matches up the BBKA standard, or for that matter really care. But if the nuc is small and weak it will be much harder for the colony to expand and collect enough honey to survive the winter. So in the worst-case scenario you could be left bee-less the following spring if you don't take care when you are buying a nucleus.

That's why we'd advise you to take along an experienced beekeeper if you can when you collect your first nuc. Would you buy a house without a survey to see if the roof is about to cave in? A trained pair of eyes will be able to give your nuc the once-over and ensure you are getting what you pay for.

Most commercial apiarists with scores of hives do not operate in cities where space is limited, so be prepared to have to drive out to the suburbs or the countryside to collect your bees. With such high demand in 2010, London beekeepers were forced to travel up the M1. The bees on St Paul's Cathedral started their long journey to the capital in the Shropshire hills.

Another option is to get together with some other beekeepers who own a car and organise a group pick-up.

One word of warning: make sure the travelling box that the nucleus comes in is wedged in tightly when you drive home.

You don't have to buy a nucleus of bees. You could start bee-keeping with either a package of bees – 10,000 bees and a queen but no brood-covered frames – or a fully working hive of 50,000 bees.

However, we wouldn't recommend either option for beginners. The lack of brood in a package of bees means that it will take more than three weeks before there are any new bees in the colony and you will have no idea if your queen is a good egg-layer. In contrast, a full colony, though strong and able to produce honey quicker, will be rather daunting for a beginner. Starting with 10,000 bees is more manageable. You will be able to build up your confidence handling bees before they expand five-fold over the summer and, importantly, you will experience the satisfaction of seeing your colony grow and thrive under your care.

The main beekeeping suppliers sell starter packs that come with bees, as well as the hive and equipment, for around £600, but check whether you are getting a five-frame nucleus or a package of bees and insist on the former.

The ideal time to start beekeeping is spring or early summer when the nectar is in full flow and your nucleus will have plenty of forage and sufficient time to expand before the nights start to get shorter. As early as 22 June, after the summer solstice, bees will gradually be preparing for winter. But however efficient you are at getting your order in early, a prolonged winter and late spring could delay your bees' arrival.

What type of bees to buy

When we got our first swarm we crossed our fingers and prayed that the bees would be well-behaved and healthy. We had no idea what race they were and how that could influence their conduct and stamina.

Beekeepers generally hope their bees will display three major characteristics: that they'll be non-aggressive, have a low swarming instinct and make copious amounts of honey. This is viewed by many as the Holy Grail of beekeeping. Almost a century ago Brother Adam, a monk at Buckfast Abbey in Devon, started to crossbreed different European honeybees with the aim of creating a gentle-natured but hardy bee, which swarmed little and was highly resistant to tracheal mites, which at that time were thought to have wiped out thousands of our native black honeybee colonies across Britain. The Buckfast bee can still be bought today and is bred in many northern US states.

In our view the perfect bee for a city would be docile, reluctant to swarm and, importantly, varroa-resistant. We would forgo the honey-making proficiency for these other three traits, but the truth is it is difficult to buy a honeybee that matches a particular spec.

There are four main species of honeybee: the small Eastern honeybee found in Asia (*Apis cerana*); the giant variety, also Asian (*Apis dorsata*); the dwarf species (*Apis florea*), common to southeast

Asia; and the Western honeybee (*Apis mellifera*), which is native to Europe and Africa but was taken to the US and Australasia by early European settlers and has subsequently been exported globally.

There are, however, numerous strains, or races, of *Apis mellifera* depending on where in Europe they originated. In Britain, the most popular is the golden-coloured Italian bee (*Apis mellifera ligustica*), first imported at the beginning of the 20th century when our native black honeybee (*Apis mellifera mellifera*) was practically wiped out. The darker Carniolan bee (*Apis mellifera carnica*), originally from the Balkans, is another favourite. Both are bred for their gentle nature and honey-producing skills.

Our first experience of honeybees was the swarm we collected. They turned out to be incredibly placid Italian bees: perfect for beginners, as they were quiet, gentle and hardly ever stung. We didn't realise how spoilt we had been until the following year when we purchased a couple of nucs from a commercial beekeeper who specialised in Carniolans. We were surprised how much more feisty they were, despite their nice-natured reputation.

In reality, your bees will probably be a local hybrid because the way that a queen bee mates naturally makes it difficult to preserve pure races and characteristics.

Italians and Carniolan hybrids are best suited to the warm, dry climate enjoyed across much of south-east England. In wetter and colder regions of the UK, we would recommend a good-tempered hybrid of the native black bee, which is better able to cope with the local weather conditions.

The black bee has evolved thick black hair and a larger body to help keep it warm. It is thrifty with its honey stores, flies at low temperatures and in high winds. So, if your bees are destined for a blustery rooftop location, more than five floors up, it may be worth considering a black bee hybrid even if you live in a town or city with a mild climate.

However, black bees are generally more defensive and poorer honey producers than their gentler foreign cousins. Apiculture professor Francis Ratnieks says: 'All things being equal it makes sense to work with what's native. Yet I have seen some very aggressive and restless black bees, so they should be bred to incorporate their better elements.'

In terms of survival rate, he points out that our native bees are less likely to starve in difficult times. 'They eke out their winter food stores for longer than their Italian counterparts and need less food in the spring because they [breed] less quickly.'

The Bee Improvement and Bee Breeders' Association (BIBBA) has argued since the 1960s against importing foreign bees and for the conservation, restoration, study, selection and improvement of the native and near-native honeybees of Britain and Ireland. Because of the popularity of foreign strains there are thought to be only isolated pockets of pure black bees around England. In 2009, the Co-operative Group launched a fund for BIBBA to map the hardy black bee's location and to develop a breeding programme to increase their numbers.

But Ratnieks warns, however, that black bees are not immune to the worst of British weather. In August 2008, for the first time in 12 years, the rain prevented his black bees in Derbyshire from collecting any nectar from heather. As a result they didn't have enough food to last them through the winter and the weaker colonies died.

In *A World Without Bees* we demonstrate how the reduction in the honeybee gene pool is a worry for bee health. When a new pest or disease attacks the Western honeybee, all hives become infected because we are using the same docile and prolific honey-making strain worldwide.

The Irish potato famine of the 1840s is a tragic example of what happens if we rely on a single variety of any living thing. Had a number of different potato types been cultivated there would have been a chance that some may have been more blight-resistant.

The most ambitious experiment to try to save the biodiversity of the black bee, which was native to much of northern Europe, took place on a small, windswept island 22 km (14 miles) off the Danish mainland. In 1989, bee imports to the island of Læsø were banned to try to preserve the original settlers. What followed was a fierce battle between professional beekeepers who favoured Italian bees and black bee-supporting conservationists. The case went as high as the European Court of Justice and is now studied by law students as an example of an international treaty – the Convention on Biological Diversity, ratified in 1993 – overriding European free trade rules.

The import ban was consequently limited to a small area on the east of the island where, of 123 colonies surveyed in 2007, 99 per cent were found to be pure black bees.

Scientists and beekeepers are now trying to breed a strain of varroa-resistant Western honeybee (see page 193), but it will be years before these are available commercially, if they are ever successful.

In the meantime, the BBKA recommends beekeepers purchase a local hybrid from a local bee breeder with some Italian or Carniolan features to improve their temperament.

You can, however, import bees from an approved list of countries which features EU member states and Argentina, Australia and New Zealand. It is not uncommon for beekeepers to receive a jiffy bag in the mail containing a caged queen bee, a handful of attendant workers and some fondant.

Because the queen lives in the dark, eating and laying eggs all her life, beekeepers argue that a few days in transit won't do her or her workers any harm. Regent's Park beekeeper, Toby Mason, swears by his New Zealand bees. Because they are Italian bees bred in New Zealand, which has a thriving bee export industry built on the reputation of its gentle *ligusticas*, he is guaranteed docility. The temperament is perfect for beginners, says Mason, and he points to the price, which at £33 a package compares favourably to purchasing a £150 nucleus in the UK.

And he is not alone. In 2010, more than 1,000 queens came from New Zealand and a further 650 from Australia according to Fera (the Food and Environment Research Agency). Its figures show the most popular European imports were Carniolan queens from Greece and Slovenia.

The government agency with statutory responsibility for bee health produces a strict guidance note about how to import bees in its attempts to prevent the spread of pests and disease from abroad and any importer has by law to notify it of any bees coming into the country and send it samples to test for disease.

While we agree air freighting bees is not exactly on a par with live veal exports, we do have a problem with beekeeping miles and with keeping bees in our back garden that are not adapted to our hemisphere. It clashes with the back-to-nature, *Good Life*-inspired set-up we were trying to create when we took up urban beekeeping.

Mason argues that it is better to buy gentle New Zealand bees, even if they die during your first winter, than to purchase feistier but hardier local ones. You can always restock in your second season with more irascible bees, once you are more experienced, he says. While this is true, he has underestimated the emotional bond many beekeepers build up with their new apian friends. We would have taken it very personally if our bees had died that first winter and may even have given up. For the one-hive novice, seeing your bees emerge in early spring after a nail-biting winter of snow, ice and sub-zero temperatures is nothing short of miraculous.

Whichever race of honeybee you purchase and from whichever country they will all look pretty much the same, the only slight variation being their colour, which ranges from golden to darkish brown for the black bees (not really black, despite their name).

The anatomy of a bee

All bees' anatomy is identical. They will all possess six legs, five eyes – three at the top of the head to orientate and two for seeing – two pairs of wings and a body covered with tiny hairs. The worker bee will have pollen baskets on her back legs, wax glands on the underside of her abdomen, glands inside her head to make royal jelly, another gland that emits pheromones to communicate to her sisters, and a special stomach, called a crop, where enzymes start turning nectar into honey. She also has a barbed sting at the end of her body. She is nothing less than half an inch of perfect precision engineering for the tasks she has to perform both inside and outside the hive.

There are three castes of bee in a hive. In the summer there are 50,000 or so female worker bees, a few hundred male drones, and one queen. The drones are easy to spot because they are slightly larger, with square bodies and big eyes. And because they have genitalia instead of a sting, they are easy to pick up and good practice for handling bees. There is nothing nicer than to stroke your bees.

The queen bee is a spindly creature with her long abdomen containing the spermatheca, the sac that holds all the sperm she acquires on her nuptial flight. We disagree on her aesthetics: one of us thinks she is elegantly regal, the other that she is frighteningly arthropodic (insect-like).

Her royal title, however, is rather misleading. She is mother to all the bees in the colony and is attended to by courtiers who feed and clean her. But she is more a slave than a monarch. Her function is to lay eggs. Once mated, she will spend the rest of her days in the dark laying up to 2,000 eggs a day at the height of her fecundity: both fertilised worker eggs and non-fertilised drone eggs. The queen also emits a variety of pheromones that tell the other bees that she is laying and all is well in the hive. If she stops producing these 'good' smells the workers take this as a sign that she is ailing and may supersede her with a new queen. The queen comes from the same egg as a worker but is reared in a special queen cell and fed only royal jelly. It is this protein-rich, white, jelly-like substance, much sought after by humans for its supposed rejuvenating powers, that bestows regal status on her.

The colony as a superorganism

Recorded apiculture dates back to the Greeks, with Virgil's famous treatise in *Georgics IV* being the original beekeeping guide. The Egyptians followed with their bee gods, bathing in milk and honey, and transporting hives down the Nile to pollinate crops. But until the 17th century the honeybee colony was always conceived of as a patriarchal kingdom. Shakespeare's Henry V even says of the hive, 'They have a king.'

Charles Butler, an English vicar and beekeeper, shattered the myth when he published *The Feminine Monarchy* and scientists backed up his theory some hundred years later.

Twentieth-century poet, Sylvia Plath, who took up beekeeping in the last few months of her life and left behind a collection of highly regarded bee poems, writes about her 'winged, miraculous women'. And there is no doubt that female bees do all the work in the bee kingdom. But we now view a colony not so much as a matriarchy but as a 'superorganism'. The term was first coined by US biologist William Morton Wheeler over a century ago (as a result of his pioneering research into ant colonies) and it means that the honeybee colony should be seen not as 50,000 individual bees but as a single integrated organism. The worker bees are comparable to the cells in a body, the queen to the heart, and the drones to the genital organs. Thinking of your colony as a superorganism helps when you accidentally squash a worker bee, or a few get left behind when you move a hive, or you see a handful dead in front of the hive. Just remember it is the health of the colony that is paramount, not each individual worker bee. The bees are all working for the continued survival of the colony.

The division of labour

The division of labour in the colony is structured according to age and physical maturity. During the first three weeks after emerging from her cell as a mature bee, a worker will do a variety of domestic duties in the hive such as cleaning, feeding and capping brood (covering over the cells of the pupae), as well as building new comb when her wax glands are developed, and flapping her wings to evaporate water off the nectar. At 21 days old, her sting fully formed, she will take her maiden flight. You can see these fledgling foragers on their orientating flights. They come out for a short time as they map their surroundings and there is a lot of activity around the hive.

Buzzing from flower to flower drinking nectar and collecting pollen on a beautiful sunny day may seem an idyllic way to spend the summer, but it is tiring work. A bee may have to travel miles back to the hive carrying her own body weight in food ten times a day and she will soon die from exhaustion. Her life expectancy once she's left the hive is estimated at three weeks in the summer, as she will fly around 800 km (500 miles) in this time. If she is born in the autumn, however, she could survive for months huddled in the hive keeping warm and eating honey stores. Only when spring arrives and she starts to forage will her days be numbered as her muscles give out.

In contrast to their busy sisters, the drones live a short life of Riley, fed and pampered and kept for the sole purpose of mating with a virgin queen. However, when they succeed they fall to their deaths, their genitals torn apart and left behind in the queen's vagina, to be ripped out by the next eager suitor. At the end of the summer, any remaining drones are evicted from the hive and left to die.

A queen can live for years, but if your bees swarm, or you split them each spring, you will have new virgin queens annually. A queen's job is to lay eggs. Without her your colony will die out. As a beekeeper, you need to be able to identify that your queen is laying well and to be able to recognise the different stages in the brood's development.

Birth cycle

It takes 21 days from an egg laid by a queen bee to become a worker bee. The process takes three more days for a drone but just 16 days for a queen. A worker bee's birth cycle follows a neat numerical pattern: three days after the egg – which looks like a grain of rice – is laid it hatches into a grub; six days later the pearly white grub, curled into a C-shape in the cell, has grow so big it looks like a Michelin man and is ready to pupate; the bees cap over the cell in which the larvae spins a cocoon and metamorphoses and 12 days later it emerges as a bee. If you can clearly see this development unfolding on the brood frames during your weekly hive inspection then you know that your bees are doing well. It is your first test of hive management.

Managing your bees in an urban environment

Clive Cohen, 81-year-old swarm collector at Barnet and District Beekeepers' Association in north London, has some extraordinary stories about where bees have swarmed. The most jaw-dropping was on a trouser leg.

'A guy sat down outside the Queen's Arms with his beer at lunchtime. The pub is next door to where I used to keep bees on the roof of a garage. His legs were under a trestle table and a swarm landed on his leg. I was called by the publican. When I arrived the poor guy's face was completely ashen. He'd sat quite still for an hour. The only way I could collect the swarm was to get him to remove his trousers, which he did very slowly in full view of everyone. I don't think he got stung.'

Other bizarre urban swarm locations include a lamppost in a busy shopping street – which made the local newspaper – the spokes of a bicycle chained to railings, the windscreen of a vehicle in a work carpark and the side of a tower block. The latter example was one of our colonies in Battersea.

Swarming is the honeybees' natural way of propagating, creating two colonies from one. The old queen and around half the colony leave the hive in search of a new home, leaving behind bees to raise a new virgin queen and develop a new colony.

It is a spectacular sight as darting bees fill the sky for 30 minutes or so. It looks like a snowstorm, but instead of the sky being filled with snowflakes it is brimming with bees. They then cluster together on a temporary site somewhere nearby. They can usually be spotted hanging in a rugby ball shape from the branch of a tree while scout bees investigate a permanent nesting site in the hollow of a tree or a wall cavity. But as the examples above demonstrate, other locations will sometimes do just as well in an urban environment.

Even with all the goodwill surrounding bees, most city dwellers with little knowledge of or contact with wild animals will be alarmed by a swarm. They won't know that the bees are filled with three days' worth of honey making them pretty soporific. In a built-up area, a swarm of bees has much more chance of coming into conflict with people than in the countryside. Pensioners at a community centre were unable to use their minibus one summer's day when a swarm of bees collected on one of the door handles. Luckily there was a spare bus or else they would have missed their eagerly awaited trip to the seaside. How long before the public's patience with bee swarms is so sorely tested that there are calls for urban beekeeping to be banned? For these reasons, swarm management has to be a crucial part of urban beekeeping.

From the beginning of April through to the end of June beekeepers have to be vigilant for telltale signs of swarming. In your first year of beekeeping you will start with a swarm or a smaller nucleus of bees, which is unlikely to want to leave, but it can happen so you need to look out for clues.

Urban Bees blog   29 May 2010

'It's been a busy old month with our bees swarming. It's certainly one way to get to know your neighbours. The ones who were around on our estate last Sunday – when a swarm decided to head for the shady side of the tower block instead of the plane tree they usually choose – were fascinated by the bees and some came into our garden to look at the hive.'

Factors that may help prevent bees from swarming include: spring cleaning the hive to give your bees a new brood box with clean brood comb or 'shook swarming' your bees onto new comb (see page 167) – this may make them think they have already swarmed; giving them ample room in the hive by adding a super box and frames before the brood box is completely full; using a young and vigorous queen to head the colony; and using a strain of bee that has been recommended for its low tendency to swarm.

Many beekeeping books will instruct you to clip one of the queen bee's wings to stop her flying off with a swarm. Many of those same books are designed for beekeepers who want to maximise honey production. Swarming will delay production often when the nectar flow is at its strongest. However, we don't agree with deforming the queen. Instead, we suggest that when you find queen cells in your hive that indicate your colony is preparing to swarm, you split the colony in two before the bees do.

Splitting your colony

During your weekly hive inspection when you smoke your hive and carefully take out each frame from the brood box to check for healthy brood development, you may see acorn-shaped cups on the bottom of the frames. These are queen cells.

Before these queen cells are sealed (capped) is the time to split your colony. You will need to get out a second brood box or a nucleus box, to find the queen – she is much easier to spot if marked – and to take the comb she is on together with the bees and place them in the middle of the second box. Transfer two more combs containing stores, brood and bees to the middle – make sure there are no queen cells on the frames – and shake off more bees into the second box. Then add a couple more new, clean foundation frames on either side. You should have five frames in all. If you are using a brood box, you will need to put dummy boards either side of the frames to stop the bees making wild comb in the gap. Place the box where a second hive would go in your apiary. Leave it for a few days before feeding the bees with sugar-syrup solution. You can then either keep this colony with the old queen to expand your apiary or you could ask around to find a new beekeeper who wants to start with a swarm, albeit an artificial one.

Queen cells will be capped halfway through the queen's 16-day birth cycle when the larvae stop eating and start pupating. Between day eight and sixteen of this birth cycle, you will need to find all the capped queen cells in the first brood box and to choose one that will survive. You will have to destroy all the others by squeezing them between your thumb and forefinger. The reason you have to do this unpleasant job is that if more than one queen is allowed to be born, the colony may swarm.

It is easy to miss queen cells so make sure you examine every frame and shake or brush the bees off the brood comb so can see right into the corners. This can be time-consuming and may agitate the bees so make sure your smoker is handy. A healthy queen cell is one that is large, placed on the face of the comb and has a dimpled surface.

Once you have left one queen cell for the colony to raise as their new queen, it is advisable not to open up the hive again for at least three weeks just in case your inspection clashes with the virgin queen's mating flight, as this will cause confusion. If she manages to mate, she should start laying 10–14 days after she emerges. From April to June there should be plenty of drones around to carry out this duty, but bad weather can delay her mating flight. If she fails to mate your colony will die. When you resume your weekly inspections you will know she hasn't mated if you see raised capped drone brood instead of smaller, flat, sealed worker brood. This means she is laying unfertilised drone eggs and you will need to replace her.

Collecting a swarm

If your bees do swarm, and however careful we are it can happen, have a second brood box, or nucleus box, ready to put them in. If you are keeping bees in a public place, make sure your telephone number is visible on signs or that relevant people can contact you if the bees swarm. If your employer is flexible, you may have to ask to take a morning or afternoon off to collect your swarm. It could even be worth taking your bee suit to work! Remember: a swarm can cluster all day before finding their new home, so when you get home they could still be there, but if they have landed in a high street or housing estate you may need to get there sooner. You will have to judge the potential seriousness of the situation.

If you are lucky enough to look out your window one fine summer's morning and see your bees swarming – they tend to leave before midday – put on your bee suit and see if you are able to catch the queen as the bees pour out of the entrance to the hive. The day our bees swarmed onto the side of the tower block they were back in the hive an hour or so later because we had caught the queen, placed her in a small cage, and put her back inside the hive. Realising they were queen-less, the bees soon made their way back home. We then found sealed queen cells and split the colony in two.

It is much more likely that you will be out when your bees swarm and the first you know of it is a phone call from a concerned neighbour or member of the public. The swarm can stay at their landing site for anything between an hour and a day until the scouts have found a new home. There will be occasions when they have left before you can get there. Other times they may be too high in a tree to get to, although that doesn't deter some beekeepers.

'I had to go up in a device call a "genie", which was a vertical lift,' recalls Barnaby Shaw, who keeps bees in central London including a hive on top of the Royal Festival Hall. He had been called to help the South Bank Centre where a swarm of bees were in the canopy of a London plane tree. 'There I was, 15 metres up in my beekeeping suit with tourists and other spectators looking up from below!' In the absence of a genie a step ladder is the more conventional tool.

The way to collect a swarm is quite simple if they are dangling from a tree branch. Wear your bee suit and gloves and give the branch a short, sharp shake so that the bees fall into a container that you are holding below. It is easier if there are two of you. One can shake while the other holds the receptacle – a straw skep, a nuc box or a cardboard box will all suffice. You can also cut the branch with a pair of secateurs.

In the case of a lamppost, bicycle spoke or car windscreen, or another favourite landing site, the gatepost of a fence, if you can get a container *above* the swarm they will move towards the darkness. You may also be able to encourage them into it by gently puffing the bees with your smoker.

If you are having problems collecting your swarm, seek help from an experienced swarm collector. Every beekeeping association will have one or two and their telephone numbers should be on the website.

Alternatively, get to know your local swarm collector before you get a call. We once saw a swarm being sucked up into a converted vacuum cleaner. Your swarm collector may have one of these 'strange contraptions.

There will probably be no shortage of people wanting your swarm – especially if it is May. An old nursery rhyme says: 'A swarm of bees in May is worth a bundle of hay, a swarm of bees in June is worth a silver spoon, and a swarm of bees in July is not worth a fly.'

You won't want a bundle of hay for yours, but you could sell it for a tidy sum or give it to your beekeepers' association who will have a list of people anxiously waiting for bees. In June there will still be takers. But by July fewer people will want a swarm. When the rhyme was written, a swarm in July was only worth a fly because the bees would have little time to make honey. Nowadays new beekeepers are less concerned with honey yield, but July is not an ideal time to start beekeeping because the main nectar flow is finished, even in cities, so a small colony will have to be fed to build them up enough to survive the winter.

Before you part with your swarm, you will first need to re-hive it on clean frames and foundation in a nucleus box and feed it for a few days. Or you could put the swarm into a new hive with frames and foundation to expand your own apiary. To transfer your swarm from the container into a nuc box or hive, just hold the swarm upside down over their new home and give them a firm shake. Make sure the queen falls in. There will be a few stragglers but if you leave the container by the entrance they will soon smell their queen's pheromones and make their way inside.

Caste swarm

Once your colony has swarmed, it may do so again. The first swarm is called a 'primary' swarm. The first virgin queen to emerge after the primary swarm has gone may decide to swarm herself. This is called a 'cast' swarm. When she has gone the next virgin to emerge may cast again. This could keep happening until there are no more bees left in your hive. You can prevent it by killing queen cells. A virgin queen will only swarm if potential rivals are about to be born in the hive.

If your bees swarm unnoticed, you won't realise until you do your weekly hive inspection and see that their numbers are depleted and the bees seem agitated because they don't have a laying queen. Hopefully there will be a virgin queen in the hive who is about to mate. Check if there are any sealed queen cells, leave one of these cells and destroy the rest, and leave the hive for three weeks.

Replacing a queen

If your virgin queen does not mate, you will need to re-queen. Introducing a new queen into your colony is also highly recom-mended in urban areas if your bees turn out to display aggressive behaviour. As we have mentioned it is difficult to know the tempera-ment of your bees before you get them home. An aggressive colony will buzz angrily during their hive inspections, bees will follow you as you walk away afterwards, and they will be more inclined to sting than docile bees.

Although Italian and Carniolan bees are bred for their gentleness, as they are hybrids you could be unlucky and get ones with a more defensive streak. As well as making your beekeeping a less pleasur-able experience, they could potentially upset your neighbours or the public if your hive is in a communal space. One way to minimise any problems is to ensure you never do a hive inspection when neighbours are using their garden, or people are close by. But this isn't always possible. You could have just taken off the roof of the hive on your allotment, for example, when your neighbouring plot holder unexpectedly arrives, or be holding up frames in a community garden when some curious people stray off the path towards you. And if your bees drink out of your neighbours' pond, there is more chance of their children being stung as they run around playing in their garden if the bees are the aggressive type.

The queen's pheromones determine the nature of her colony, so as one beekeeper put it: 'If she's nasty, she's got to go.' It seems a brutal solution, and one that many bee lovers like ourselves have been reticent to take but with the rise in urban beekeeping increasing the risks of conflicts between people and bees, it is one we would now seriously consider.

The BBKA produces a detailed leaflet on queen introduction. The basic principles are that you have to remove and kill the aggressive queen, and place a new queen in a special sealed introduction cage which you put in the brood-rearing area of the hive so the bees can familiarise themselves with her smell, and touch her through the small holes in the cage, before she is released into the colony. The cage comes with a wooden plug, which you will replace with a plug of candy before inserting in the hive. When the bees have eaten through the candy, the queen will be able to escape the cage by which time, with luck, they will have become accustomed to her. Sometimes bees don't take to the new queen and kill her. You won't know if your introduction has been successful until your next hive inspection – a recommended nine days later – at which you will be looking for evidence of egg laying.

If you have more than one hive, you may be able to rear a new queen to put in the troublesome colony. But more often than not you will have to ask around your local beekeeper association to see if any members have spare queens or order a new queen from a bee breeder. If you explore the latter option, your queen will probably be sent in the post in a travelling cage with a few attendants and some food. Don't be tempted to put this travelling cage into the hive. The attendants will antagonise the new colony and the cage could transfer disease. Young queens not in lay are liable to fly so make sure you do the transfer from travelling cage to introduction cage in a room with the windows shut.

Disease control

One of the other reasons why urban beekeeping requires such careful and regular husbandry is to ensure your bees are strong and healthy and to prevent the potential spread of disease to other nearby colonies.

We go into detail about the many foes our bees face and the best way to fight them off on page 156, with a summary in the month-by-month guide starting on page 202.

Whatever problems your hive may face, the only way you will be able to find out about them and solve them is by carrying out a weekly hive inspection. In your first year this will be your main management technique. From April onwards, pick a warm day once a week – don't open the hive when it is raining or below 13 or 14°C (55-7°F) – and look through each of the frames in the brood box. You are looking for eggs, larvae, sealed brood, pollen, honey and sealed honey. Don't forget to also keep an eye out for signs of swarming, with queen-cell building the telltale sign.

How to do a hive inspection

1. Light your smoker, put on your protection gear and give the hive entrance a few gentle puffs of smoke.
2. Wait for five minutes and then, standing behind the hive so as not to block the entrance, lift off the roof.
3. If you just got your bees a week earlier there will be a feeder in an empty super above the crown board which you then remove. If the feeder is not empty you can give it back to the bees at the end of the inspection.
4. Run the sharp end of your hive tool around the underside of the crown board which will be stuck with propolis, then prise it off gently. There will probably be lots of bees on the underside. Lean it against the entrance so the bees can walk back into the hive.
5. Use the curved end of your hive tool to lever an end frame out of the hive. You may find it is an empty frame of foundation that the bees have not yet drawn out into wax comb cells. That's to

be expected as most of the action takes place in the middle of the brood box.

6. Place the first frame in the upturned lid on the ground and lift out the next frame from the box. The foundation may have been drawn out but little else. Also place it in the lid to give you more room to slide out the remaining frames.

7. As you get nearer to the centre of the brood box the frames will have lots of bees on them that you need remove with a firm shake above the hive in order for you to be able to see the brood.

8. You should see large, pearly-white C-shaped larvae, smaller larvae and tiny white eggs like rice grains. Some of the cells will be covered with a brownish wax capping – this is sealed brood. The white, wax-covered cells on the edge of the frames is honey. There should also be cells containing different-coloured pollen and liquid nectar.

9. You may see the queen on the frame where there are eggs, but it doesn't matter if you don't see her. If there are eggs you know that she is laying.

10. If the bees buzzing around your veil are getting agitated – their buzz becomes high-pitched and louder – give them a few puffs of smoke.

11. Make a quick note of what you have seen on each frame. It is easier if there are two of you as one can be making notes or taking photos while the other does the inspection. We keep a notebook in the top of the hive in a freezer bag.

12. Put your frames back in place, scrape off any wild comb the bees have made on the crown board and replace it gently to avoid crushing lots of bees. When a bee is crushed it emits a pheromone alerting the colony it is in danger so mask that scent with puffs of smoke.

13. Replace the lid. Open the entrance by a few centimetres if they seem to be doing well and the weather is fine.

14. Walk away. Make sure there are no stray bees on your veil or suit before taking them off. Put out the smoker by sticking a cork or grass in the snout.

15. Write up your notes with the time, date, weather conditions, temperament of the bees, details of what you saw on each of the frames, your actions (if you fed the bees or gave any medication) and required action before the next inspection. If, for example, the brood had expanded beyond the middle frames to almost fill the box you will need to add a super and frames in a week's time where your bees can store honey, so you will need to make them up and have a queen excluder ready.

If the brood does not seem to be developing correctly (see page 195 for brood diseases) you should speak to an experienced beekeeper who may advise you to contact your local bee inspector. Even if all looks well, you should incorporate varroa monitoring (page 189) and drone brood removal (page 190) into your hive management regime.

Replacing old comb

In your second year of beekeeping and thereafter, you should always start the season by giving your hive a spring clean. In March, when the temperature hits 13 or 14°C (55-7°F), you can begin what is called the Bailey method of brood comb change. It allows you to remove old, potentially diseased brood comb and replace it with clean, healthy comb for the queen to lay her eggs in.

You will need to make up five new brood frames, have a second brood box ready, four dummy boards and some feed. This will be placed on top of the old brood box.

First, open the old brood box and take away the frames that have old stores or are empty. Leave five frames, which will include brood and bees, and centre these frames in the box.

Place the new box and five new frames on top of the old box, making sure the frames line up. Put in a dummy board at each end. You have just created a tall, thin nest.

Close up the hive and give the bees a feed to encourage them to draw out the new foundation above. What you want is for the queen to lay in the new foundation in the upper box, so leave them for a week and then have a look in the upper box for brood. You will more than likely see the queen on the new frames. This is the time to exclude her to the upper box by putting in a queen excluder between the two brood boxes.

You may need to add new frames to the top box as it expands but after 21 days all the brood that was in the lower box will have become adult bees and moved upstairs to look after the new brood. You can then take away the bottom box, queen excluder and clean the floor and area under the hive.

You now have a new clean box, comb and home for the bees.

Removing old comb using the 'shook swarm' method

If a varroa count in February and March reveals that your colony has a critical level of varroa infestation, you should practise the shook swarm method of spring cleaning instead of the Bailey method. How it differs is that instead of allowing your bees to migrate from the old comb to the new comb, this method gets rid of the old comb – and with it the varroa-infested brood – immediately.

Start by removing the old brood box and put your new brood box and 11 frames of foundation in its place, then find the queen, isolate her and put her in the new box before shaking all the other bees from the old box into the newly positioned one with her. Leave the old box by the entrance of the new one for a few hours to let the stragglers find their new home. Then take the box away to clean with a blowtorch and destroy the old comb. Your bees will need a feed after a shook swarm as there will be lots of work to do drawing out foundation before the queen can lay. The colony has lost all of its brood – as if it has swarmed – so it will be anxious to expand quickly. If the weather is poor you may need to keep feeding the colony until warm weather persists.

Because, as its name suggests, this method of varroa control does mimic a swarm, it will reduce your bees' swarming instincts at least for the few weeks while they are busy drawing out foundation and expanding the colony.

Making sure your bees have enough space for their honey

At the same time as checking on the health of your bees and curbing their enthusiasm to swarm, you will also have to ensure your hive is equipped for honey production.

Even though many urban beekeepers are not primarily keeping bees for the sweet, golden substance, if you don't give your bees enough space to store their honey they may swarm. So knowing when and how to add a super (a box full of frames for honey) is an integral part of managing bees in an urban environment.

You add the first super of the year with frames of shallow foundation (or their old honey wax comb from last year that you have stored over the winter) when the outermost frames in the brood box have been drawn out. If they have, the colony will soon need more space. You take off the roof and crown board and place a queen excluder on top of the brood box, trying not to squash any bees. Use a puff of smoke to shoo them off the top of the brood frames. Put the super on top of the brood box, making sure that the frames are aligned with the frames in the brood box below.

You can add a second super when all the frames of the first super are full of bees. This could be in one week if the weather is fine and the nectar flow is strong, or in one month if it rains or is cold. You can add the second super above (top supering) or below (bottom supering) the first. Putting it on top is easier for the beekeeper, but it is easier for the bees to get to new empty frames if you bottom super.

You may have to add as many as four supers to your hive over the course of the early summer. If you harvest frames or supers of honey as they are ready rather than waiting until the end of the summer, you can reuse supers and honeycomb as you go. This will save you having to buy four supers and 44 frames of foundations per hive. How to harvest your honey is explained on page 178.

By July your queen will be laying fewer eggs, so there will be more room in the brood box to store honey. You can encourage your bees to store honey down there for their winter stores by not adding any more supers.

Children and beekeeping

Sometimes you can lose sight of the joys of urban beekeeping with swarm management and disease control at the forefront of your mind. Involving your children, or other people's, in your hobby can quickly restore the magic. Take most children to a museum with an observation hive and their faces will be glued to the glass, mesmerised by the inner workings of a colony.

For some city beekeepers the rationale for keeping bees is to introduce their computer-bound, gadget-obsessed urban offspring to an aspect of nature. The experiences of Charlton Manor School illustrate the calming influence bees can have on even badly behaved young people. And beekeeping can be a pastime enjoyed by the whole family. Children's bee suits start at age six and the monthly beekeeping magazine, *BeeCraft*, has a children's page.

We don't have children, but beekeeping parents we have approached for advice on this subject suggest that eight and over is a good age to get kids opening up the hive. That said, parental perceptions of risk vary greatly so if you have children and are thinking of keeping bees you need to work within the boundaries of what you are comfortable with. Some parents may prefer limiting their children's involvement in their newfound hobby to harvesting the honey and candle making. Other parents let their children watch the hive inspection from a safe distance away of about 2 metres (6 feet).

'I've had bees that I've been happy to take my two-year-old right up to when they arrived, so gentle were they. My other bees are more snappy and I would make sure he was in the house and unable to wander up to me when I work on the hive,' says Rowena Young, who has two young children and two beehives. 'You also need to take into account your children's temperament. If they are timid, managed exposure, a little at a time, might be suitable. If they are fearless, they often dive in with oodles of curiosity and a matter-of-factness many new adult beekeepers lack. My then seven-year-old daughter was right in with the mature colony, spotting the queen before I could, damn her. She needs holding back a bit – she has a habit of picking up bees in her hands, and getting stung – though she just brushes that off. What's bothered her more is how hot you get in a suit on a warm day. For her, keeping sessions short or working the hives at the beginning or end of the day helped.'

'I would not hesitate to show my children bees even if they were quite small,' says one-hive Chantal Coady, whose children are 11 and 14. 'Most people's homes and gardens are full of hazards, so it just needs to be thought through in each case. Clearly bees can sting, and some people have bad reactions, but I think we should all be much more sensible and teach kids about bees, swimming, cycling, crossing roads, sharp knives and other potentially dangerous things so that they feel empowered to do stuff.'

Esther Coles, whose nine-year-old daughter Jeannie enjoys hive inspections on her mother's allotment, says: 'Keeping bees is a real treat for us all. I think keeping any animal is confidence-building for children (and adults) and the more they can be involved on all levels the better. I thought my kids would flap and run off but they were so calm I hope they'll come to every inspection because it makes me stay calm too!'

Kate Griffiths-Lambeth agrees. 'My youngest son Hamish, 12, has taken a real shine to the bees – after initially just observing me, he has become increasingly involved and is confident, careful and gentle. Having his own suit helps with his confidence. He is not fond of insects as a rule, but the bees have become an exception and he finds them fascinating. He is excellent at spotting the queen amongst her workers and seeing eggs in cells, etc … He understands the importance of bees to the environment and is proud to be doing his bit.'

But all the parents we spoke to agree that there is no one-size-fits all answer to questions around beekeeping and children. Only you know if your children or their friends are inquisitive enough to try pushing over the hive.

'One of my friends, as a kid, prodded a beehive with a stick and recalled getting hundreds of stings on her head,' says Coles. 'Kids are curious and really need to be educated. I do think under-fives don't always do what you tell them and I would certainly protect the bees from them and vice versa with a fencing.'

If you do decide to allow children to accompany you on a hive inspection, follow these simple safety tips:

- Show children pictures of what to expect beforehand and explain how to handle the hive tools safely and how they should act around the bees.
- Wear protective clothing and explain why you need it. Rubber gloves are usually too big for a child but you can stop them from falling off by using string or even Sellotape to stick the gloves to a sleeve.
- Keep children with you behind the hive, out of the flight path.
- Explain what you are doing and why and, where appropriate, let them have a go, as that makes it more interesting/memorable for them.
- Avoid letting young children play with hive tools, or be close to smokers (which often don't look hot but can provide a nasty burn).
- Little and often is probably better than a single very lengthy session, but don't force viewings on a child after the first time if they don't want to do it again.
- The most important thing is to make it interesting and at the same time to make the child appreciate that bees are not a game and that there are risks.

Remember, there are other ways of getting children involved even if you don't feel they are ready to accompany you on a hive inspection. Jill Mead says: 'Other ways to involve them can include: drawing pictures of colourful bees; making recipes with honey; honey tasting from the frame; and jarring honey, especially if it's a gift for someone.'

Urban honey and other bee products

For many urban apiarists, keeping bees at the bottom of the garden, on the roof, or on the allotment is a way of feeding their family locally produced, unadulterated honey all year round to ward off colds and hay fever. It is part of a drive for self-sufficiency and a personal crusade against the stranglehold the supermarkets have on our food supply. For city dwellers like ourselves who had become totally divorced from how our food is produced, keeping bees has also made us appreciate what it takes to make this golden liquid that has been revered for thousands of centuries.

Ancient civilisations venerated honey both for its sweetness and its medicinal properties. Cave paintings in South Africa dating back 20,000 years show honey hunters smoking bees out of their nest. Pharaohs made honey offerings to their gods and their mummified remains have been found with containers of 3,000-year-old honey designed to sweeten the afterlife. For the Greeks and Romans, honey was the food of the gods. The great poet Virgil describes it as an 'air-born gift of heaven'. And one of the oldest alcoholic beverages is honey wine, or mead.

Until modern medicine came along, honey's antiseptic and anti-bacterial qualities healed wounds, treated stomach disorders and cured colds. The Qur'an even has a chapter called 'The Bee' in which it extols the health-giving properties of honey. 'There comes forth from their [bees'] bellies, a drink of varying colour wherein is healing for men,' it says.

Manuka honey from New Zealand is cleverly marketed as today's cure-all, but in *Honey and Its Many Health Benefits*, author Margaret Briggs lists an A-Z of illnesses that all types of honey have been used to treat over the years, from arthritis to ulcers.

Research suggests the darker the colour of the honey, the higher its antioxidant content, so black-coloured buckwheat honey from the US, dark-brown chestnut honey from France, and Greek pine honey should all be highly prized.

Even our lightest honey is a hit with hay fever sufferers who swear that eating local honey helps their pollen allergy. The thinking is that because the honey contains minute quantities of the specific pollen to which they are allergic, eating it may help to desensitise the body.

Any fears about urban honey being polluted can be allayed because many flowers only secrete their nectar for a short period during the day from glands deep inside the flower. So while bees themselves may contact pollutants when they land on flowers, the honey they produce is pretty much pollution-free.

If you don't keep bees yourself, you may be able to buy locally produced urban honey at a local deli or farmers' market. It will be more expensive than the imported, blended varieties for sale in the supermarket but it is one way to support urban beekeepers.

One of the joys of urban beekeeping is regularly harvesting and tasting your honey during the summer. Every month will bring a different consistency, aroma and flavour depending on which combination of flowers are in bloom and have been visited by your bees.

Beekeeping books will tell you to harvest your honey-filled supers at the end of the summer. Yes, you can stack full supers one on top of each other in the hive until it is over six feet tall and then remove them all in one go in August, but why wait? Urban beekeepers can have their honey fresh off the comb every few weeks. We don't even wait until each of the 11 frames in a super is perfectly capped before we harvest ours; we harvest individual frames of capped honey.

In our front room, 35 small jars sit side by side in chronological order on a shelf on top of the bookcase. They are a reminder of each

Urban Bees blog   2 September 2006

'We couldn't wait any longer to taste our home-grown honey, so we selected one frame from the full super. Because there are still bees on the frame Brian made a box to put the frame in with a porter bee escape fitted at the top. This little plastic device allows the bees to escape from the box but they can't get back in. When we were sure all the bees had buzzed off, we took out the frame and prepared to scrape off the wax and the honey.'

batch of honey we have harvested since our first in west London in the hot summer of 2006. Some are palest straw, others a deep amber colour, some are still as runny as the day we span the honey off the comb; a few have crystallised and gone hard.

All urban honey is polyforal because of the rich variety of flowers in gardens, parks, railway sidings and growing on bits of wasteland. But you can sometimes detect strong differences in flavour according to the dominant nectar source.

Frequent visits to the horse chestnut tree, for example, will give your honey a toffee taste and lime trees will ensure that much late June honey in towns and cities will have a slight citrus flavour. But unless you have a very sophisticated palate, it is difficult to decipher many of the other subtle variations.

Broadcaster and amateur apiarist Martha Kearney attempted it when she was asked by the *Evening Standard* to judge the best London honey by their taste. She sampled 14 jars from central London to far corners of the capital and found a rich assortment of flavours. She described Regent's Park honey as having 'a strange aroma – cat's wee – but the taste was pleasant, with a touch of lilac'. Kennington honey 'smelt and tasted of jasmine flowers, beautifully fresh,' said Kearney, and honey from Hampstead Heath was 'an interesting, almost maple syrup flavour'. As we have seen it was the Kairos Community Trust in Streatham (see page 62) who were the winners of the tasting, with their Scottish tablet-flavoured honey.

It is rare for urban bees to produce insipid or flavourless honey. Unlike their rural counterparts, they are never exposed to the two crops that are an occupational hazard for beekeepers in the countryside.

Oil-seed rape and borage are ubiquitous on arable farmland, where the rape turns the fields a sea of yellow. Bees quickly devour their plentiful supply of nectar, filling up supers in a matter of days. But the honey is really as dull as ditchwater and oil-seed rape honey quickly crystallises on the comb.

Despite our cities' diversity of flora, which gives a continuous nectar flow throughout the summer and into the autumn, this doesn't mean you'll be harvesting honey in October. By July your bees will need to start keeping the honey they make for their own winter stores and by mid August the taste of any honey in the hive will be tainted by the thymol-based varroa treatment (see page 191) you have to apply at this time of year.

How much honey you will get from one hive depends on a number of factors: the weather, available forage, competition for sources of nectar, and how productive your bees are. You as a beekeeper can also influence the outcome by careful husbandry. The average honey yield per hive is estimated at 18 kg (40 lbs) of honey, which is equivalent to about two full supers, but a warm, dry summer from May through to August could double that amount especially if your bees don't swarm – swarming slows down honey production. Conversely, in a wet summer bees can't get out much to collect nectar, and what little honey they do make they may need to eat themselves because food is scarce, so you could have no more than one super's worth.

When you understand the effort bees put into producing just one jar of honey you will be thankful for receiving any.

One of the many fascinating facts about bees is that they are thought to fly some 55,000 miles – the equivalent of one and a half times around the world – to make a pound of honey.

German apiarist, Michael Weiler's own calculations for the production of 1.5 kg (3.3 lbs) of honey are mind-boggling.

'On the foraging flight which lasts 30 to 45 minutes, a bee visits 200 to 300 flowers of a plant species,' he writes. 'In doing so she accumulates in her [honey] crop about 0.05 g (0.001 oz) nectar; that is half her body weight. In really good weather a bee will manage about ten sorties a day, which yields 0.5 g (0.01 oz) nectar. On a good day, 10,000 foraging bees on 100,000 foraging flights will visit 20–30 million flowers and in doing so may bring in about 5 kg (11 lbs) of nectar. This is processed into 1.5 kg (3 lbs) of honey in the hive.'

If you factor in the processing, where the bees evaporate off the water content to turn the nectar into honey and then seal it with a wax cap, Weiler estimates it takes 12,000 bee-hours to make one jar of honey.

Many beekeepers find their first honey harvest a deeply emotional experience. At Camley Street Nature Park on the evening of 3 August 2010, trainee apiarists shed tears of happiness and hugged each other for joy as together they uncapped, extracted and jarred the fruits of their bees' labours.

Harvesting honey is always a delight, albeit a sticky one. Unlike picking fruit or digging up vegetables, it is not back-breaking work, nor does it have to be done on a specific day to prevent the produce rotting.

Kids love it, especially if you spin off the honey in an extractor. Ideally you'd have a separate utility room, but in a small city town-house or flat that is unlikely, so you need to make sure you've kept lots of old newspapers to cover the kitchen surfaces and that the kitchen is free for a few hours.

It can be a bit tricky at first. Getting the hang of removing the wax cappings with your special uncapping fork, for example, takes a bit of practice before you can do it quickly without removing chunks of the honey.

Here are some of tools you'll need for the job:

Bee escape: This is an ingenious bit of plastic with a one-way valve that allows you to take away a super full of honey without any bees. You attach the bee escape to the hole in the crown broad and place the super above the crown board. The bees can leave the super but they can't go back up into it, so 24 hours later your super is bee-free.

An uncapping fork: This is a special fork you buy from your beekeeping supplier to remove the white wax cappings from the honey. This is the same fork you can use for removing drone brood earlier in the summer, so make sure you have given it a good wash in soda crystals.

Sieves: A coarse sieve and a finer sieve are necessary for filtering, so that pollen, bits of wax and even the odd bee body part doesn't end up in your honey.

Honey buckets: We use these for collecting the honey in. They come in a variety of sizes from your beekeeping supplier. It's important that they have a valve (honey-gate) at the bottom so you can transfer the honey straight into jars. We have also started buying smaller buckets with lids, but without the valve, from pound shops which we find are good for storing honey if you don't need to jar it all at once.

Extractor: These are costly and bulky, so if you only have one hive it's worth either chipping in with other local beekeepers and sharing a communal extractor, seeing if your local association has one you can borrow, or scraping the honey off the comb instead. An extractor does, however, make harvesting quicker and less messy, and it allows you to reuse the honeycomb. We have a plastic, manual four-frame tangential extractor but you can also buy more expensive stainless steel, electrical models. Make sure that you get one that holds a minimum 9 kg (20 lbs) of honey – one super's worth.

Small, sharp knife: Taken from the cutlery drawer, a knife is used to slice small chunks of comb from the frames to make chunk honey. If you are using wired foundation, make sure you cut around the wire.

Spatula: This broad-bladed implement will allow you to scrape off honey from the comb while keeping the foundation intact if you do it gently.

Jars: People are forever giving us their old jars. Unfortunately, the lids harbour the odours of the previous inhabitant however well you scrub them, so unless you want your honey smelling of raspberry jam, marmalade or mayonnaise, it is better to buy new. We like hexagonal-shaped jars and use two sizes: 230 g (about ½ lb) and 130 g (about ¼ lb). They make great sizes for presents, or to sell. We found a cheap mail order supplier on the internet.

Labels: There are strict rules about labelling if you plan to sell your honey. But even if you give it as gifts to friends and family, they will probably want to know the location of the hive, and the month and year the honey was jarred. We design our own labels on the computer and print them onto sticky labels, but some beekeeping suppliers have a range of ready-made labels and others that you can customise with your own text and a photograph (also see below).

How to harvest your honey

Scraping

The advantage of harvesting a frame, or a few frames, of honeycomb at a time is that you don't have to lug a heavy super weighing 9 kg (20 lbs) up the garden, down through the hatch in the roof or across the office. This is particularly useful if there is just one of you.

It is best to remove the frame(s) during the day when most of the bees are out. Wear your bee suit, open up the hive, remove a capped frame of honeycomb, shake off the bees and brush off any stragglers, and replace the comb with an empty super frame of foundation. If there are too many bees, use a porter bee escape and come back 24 hours later. Carry the frame into your kitchen making sure you are not being followed by a group of angry bees. Quickly close any doors and windows to prevent bees and wasps getting in. Now the fun starts. Even one frame of honey can drip everywhere once uncapped. Uncap your frame on both sides using your special uncapping fork, by running it just under the surface of the cappings.

Place the white wax cappings in a bowl (we'll come back to those on page 184). Place a coarse sieve over a honey bucket and scrape each side of the frame(s) into the sieve with a spatula. If you do this gently the honeycomb foundation may still be intact and you can give this back to the bees in the evening to clean up and reuse. Leave the honey to ooze through the sieve into the bucket.

When it has collected in the bucket below, you can then filter it again into another bucket using a finer sieve. This whole process could take a few hours. Once it is filtered put a lid on the bucket and let it stand for a couple of days so that air bubbles rise to the top and form a scum that can be skimmed off before you pour it into the jars. One frame of wax comb filled with honey will contain just under 1 kg (around 2 lbs) of honey, enough for a few jars depending on their size.

When we had just one hive and a couple of supers, honey harvesting consisted entirely of scraping our frames into large sieves and buckets and waiting patiently for it all to ooze through. It was fun, physical, time-consuming work and of course we had to keep wiping up any drips with our fingers and licking them clean.

Using an extractor

The main drawback with scraping off the honey is that can easily destroy the honeycomb. So when we got a few more hives, we decided to invest in an extractor. Although bulky to store, it does make the harvest quicker and less messy, but no less enjoyable.

Our extractor takes four frames at a time. It sits on the kitchen table and once you've uncapped the frames of honey, you place each one in the drum and turn the handle slowly at first and then faster and faster until all the honey has flown out of the comb on to the sides of the extractor. Make sure the lid is on or it could splatter all over the kitchen. It's difficult to see when no more honey is coming off the frames, but the spinning will feel lighter. This will only take a couple of minutes. Because we have a tangential extractor, we have to take the frames out and turn them round and repeat the process again. A more expensive radial extractor will empty honey from both sides of the comb at once. Children squeal with delight when you let them turn the extractor handle and they can see the centrifugal force pushing out the honey. For one National super with 11 frames of honey, you will have to repeat this process six times. The first two lots of four frames you spin out twice, once on each side. You are then left with three frames. But the extractor needs to be balanced to work effectively, so you just put in two of the frames opposite each other and spin out on both sides. That leaves you with an odd frame. You can either put it in the extractor with three empty combs, although it doesn't work very well, or you can scrape this final frame over a sieve. Once you've got the hang of uncapping and extracting, you can harvest one super in less than an hour, but for a beginner it is probably best to set aside a morning or afternoon.

After you've extracted the honey, put the empty honeycombs back in the super to give to the same bees to clean out and recycle. It may be tempting to give the honeycombs to the nearest bees, especially if you have a hive in your garden while others are scattered around like ours, but that is a sure way to spread disease and best avoided. So if you are harvesting a few supers on the same day, be sure to remember which super frames come from which hive by marking them in some way.

If you are planning a harvesting day, keep honey from each super separate since they will each taste slightly different.

Jarring your honey

Whichever jar you use (see page 177), it's best practice to sterilise them first. If you do decide to reuse old jars, discard any that have cracks. Wash all jars in hot, soapy water and rinse in freshly boiled water, then drain upside-down on a clean tea towel. You can sterilise them in a preheated oven by standing them on a baking sheet for 10 minutes (Gas 3/170°C). Or you can put them in a deep saucepan, cover them with boiling water and boil for 10 minutes. Alternatively you can half-fill the jars with fresh water, place them one at a time in the microwave and heat on full power until the water boils. Wait until the jars have cooled before you add the honey.

The trick with jarring honey is knowing how wide to open the valve at the bottom of the bucket; too wide and the honey will escape too quickly and air will get trapped, too narrow and the trickle of honey will take ages to fill even a small jar and will get lots of air bubbles. Fill the honey to the neck of the jar then put the lid on each jar immediately. The lids should be tin-plated with a flowed-in seal on the underside of the cap that prevents air and moisture getting in.

Labels

There are as many honey labels as there are beekeepers and different types of honey. Some are homemade, others are professionally designed and printed. Our Urban Bees label aims to convey a sense of bringing nature into the city with a cartoon-like blue WBC hive and bees reminiscent of the famous E H Shepard Winnie the Pooh illustrations. In contrast, the London Honey Company has cleverly created the London skyline out of dripping honey. What the labels should all share is details about the location of the hive, the month and date the honey was made and your contact details. If you sell your honey other legal labelling requirements are:

1. The word 'honey' is required.
2. The weight must be on the label.
3. You can specify the type of honey.
4. If you are selling the honey through a third party, you must have a lot number.
5. You must have a 'best before' date on the jar (two to five years from now) – even though honey never goes off!

Selling your honey

Anthroposophist Rudolf Steiner said honey 'is something so valuable that it is impossible to put a price on it'. But of course people do, and the more pure and local it is, the higher its price tag.

At the top end of the market, a 227 g (8 oz) jar of Fortnum's Bees honey sells for £12.95, closely followed by Regent's Park Honey at £11.95. Mid-range honeys are Urban Bees Battersea Honey, retailing for £6.99 and Capital Bee Greenwich Honey for £3. At the lower end of the scale, your local deli or famer's market may sell jars of locally produced honey for less.

A farmers' market will take a percentage of your earnings, while a posh deli will pay you a wholesale price and then put a mark up on the retail price.

Don't be fooled into thinking that a few hives will pay for themselves in honey sales or even make you a profit. If you take on board the time it has taken you to produce the honey and the costs involved – not just for honey harvesting but caring for your bees each week – you will never break even unless you have a large-scale honey operation.

Bear in mind you will also need to be aware of food standards and hygiene regulations if you plan to sell your honey to a third party. Your local council or food standards agency will be able to advise on specific criteria.

Different types of honey

Blended: A mixture of two of more different honeys, often from different geographical locations. You will often buy this in the supermarket. Check the label to see if the product is from more than one country.

Chunk: A piece of the beeswax comb filled with honey cut out off the comb and put in a jar with liquid honey poured around it.

Comb: A slab of honey-filled beeswax comb cut off the comb and put in a presentation box. Honey on the comb is viewed as a delicacy by some people and can fetch a premium price, but beware: the chewy bits of beeswax have a habit of getting stuck in your teeth.

Creamed: Processed by controlled crystallisation to a smooth spreadable consistency.

Crystallised: When part of the glucose content has spontaneously crystallised and gone hard. Oil-seed rape honey can crystallise while still on the comb. A jar of crystallised honey can be re-liquified by heating in a double boiler.

Raw: Honey obtained simply by extraction, filtering and settling, during which process no heating takes place. Most locally produced urban honey will be raw.

Organic: Urban honey is unlikely to ever be certified organic because it would be difficult to prove that within a 5 km (3 mile) radius of, say, south-east London, your bees only foraged on plants that met a strict 'organic' criteria. If you want organic honey, you may have to look further afield to the Scottish heather moors, or compromise on food miles – the world's first certified organic and fair-traded honey came from a tropical forest in north-western Zambia in 1983.

Showing honey

We thought entering our local association honey show would confirm the positive feedback we'd received from friends and customers. Yet we found to our surprise that taste isn't the most important factor when it comes to showing honey. Key qualities for a technical honey judge are aroma, viscosity and clarity. So if you ever go to a honey show you will be confronted by the strange sight of old, bearded men inspecting jars of honey through magnifying glasses and shining a large torch at them. They are looking for any impurities such as air bubbles, which are the telltale signs of 'insipid crystallisation' – and something no prize-winning jar of honey will ever possess. We're no connoisseurs or experts but it does strike us as a rather anachronistic way to assess the quality of honey, like evaluating a marrow by its size rather than its taste.

You can also show other products made from honey such as cakes and mead, and candles made from beeswax. The BBKA produces guidance for judges that will give you a heads-up on what makes a prize-winner.

Other hive products

Propolis, pollen, royal jelly and beeswax are other products than can be harvested from a hive. However, we'd advise you to leave pollen for the bees to eat and, unless you are going into commercial bee breeding, collecting the royal jelly that the larvae bees feed on will be impossible. In contrast, propolis, the dark tree resin that bees use to stick parts of the hive together and fill up holes, can be easily scraped from the hive with your hive tool a little at a time and put in a small container. By the end of the summer you may have enough to sell or give away to friends.

Because it has antiseptic, antibiotic and antibacterial qualities there are claims that bee propolis boosts the immune system and fights infections. You will often find it in toothpastes and eczema creams. But remember the bees use it to maintain a germfree hive so don't take too much.

Beeswax

Bees have not only always been associated with sweetness, but also with light, because beeswax was important for candle making right up until the 20th century, when the Catholic Church finally permitted the use of non-beeswax candles. Today our light comes chiefly from electricity and most of our candles are made from paraffin and perfume. But beekeepers can still use the white wax cappings removed before extracting the honey to make subtle-scented beeswax candles, or even cosmetics or polish.

It takes about 4 kg (9 lbs) of honey to produce 450 g (1 lb) of beeswax. Worker bees secrete scales of wax about the size of a pinhead from their wax-secreting glands under their abdomen. It takes 500,000 of these scales to make 450 g of beeswax.

You'll have to use dedicated utensils for making wax as it is extremely difficult to extract. You will need a double boiler or bain marie (a pot within a pot). Put the wax cappings in the inner pot and indirectly heat them by boiling water in the outer pot. Add some water to the wax so that any debris contained in the wax can sink to the bottom of the pot.

Don't be tempted to heat wax directly as it has a low melting point of between 63 and 65°C (145 and 149°F) so it gets hot quickly and can easily burn and ignite. Use a metal strainer to coarse-strain the melted wax into a dedicated collecting pan. Melt the wax for a second time and then fine-strain it through nylon tights or muslin. You melt the fine-strained wax for a third time with some water and let it cool for a day or two. You will then have a block of light yellow wax floating on top of the water. It is yellow, rather than white, because of pollen and propolis.

There are plenty of recipes for beeswax polish, beeswax cosmetics and whole books on how to make beeswax candles, so we are not going to duplicate them here. Suffice it to say they all make great gifts or, like honey, are a good way to involve children or the community in your beekeeping hobby. Alternatively, they can be sold to generate income or to teach business skills.

Utilising more than just honey from your hive to meet some of your basic household needs also adds to that sense of self-sufficiency that beekeeping can bring. However, if you don't have the time, space or inclination to explore the treasures of beeswax, you can go to your beekeeper supplier and exchange your block for new beeswax foundation to put in your hive for the following year.

Pests and diseases

Even though anecdotally honeybees seem to be doing better in cities than the countryside, it doesn't mean we can take a lackadaisical approach to pests and disease. It is easy to miss early warning signs that something may be wrong with your bees and, left to flourish, disease can weaken your colony and eventually kill it. Conditions beyond your control can rapidly change to turn your healthy bees into sickly specimens. Nowhere is this more true than in a city where a densely populated area of hives means that if a neighbour's becomes riddled with a virus it can quickly spread to your colony.

Chief disease spreaders are infected bees who may drift into a healthy hive, and beekeepers themselves. If you transfer combs, honey or equipment from infected to healthy hives they will transmit disease.

Carelessly discarded honeycombs in an apiary can also attract infected robber bees. Simple steps such as always washing gloves and suits before you visit another colony, having a separate hive tool for each hive you manage, and never feeding your bees with honey taken from another hive can all help keep disease at bay.

Like us, bees are at their most vulnerable when they are stressed, aren't eating a balanced, nutritious diet and have become weak. So the best way to ward off ailments is to keep your bees strong so they are able to fight pests and parasites themselves.

In towns and cities the diversity of forage should provide your bees with a nourishing intake of food and prevent the malnutrition associated with monocrop farming, but if there is increased competition for food sources within a 5 km (3 mile) radius of where you live because of an influx of urban beekeepers, the best way to help your bees is to plant a bee-friendly tree and lobby your council to make its green spaces more bee-friendly (see page 87).

If it rains all summer, however, your bees won't be able to get out to collect pollen and nectar no matter how abundant the source. Feeding them sugar syrup will prevent starvation but a lack of protein will make them weak. Feeble bees cooped up inside a hive where disease can spread may succumb to various ailments.

In 2008, when average bee mortality reached 30 per cent in the UK, the National Bee Unit attributed the unusually high winter bee deaths to a wet summer in 2007 and in the early part of that spring, which confined bees to their hives. This meant they were unable to forage and this stress provided the opportunity for pathogens to build up and spread. However, in a report the following year from parliament's spending watchdog, amateur beekeepers were partly blamed for almost one in three hives perishing because it said they didn't know how to spot and combat disease.

Since then, government money has gone into better training for beginners, and The Food and Environment Research Agency (Fera) and the BBKA both produce very helpful leaflets, which are worth seeking out. In the meantime, here is a short guide to help you identify and tackle some of the most common honeybee pests and diseases.

The varroa mite

You have probably heard of the honeybees' nemesis, the varroa mite, which has killed millions of colonies worldwide.

Even the most robust honeybees can fall prey to this external parasite. The mite happily co-existed for millions of years with the eastern honeybee (*Apis cerana*), but proved lethal to its western cousin (*Apis mellifera*) when they were introduced in the early 20th century as man transported western honeybees to Asia. Our bees had no defences against the canny mite as it adapted to live on the new arrival.

By the late 1970s it was spreading across mainland Europe. In 1987, despite stringent efforts to keep it out, varroa arrived in the US and by 1992 it was reported in the UK. Now only Australia and the Antarctic are varroa-free.

The aptly-named *Varroa destructor*, under a microscope, looks rather like a cross between a jellyfish and a frisbee with hairy legs. Most books refer to it as spider- or crab-like because it has eight legs and is most closely related to the araneidae (spider) and argasidae (tick) family. To the naked eye, it is a reddish-brown dot, 1.1 mm ($\frac{1}{24}$ in) long and 1.5 mm ($\frac{1}{16}$ in) wide, hard to make out on adult bees but clearly visible on the pearly white larvae on which they also feed.

The reason these mites are so troublesome is not just that they weaken their host with their vampire-like feeding habits, but that as they move around the hive from bee to bee they spread nasty viruses, in the same way a dirty needle can spread HIV/Aids.

There are 14 identified honeybee viruses from the five-day killer, acute paralysis virus, to slow paralysis virus, which takes 12 days, and the less virulent deformed wing virus which clearly manifests itself in stumpy bodies and shrivelled wings. If your bees go into winter carrying one of these viruses they can die before enough new bees have been born to sustain the colony. As leading varroa specialist Dr Stephen Martin at Sheffield University explains: 'A significant proportion of over-wintering bees die prematurely and the rest of the colony gradually disappears as the balance of the colony is shattered.'

There is serious disagreement, as with most things in the beekeeping world, about the best way to tackle varroa. There are those who think nature should be left to take its course and any bees that survive will build up a natural resistance, and those who favour preventive measures. In an urban environment, we believe the mite must be controlled because it is irresponsible to let you bees potentially spread varroa and viruses to neighbouring hives.

We don't, however, endorse the use of 'hard chemicals' in the hive, preferring to take what is called an integrated pest management approach. This involves doing a variety of things throughout the year to try to reduce the mite population.

Counting your mites

First, you need to be able to find out if varroa is a problem in your hive. You can't tell just by looking at your bees. Luckily, we have never had the misfortune to see a mite on one of our adult bees. If you ever see this distressing sight then your colony already has a serious infestation. But we do know that varroa is present in most hives in Britain. We can assess the level by monitoring the 'mite drop' – this is the number of mites that fall through the varroa-floor mesh in your hive each day, either because they are picked off a bee by her sister, pulled off a pupae in a cell, or have come to the end of their natural life. To count the mites requires a varroa-floor with a drawer or tray underneath, which you order when you buy your hive. When you pull out the drawer it will be covered in debris, mainly bits of pollen, and the mites can be tricky to spot. But some will still be alive, so if you take your time looking at the tray you should eventually see brown specks moving around.

The National Bee Unit recommends you monitor your colonies four times a season: early spring, after the spring honey flow, at the time of the honey harvest and late autumn.

However, since we harvest our honey throughout the summer, and in cities it's not easy to know when the spring honey flow is over, we find it easier to monitor our mites once a month. We count the number of mites on the tray and convert this figure into a daily mite drop by dividing it by the number of days that the tray has been in. This requires meticulous record keeping.

UK research suggests that colony collapse is very likely before winter if the average daily mite drop for a colony exceeds the following: 0.5 mites in early spring, 6 mites in May, 10 in June, 16 in July, 33 in August and 20 in September. BeeBase has an online varroa calculator that you can use to assess the seriousness of the situation and it also recommends what action to take.

Because of the way the mites reproduce in sealed brood cells, ironically some of the strongest colonies with lots of brood often have the highest mite population.

We didn't realise we had a varroa infestation until one September we counted a hundred or so on the tray in a two-week period in a vigorous colony. This number equated to something approaching ten a day, still below the collapse level for that time of year but worrying nevertheless.

Even if your mite drop does not sound alarm bells in early spring and you can't see any varroa on your bees, the mites can build up very quickly during the summer as the queen starts to lay more eggs, so take precautions throughout the year.

Sacrificing drone brood

The female mite prefers to lay her eggs in sealed drone brood because drones take longer to develop (24 days) than worker bees (21 days) and those extra three days give her newly born daughters more time to mature and mate. So we give the colony a separate place to produce drone brood, which we then remove from the hive and kill before the drones and the mites have emerged from their cells.

To do this, we replace one brood frame with a super frame in the brood box in early spring when the queen is first beginning to lay drone brood. The worker bees will build natural drone comb beneath the shallow comb you have given them and the queen will lay drone eggs in the cells. When the drone cells are fully sealed, we remove the frame from the hive and then uncap it ourselves to see how many of the larvae are infested. Using a honey uncapping-fork, we slide the prongs under the cappings and scoop out the pupae.

If you are squeamish, you may find the sight of huge white pupae hanging from your fork nauseating. One of our beginner beekeepers retched when she saw the squidgy mess. It is certainly not an aspect of beekeeping we relish. We didn't take up this hobby to kill male bees, but it is one of those activities where you have to remember that a honeybee colony is a superorganism and sacrificing a few drones to aid the health of the whole is a case of the ends justifying the means.

Many beekeeping books recommend that you repeat this process several times throughout the summer. We usually do it twice, replacing the super frame we take out with another. We hesitate to do it more frequently, because we appreciate that depriving the colony of drones probably isn't good for the long-term genetic diversity of our bees.

Count the infested cells rather than each varroa mite – there could be five in one cell – and use the BeeBase varroa calculator to check if the level of infestation is serious.

If you find that more than 5–10 per cent of the 100 pupae you uncap and examine are infested with the reddish-brown mites, clearly visible against their pearly white bodies, you have a serious problem and will need to 'shook swarm' your bees (see page 167).

Icing sugar

Natural beekeeping disciples, if they do any varroa control, favour the icing sugar treatment. This involves liberally sprinkling your bees with icing sugar throughout the summer. It is thought to encourage the bees to preen each other and as they clean off the sticky substance from their sisters, it is hoped that they will damage and dislodge the mites who will fall through the varroa-floor onto the tray below.

Thymol-based treatment

At the end of the summer after we have harvested the last super of honey, we put a gel in the hive which kills mites. Beekeepers have been rightly criticised for adding a 'toxic soup' of chemicals to hives in their attempts to kill varroa. Researchers in the US investigating the role of pesticides in colony collapse disorder uncovered high levels of fluvalinate and coumaphos in old comb where the residues build up and suggested that this may be damaging the bees.

After enduring years of chemical warfare, the mites built up a resistance to varroacides such as Apistan, whose active ingredient is the synthetic pyrethroid, fluvalinate. This was just as we took up beekeeping, so we never had to make the difficult decision about whether or not to use them. Instead, thymol-based Apiguard gel became the most effective varroa treatment in the UK. It comes in small trays and you need two per hive. You peel back the lid and place the first one on top of the brood frames for two weeks, then replace it with the second.

The strong thymol fumes can make the colony want to vacate the hive so put a queen excluder on below the brood box and above the entrance to keep the queen in just in case the bees have the urge to leave.

Follow the instructions carefully since misadministration of medication reduces the efficacy of the treatment. Keep the varroa tray in while you are giving the varroa treatment to keep the fumes in the hive. Count the number of dead varroa that drop on to the tray. You may be shocked. Often the seemingly strongest colonies can be infested with varroa and the impact wouldn't be seen until next spring when they come out of winter weak and depleted.

How it works, according to the manufacturer Vita Europe, is that the bees don't like the fumes, try to remove the gel and in doing so spread it around the hive where it comes into contact with the mites. Pyrethroids kill mites by acting on specific nervous channels, and thymol disrupts cell membranes and affects all cellular processes, which Vita Europe says makes it more unlikely that the mites will be able to build up a resistance. We shall see. In the meantime, watch out for the pungent whiff coming from the hive and don't be surprised if your bees are hanging around outside.

If you have a varroa infestation in early spring, you can try using Apiguard then. But thymol can make the queen stop egg-laying for a short period, and in the spring she needs to build up the colony, so only use in an emergency. Also, make sure you don't apply it too late in the autumn as once the temperature drops it won't fully vaporize.

Oxalic acid

This is the final weapon in the beekeepers' anti-varroa armoury. A naturally occurring substance, found in rhubarb leaves and spinach, it nevertheless conjures up images of burnt bees and frizzled mites, and, certainly, too high a concentration can harm the bees. Only use it as a last resort if you have identified a serious varroa infestation at the end of the summer.

You apply it either side of the winter solstice (21 December) when there is little, if any, brood so any varroa will be on the bees themselves. This means you will have to open the hive on a cold day and upset the temperature inside.

To ensure you administer the right dose, buy a ready-prepared solution of oxalic acid in sugar syrup. We purchased a 3.2 per cent solution in a squeezy bottle with a special dispensing chamber that allows you to trickle just 5 ml (1 tsp) on each seam – the space between the top of the frames – of bees. The promotional literature says that in winter there may only be bees on five or six seams, but the one time we used oxalic acid we had bees on eight seams. It did take a bit of practice to get the hang of applying it, resqueezing the bottle to get the solution in the upper chamber and then turning it over and squeezing it out.

The solution should be lukewarm to avoid chilling the bees, so you may need to stand the bottle in hot water for a few minutes or put it in your pocket. Although you apply it in midwinter you should still wear your bee suit and gloves.

The acid works by damaging the mites' respiratory system and also their claspers, which prevents them from sucking the haemolymph (the fluid in the bees' circulatory system, rather like their blood) from the bees.

Varroa-resistant bees

None of the varroa treatments are a panacea. If natural selection was allowed to occur, an experiment carried out on the Swedish island of Gotland, in the Baltic Sea, suggests that varroa-resistant bees would develop. Bees were left to fend for themselves, and as you'd expect, initially most of the colonies died. But after six years mortality rates decreased to 19 per cent. The bees that survived evolved to live in small colonies, with a short breeding cycle and produced few drone brood.

Scientists and beekeepers are trying to breed a strain of Western honeybee that is varroa-resistant. Professor Ratnieks at Sussex University is breeding a 'hygienic' bee. These are worker bees that have been selected for their genetic trait of removing dead pupae and larvae afflicted with mites from hives.

Veteran UK beekeeper Ron Hoskins hit the headlines in 2010 with his Swindon 'super bee'. For a number of years he has been breeding queens from colonies that he discovered had a propensity to damage mites and to uncap brood cells to remove varroa-afflicted pupae.

Researchers in the US developing their own hygienic bee found that it was a less profilic honey-maker, which raises the question of whether selecting for one beneficial characteristic might at the same time unwittingly select against others.

The latest breakthrough in the war against varroa has been made by researchers at the National Bee Unit (NBU) and Aberdeen University who have worked out how to 'silence' natural functions in the mites' genes to make them self destruct.

All these possible scientific solutions to ridding our bees of their most lethal foe are exciting. But it will be years, if ever, before varroa-resistant bees or self-destructing mites are a reality for most beekeepers. Until then the best way to help your bees is to follow an integrated pest management regime and to keep up to date with the latest varroa control techniques from the NBU or your local beekeeping association.

Wax moth

A pest that has been around a lot longer than varroa is the wax moth. Aristotle in his animal books observes: 'There is another insect resembling the moth, called by some the "pyraustes", that flies about a lighted candle: this creature engenders a brood full of a fine down.' And he writes of a disease attacking prosperous beehives that consists of 'a growth of little worms on the floor, from which, as they develop, a kind of cobweb grows over the entire hive'.

Wax moth is still common in hives today, laying its larvae among the bee brood in a straight line. It is easy to spot because the larvae chews the brood cappings, so if you have a straight line of what looks like uncapped brood in a frame of sealed brood, chances are it is the wax moth. Tapping the frame should bring the larvae to the surface, where you'll see they look horribly grey and wormlike compared to the bees' pearly white grubs. If tapping doesn't work, try pulling them out with a pair of tweezers. Not nice, but it is the only way to get rid of them. If you don't eject them from the hive, they will eat away at the bees' wax comb and spin silk webs that can ruin the comb just as Aristotle witnessed.

Mice and other large pests

For other large pests, such as mice and woodpeckers, barrier methods will deter them. A mouse guard is a thin strip of metal with very small holes in it which, applied to the entrance of your hive in the autumn, will prevent mice getting in to make a dry, warm nest. In the suburbs or the edge of towns woodpeckers may make holes in the side of your hive and feed on juicy bee larvae, so loosely wrap the hive in chicken wire to stop them. If there are reports of badgers encroaching into your neighbourhood be sure to erect a tall fence around the hive. Badgers are strong enough to topple over the hive, rip it open and wolf down the protein-rich larvae and sweet energy drink they find inside.

Brood diseases

There are a number of diseases that just affect the brood. So giving your hive a spring clean in March to replace old brood comb, where bee pathogens can fester, with new foundation (see page 166) is considered good beekeeping.

Chalkbrood
Caused by a fungus that invades and kills the larvae, this is the most common brood disease. It turns the dead larvae into hard, chalky-white remains, hence its name. The adult bees remove these so-called 'mummies' from the hive. It is not unusual therefore to find a pile of chalkbrood mummies at the entrance of the hive in the spring. It is distressing when you see it for the first time. But don't panic. The bees are dealing with it themselves and it usually only affects a small proportion of the brood, so it is rarely a serious

disease. However, it is a sign that a colony is weak. This may be because there is little pollen around at the beginning of spring and the larvae are hungry, so feed your bees fondant. As spring progresses, and more food comes into the hive, the colony should grow stronger and chalkbrood will no longer be a problem. But larvae affected by chalkbrood can release millions of spores with a sticky coating that can stick to combs and remain infectious for three years or more. This is another reason why replacing old comb with new brood foundation each spring is critical to prevent disease.

Sacbrood

Also called Chinese slipper, this is a common virus affecting brood. The Fera guidebook on how to recognise and control brood diseases mentions that it is an easy one to spot. You can refer to the gruesome photos in the book if you're unsure of its presence. Larvae die from the virus in their sealed cells and become like fluid-filled sacs, stretched on their back with their heads towards the top of their cells. The worker bees uncap the cells to reveal pale yellow larvae with their head curled up like a Chinese slipper. There is no treatment for sacbrood; getting a new queen is recommended in a bad case. You can remove the larvae in one piece from the cells using tweezers. The virus becomes non-infectious within a few weeks. Like chalk-brood, relatively few larvae will be affected and it rarely causes measurable harm to colonies. It can however sometimes be mistaken for a much more serious disease, American foulbrood.

There are two notifiable honeybee diseases in the UK under the Bee Diseases and Pests Control (England) Order 2006 (there are separate orders in Wales, Scotland and Northern Ireland); they are American foulbrood and European foulbrood. Like foot-and-mouth or bluetongue in cattle, if your hive has an outbreak of either of these brood diseases you have a statutory duty to notify the govern-ment. You can do this by either contacting the National Bee Unit in York or by speaking to your regional bee inspector. They will send out a local inspector to do some tests and assess what action to take, which in the worst-case scenario could be torching your hive and bees.

Both of these brood diseases are caused by bacteria. One is much more prevalent than the other and if there is an outbreak in your area it can spread very quickly.

American foulbrood

This is the less common of the two notifiable diseases and hopefully you will never see it. But you need to be aware of the telltale signs in the unlikely event that your colony has the disease. We have only seen it once, when we were holidaying on the island of Crete. A friend who lives on the north of the island and had recently taken up beekeeping invited us for dinner and to look at his apiary. We had read about the sunken, perforated and greasy-looking dark wax cappings, but we couldn't believe it when we actually saw this in one of his hives. To make sure our diagnosis was correct, we found a matchstick and inserted it into the cell to do what is called the 'ropiness' test. If, when you pull out the matchstick, it is covered in a brown mucus-like thread, or rope, up to 30 mm (1 inch) long then you can be sure it is AFB. While part of us was excited to have detected AFB, we were concerned for the bees and how our host would take the news. We didn't know the rules for AFB in Crete, but we advised him to destroy the bees and frames and to scorch the hive. Thankfully, he was grateful that we had identified the disease. He said he had heard there was an outbreak on the island and he would follow our advice and burn the frames in a few weeks when it rained and was considered safe to start fires on the island.

Control of AFB in the UK by compulsory destruction of infected colonies has been highly effective since it was first introduced in the 1940s and has brought the incidence down from several thousand infected colonies to just 31 in 2010.

European foulbrood

You are more likely to come across this notifiable disease, which is also caused by bacteria in the gut of the larvae. However, unlike its American namesake, EFB kills the larvae before they are capped. You will see yellowish-brown larvae lying stretched out or twisted in cells, rather than the pearly white C-shaped larvae that a healthy colony produces. The brood pattern may also appear patchy, as dead brood is removed by the bees. Fera says that EFB 'cannot be reliably identified visually, as the disease signs can easily be confused with various other brood abnormalities'. So if you have any doubts, call out the bee inspector. An unpleasant odour may sometimes accompany severe EFB infection. If caught early enough it may be treatable with antibiotics administered by the bee inspector, but if not the colony and hive will have to be destroyed to avoid it spreading to other hives.

Adult diseases

Even if your brood is in fine fettle, your adult bees could be sick.

Nosema

This is a single-cell organism that multiplies in the mid gut of adult bee and impairs digestion. The first you'll know of it is when you see patches of brown splattered on the hive. This is bee excrement and it means that your bees have diarrhoea and dysentery. It may also be visible on brood comb. Young house-proud bees will try and clean up the faecal material on contaminated combs but unfortunately this action spreads the spores. Because the lifespan of infected bees is shortened, it increases the likelihood of your colony perishing in the winter. There are two types of this gut parasite: *nosema apis* and its more virulent cousin, *nosema ceranae*, which like varroa crossed the species barrier from its Asiatic host, the eastern honeybee, to our western honeybee. Unfortunately, *nosema ceranae* does not show the tell-tale signs of dynsentry.

An antibiotic called Fumidil B can provide temporary respite. It comes in powder form and can be mixed in sugar-syrup solution to feed to your bees in either spring or autumn. Some beekeepers give it to their bees in a just-in-case way, regardless of whether or not they actually have nosema. This could actually lead to nosema developing a strain that is resistant to the treatment, so only give your bees Fumidil B if it is 100 per cent necessary.

To be sure any signs of dysentery are caused by nosema, you should take along a sample of bees to your local beekeeper association's diagnostic clinic. Each year, your association will hold a number of these clinics where they will test for a variety of ailments.

To participate, you will be required to take along about 30 dead bees. Killing bees is never nice, even though we know it is for the good of the superorganism. The best way to do it is to scoop them up into a household-sized matchbox and put it in the freezer.

At the clinic, experienced beekeepers will mash up your dead bees' abdomen in a pestle and mortar with a few drops of water. They will take a drop of this bee soup and put it onto a slide under a microscope. Under the lens, they are looking for little, pale, rice-shaped grains that are nosema spores. You could do this at home if you have a microscope with x 400 magnification, but it is best left to someone with an experienced eye.

All the bees we have had checked out have been given a clean bill of health, so no antibiotics were needed for those colonies. But the spores can persist on contaminated comb and trigger more severe infections the following winter, so remember to do your spring clean.

Tracheal mite

Also known as acarine or Acarapis woodi, this is another blood-sucking parasite. This one, however, lives in the adult bee's windpipe, or tracheal tube, which is the thickness of a human hair. The female mite lays her egg in the tube and the baby mites pierce through it and feed on the bees' haemolymph (body fluid). Like varroa, it will shorten the bees' lifespan and can lead to a colony dwindling and dying in the spring. In the worst-case scenario you may see crawling bees that are unable to fly. It can be diagnosed at your association's bee clinic. Some associations test for nosema and tracheal mites at the same clinic. However, there is no approved medication in the UK for these mites, so prevention is the best cure. By making sure your bees are healthy and stress-free, you will help them fend off these unwelcome predators.

Future threats

Globalisation is killing bees as bee pests and diseases are being passed swiftly around the world, a United Nations study reported in March 2011. It predicted that it is only a matter of time before our beleagured honeybees will have to contend with three more pests that have yet to reach UK shores.

Asian hornet: This is a south-east Asian species of wasp (*Vespa velutina*) that was first recorded in France in 2005. It is thought to have arrived in the port of Bordeaux in a container of pottery from China. It has spread quite rapidly over the country but has so far not been spotted in the UK. It is capable of wiping out colonies of bees but government scientists say that the impact on honeybees can be limited by reducing the hive entrance to a narrow slit. They are asking people to be vigilant and report any sightings of this hornet, which is 25 mm (1 in) long, has a dark-brown thorax and abdomen with yellow at the tip.

Tropilaelaps clareae: This is another mite similar in looks and behaviour to varroa which has been found infesting colonies of *Apis dorsata* and *Apis mellifera* in the far east.

Small hive beetle: This is native to southern Africa and since it was found in the USA in 1998 has been causing widespread destruction and damage to western honeybee colonies.

You can read more about these future threats in Fera booklets.

Sources of help

BeeBase

The government's online database for beekeepers provides a wide range of information for beekeepers to help keep their bees healthy. All beekeepers should register and request a visit from a local bee inspector.

When we had our first hive, we met our local bee inspector at an association meeting and asked her if she wanted to have a look at our bees. She was more than happy to make an appointment and when she went through the hive with us, her inspection helped to reassure us that our bees were healthy and we were doing the right thing.

Knowing the distribution of beekeepers and their apiaries across England also helps the National Bee Unit to effectively monitor and control the spread of serious honeybee pests and diseases. If AFB or EFB is reported in an area, all the registered beekeepers locally will be contacted and visited by an inspector.

Between 2008 and 2010 the number of colonies with EFB in England almost halved from 806 cases to 434 according to inspectors' reports, while AFB was detected in 31 colonies compared to 58 three years before.

BBKA
The British Beekeepers' Association produces a number of useful leaflets about pests and disease.

Your local beekeeping association
This will disseminate the latest techniques that Fera and the National Bee Unit have devised for tackling bee ailments and controlling varroa. You will probably be able to attend demonstrations on applying oxalic acid, spring cleaning your hive, and diagnostic clinics.

Sometimes beekeeping can seem little more than pest and disease control. It can get a bit overwhelming and scary. When this happens, take a deep breath and try to develop a Zen-like calm about any possible setbacks. Remember that honeybees have been around for millions of years and had seen off a host of foes before we were even around to give them a helping hand.

A month-by-month guide to urban beekeeping jobs

Beekeeping is a fair-weather pastime. Your bees will fly from March to October and the odd winter day when the temperature climbs above 11°C (52°F). But to make the most of what beekeeping has to offer requires preparation during the colder months. For younger city beekeepers with busy jobs, full social lives and little space, planning is paramount. You can't take a day off work if your bees are preparing to swarm early, or run out of storage space in the hive quicker than you expected, or suddenly need a feed. So we've included 'guidance at a glance' as to what you should aim to do each month to make urban beekeeping as painless as possible.

The type of bees you have and the weather conditions where you live will influence the timings of some of the jobs we recommend, but we are writing with city centres in mind, which tend to be a few degrees warmer than the surrounding countryside.

January: Courses, order new equipment, heft your hive

January is the month for New Year resolutions. If yours is to become an urban beekeeper now is a good time to get onto a beginners' course. You may want to start with a day-long taster course to get a feel for what beekeeping entails. If you are then convinced that it is the hobby for you, you can book a place on an introductory course run by an association or commercial trainer that will cover both theory and practical beekeeping.

If you already keep bees, think about using this month to improve your knowledge by taking one of the many BBKA beekeeping modules on offer. Some may be taught one evening a week at your local association, or you can take a correspondence course if your timetable clashes with the classes. The BBKA website has a full list of modules.

January is also a great time to get ready for the beekeeping season ahead. Take stock of your equipment and put together a list of what you will need to buy. If you are going into your second year of beekeeping, you will have a long list, including a new brood box with frames and foundation, a blowtorch to clean the old brood box you will be removing in the spring, a new cover board and open-mesh floor, and another super for extra honey production. Remember to order the frames and foundation to go in the super and jars and labels for your honey.

You may also want to consider whether your honey harvest would be easier with an extractor. If so, ask around your beekeeping network to see if there is anyone who lives nearby who you could share an extractor with to reduce the costs and storage problems. You may also want to think about increasing the size of your apiary and buy a second hive for when you split your colony in early summer to manage swarming. By getting your order in early you won't have the risk of the suppliers being sold out or having a backlog. Don't forget to order varroa treatments that you apply later in the year.

You can't open the hive in January but you should keep an eye on the entrance to make sure it has not been blocked by dead bees. Don't panic if you see lots of dead bees around the hive during the winter. When they die naturally in the hive, the surviving bees will drag them outside so as not to clutter up the hive or spread disease. But sometimes they clog up the entrance and trap the live bees inside the hive, who will want to come out on a mild day to defecate and hunt for any early pollen from snowdrops, winter aconites and white deadnettles. Clear any dead bees with the hook end of your hive tool.

While you are at the hive check its weight for an indication of the amount of stores in the hive. You do this by 'hefting' the hive – lifting it with one hand at the back of the hive just slightly off its stand. If it tips easily then there probably isn't enough food. If it is hard to lift then there will probably be enough. Knowing where the balance lies comes with experience, so heft hives at intervals during the winter. Remember how heavy it was when you first hefted it in September. If you left the colony more than 13 kg (30 lbs) of stores in the autumn they should have enough for winter, but sometimes the cluster of bees can't get to the food or the honey may have crystallised and be difficult to eat.

This is an anxious time in beekeeping calendar. The queen has started to lay again and there will soon be hungry mouths to feed, so you may want to feed your bees. It is best to feed them fondant, not syrup, at this time of year because they can use it as instant energy rather than trying to turn it into honey. Place a block that you have bought from your beekeeping supplier over the crown board holes and the cluster will soon find it. Once you start to feed your bees you can't stop until there is a good source of natural forage available that they can get out to eat, which if we have a particularly cold and wet spring may not be until May.

February: Build new equipment, feed and read

The days are getting longer and on the milder ones the bees will be out looking for that early pollen to feed the young from the crocuses and hazel trees. It is still too early to open the hive, but keep hefting when you occasionally visit to gauge the amount of stores and feed the fondant if necessary. This is the month when the bees are most vulnerable to starvation as the growing brood will probably need more food than the remaining stores can provide.

All the new equipment you ordered should arrive and can be built this month and stored, so find some spare evenings or weekends to construct your flat pack brood boxes and frames of foundation.

Buy a few kilos of cane sugar. You will need this to make a sugar-syrup feed to give your bees after you do the spring clean next month. Don't forget to get soda crystals in preparation for cleaning your equipment too.

There is always plenty to read about keeping bees and plenty of sources. Go online and register on one of the many growing beekeeping forums. This is a place where you can ask the questions that have been going through your mind and get answers from your peers. More traditional sources of information are your local association or *BeeCraft* magazine.

For beginners, if you've done a taster course, get on an introductory course and begin your theory lessons, keep reading and order equipment.

March: Spring clean, varroa control, scorch old equipment

With luck your bees will have survived the winter and are out foraging on warm days. This is the month for both spring cleaning your hive and starting your integrated pest management approach to varroa control.

When the temperature hits 13 or 14°C (55–57°F) you can begin the Bailey method of brood comb change, which will allow you to remove old, potentially diseased brood comb and replace it with clean, healthy comb for the queen to lay her eggs in (see page 166). You can put the old brood comb on the compost, but burning the whole lot is best. We give ours to a friend who has a wood-burning stove still going at this time of year. If you don't have a fire or compost then they just have to go out with the rubbish. Keep detailed notes so you know when you can return to the hive to finish the process three weeks later. Once the brood change is complete you will put on a clean cover board and open-mesh floor.

Clean up the old brood box you have taken off. A good scrape with the hive tool and then scorching the woodwork with a blowtorch is the most effective way to clean your equipment. The heat will get rid of all the pests and disease that might be lingering.

In your new brood box, you should insert a short super frame of foundation as your varroa trap (see page 189). Use the BeeBase varroa calculator to check if the level of infestation is serious. If it is severe you should shook swarm your bees (page 167).

The weather in March is highly unpredictable, so you will have to be prepared for beekeeping in both cold and warm conditions. If there is a cold or wet snap, the colony will need feeding because by now there will be many mouths to feed and brood to keep warm, which takes lots of food and energy. Candy or syrup, if it is warm enough, can be fed on top of the crown board.

If there is a warm spell, your bees could think about swarming, so you will need to look for queen cells. But a comb change for your spring clean and a shook swarm will both greatly diminish the chance of your bees swarming now, since they will be too busy drawing out the new foundation comb you have given them.

Beginners can put together their hive and frames and foundation and order some bees for May.

April: Swarm watch, weekly hive inspections, varroa monitoring

This is the start of the busier hands-on period for the urban beekeeper. It marks the beginning of the swarm-watch season. Have your spare equipment ready to split a colony as a method of swarm control if you see queen cells.

If you are going away for Easter you might want to arrange for a beekeeping friend to come and have a look at your colony while you're on holiday. If not, put into place strategies that may prevent the swarming urge such as adding a super to give your bees more space or splitting the colony before you go. You can always reunite them when you're back.

Queen cells don't always mean swarming. They can also signify 'supersedure' or an emergency queen replacement – maybe the queen was damaged in the previous inspection – so you need to know the difference. Many acorn-shaped queen cells hanging at the bottom of the frames suggest swarming, whereas a few of these cells in the middle of the frames indicate supersedure, in which case the colony is best left to carry on by itself.

As the weather becomes warmer you will begin your weekly routine hive inspection. Pick your time during the day and make sure your neighbours are not out in their gardens if your hives are close to them.

Start your varroa monitoring this month too. Put in your clean varroa tray for a set number of days and count the number of dead varroa. Use the BeeBase varroa calculator to check the level of infestation. You can also trap more drone brood as part of your varroa control.

If the weather is particularly warm in April and there is plenty of forage you may need to add a super as the bees will be ready to store extra honey. So make sure you have both a super and frames and foundation made up. Or, even better, if you kept frames of honey wax comb from last year that your bees cleaned out, stored in old supers, give these to your bees. It will save you and your bees much work.

If April is cold and wet, think about feeding your bees again. The colony is not safe from starvation until May.

Beginners should aim to get some hands-on practical training and have your hive in location for when your bees arrive next month.

May: Add supers, collect swarms, harvest honey

This is the bees' favourite month. They have got through the winter and the chilly spring when food is scarce. Now the weather is warm most days and there is a strong flow of nectar and pollen as a huge variety of flowers and trees burst into bloom. The queen is laying up to 2,000 eggs a day to build up the colony and there will be plenty of drones around waiting to mate with virgin queens. By the end of the month you may be able to harvest the first honey of the year.

But it also means that May is the beekeepers' busiest month. You will have to have supers with frames and foundation ready to add, be vigilant for swarms and be ready for honey harvesting.

Have your honey harvesting equipment and your jars ready for the end of the month. If you need to borrow an extractor, book a time a few weeks ahead.

If you decide to harvest your honey a few frames at time instead of removing a whole, heavy 11-frame super, remember to replace the frames you are taking away with new ones. Don't underestimate how quickly the bees may fill them with honey. If the nectar flow is strong they can fill and cap a super in just a week. Make sure they have enough room for their honey stores, or else they may decide to swarm.

If your bees weren't getting ready to swarm last month, chances are they will want to swarm in May when the warm weather and plentiful supply of food means they have a strong chance of survival. So you will have to be even more vigilant for signs of swarming and have spare equipment ready to split the colony as a management measure. If you don't want to keep the second colony you've created, ask at your local association if anyone wants a nucleus of bees.

If your bees do swarm, and however careful we are it can happen, have a second hive or a nuc box ready that you can put them in if you can collect them. If you are keeping bees in a public place, make sure your telephone number is visible on signs. It may be worth taking your bee suit to work.

Keep up your integrated pest management systems. You varroa tray should be kept off the hive unless you are monitoring the varroa drop count for a few days a month.

Keep writing up your records with information about how much brood there is in the colony and how much honey you take off.

Beginners, this will be a very exciting month if your nucleus of bees is ready to collect. Make sure you have a welcome meal of sugar syrup made up for them after you have transferred them into their new home. Wait a week before you do your first hive inspection.

June: Harvest, swarm management and varroa control

There may well be quite a few frames of honey ready for you to take off. If you take off frames regularly you should start to taste the difference in the flavour, consistency and colour between batches.

Don't be greedy though, as the bees still need a lot of food for themselves. You will see fresh protein-rich pollen being carried into the hive on the bees' back legs as food for the young grubs, but the colony also needs the honey as its energy fuel. Leave them enough so they don't get hungry, especially if the weather turns wet and they can't get out to forage.

The colonies will be large at this time of year and you may have two or three supers on top of the brood box, so having a beekeeping buddy will help with the heavy lifting that is required to get to the brood box for those weekly hive inspections you still need to do.

Swarming is still likely as well as supersedure, so be on the lookout and take the necessary actions.

Keep up your integrated pest management systems and write up your records.

Beginners will be getting the hang of hive inspections, making notes and recognising what a good brood pattern looks like. If your bees are building up well and have nearly filled the brood box, you will be able to add a super for honey production. Make sure you give your bees enough space or they may swarm. Swarming is unlikely in your first year of beekeeping but it can happen, so make sure you know how to check for queen cells and have a mentor who you can ask advice from regarding swarm management if necessary.

July: Honey harvests, inspections, and not adding supers

Amazing as it may seem, just as we are getting ready for the school holidays and thoughts turn to the beach, the bees are doing the opposite and gradually preparing for the onset of winter. In fact, after the summer solstice on 21 June, the queen begins to reduce the number of eggs she lays.

You'll still want to make sure the bees have enough room for the incoming food but later on in the month you will want the bees to start storing the honey in the brood box instead of supers by filling up the spaces left by the emerging brood. So you probably don't want to be adding supers now. If you leave the honey supers on the hive during the summer with the intention of taking them all away in one go in August, you will find that if it turns rainy in July some of the honey destined for your kitchen table will be eaten by the bees.

If you have taken off some honey but not had time to extract it make sure it is in a place the bees can't get to it. Their sense of smell is so good they will find any honey that is around and will do everything they can to get at it. We wrap our supers in newspaper and store them in the house but the bees still come in searching for the food. We find it best to harvest it quickly, storing it in plastic buckets with secure lids.

Swarming is less likely later on in the summer but the bees can surprise us, so again keep looking for the queen cells. Supersedure can still take place as there will still be some drones around to mate with a queen if necessary.

If you forgot to order thymol-based varroa treatment earlier in the year, you must buy it now in preparation for next month's application.

Beginners will be building up confidence around the hive and getting sticky at their first honey harvest. They will also have to order the varroa treatment.

August: Final honey harvest, start thymol treatment, unite weak colonies

It's safer to take your summer holiday at this time of year as there is little danger of your bees swarming now. As the nights get noticeably shorter, the bees are getting ready to batten down the hatches.

Before you go away, reduce the entrance block. Wasps can be a nuisance as they try to steal the bees' honey, so the smaller the area the bees have to defend the better.

It's even worth making a wasp trap or two to attract them away from the hive. We find a plastic bottle containing some fruit and bits of meat usually does the trick.

If you plan to go away in late August, you should enjoy your final honey harvest and apply your first thymol treatment before you go. The warmer the weather the better the chance that the treatment will work against the varroa mites and since most treatments are at least 28 days long you need to start it before the temperatures drops in September (see page 191). Any honey that is in the hive after you start the treatment will have to be left for the bees as the strong smell of thymol taints the flavour.

Unite weak colonies this month. Two weak colonies going into the winter may leave you with none in the spring but one strong colony has a much better chance of surviving the winter.

If the colony is short of stores because it has been a cold, wet summer you can give it some sugar-syrup feed this month. The temperatures will be warm enough for the bees to evaporate the syrup and turn it into the honey they need for the winter.

Often, beginner beekeepers will not receive their nucleus of bees until late June or even July, which will not give the bees enough time to build up into a strong colony during the summer and make enough stores to see them through the winter. So beginner bee-keepers should take very little honey from the hive in the first year and feed their bees sugar syrup going into the winter.

September: Finish varroa treatment, check food stores, reduce hive entrance

Even though we can often enjoy an Indian summer and the bees will still be out most days collecting pollen and nectar, they and you will be preparing for winter. You will finish the thymol treatment and be ready to close up the hive in preparation for winter.

If you want to overwinter with just a brood box, check that the bees have at least 13 kg (30 lbs) of stores in the brood box: that is equivalent to six National brood frames filled with capped honey. If they don't, then feed them a sugar-syrup solution or give them back a super of their own honey. Never give them honey from another hive as it harbours bacteria that can be harmful to bees.

We always leave each of our hives a super full of honey – this is called a brood and a half – in the hope that it will improve their chances of winter survival. This extra 9 kg (20 lbs) of honey gives us peace of mind that the bees will have plenty of food for late winter.

Heft your hive now so you know what a full hive feels like and you will be able to gauge how much stores are in a hive without opening it up when it is cold.

Keep your entrance small just in case there are still wasps around or bees from other colonies wanting to rob your colony of its stores.

If you go into winter with a brood and a half it is a good idea to move the super to below the brood box and to take away the queen excluder to give the queen and the bees full use of all the hive. The bees will still be able to get to all the honey and having the super at the bottom will make next year's spring clean and brood comb change a lot simpler.

Beginners will need to follow the procedures above.

October: Mouse guards, candle and cosmetic making, and clean supers

If you are feeding the bees to top up their stores, this needs to be completed while the weather is still warm enough for them to turn the syrup into honey.

Mouse guards should be on the small hive entrance before the first frosty evening to prevent rodents from getting into the warm hive to hibernate.

Make sure you have open-mesh floors to provide ventilation within the hive, with the varroa tray out.

If you have green woodpeckers in your area, wrap the hive loosely with chicken wire mesh.

You can continue monitoring for varroa during the autumn months by counting the fall on the varroa tray – which should only be in when you are monitoring the varroa count. If the count is high think about applying oxalic acid around 21 December.

Away from the hive, your supers need cleaning with a blowtorch and storing. We stack ours outside with a roof and a floor to keep the damp out but enough air inside to allow for ventilation. You can stack the supers off the floor by putting them on a hive stand. If you don't have one, bricks, blocks of wood or milk crates will do. In the supers we store the wax honeycomb that the bees cleaned out and we want to give back to them next year. The cold over winter will kill any wax moth larvae that may be lurking inside the wax.

If you have kept all the wax cappings from the honey harvesting, you will now have time to render them down. You can then use the wax to exchange for new foundation at your beekeeping suppliers, or make candles, furniture polish or cosmetics.

You can also clean your smoker and other tools and sort out your storage area.

Beginners can follow the procedures above.

November: Sell bee products, read and rest

The winter months are the quietest for the beekeeper and the bees. While they are clustered in the hive, keeping warm and eating their winter stores, you too will be inside reading books to increase your knowledge of apiculture and just enjoying time off from your all-consuming hobby.

If your hives are in a windy spot on a roof-top put something heavy over the hive stand legs or on the roof of the hives to weigh it down such as a brick or slab of concrete. And every so often you will want to check that the hive has not been blown over by the wind and that the entrance is not blocked by dead bees that have been ejected from the hive.

If you have any honey left you may decide to sell it at the local farmers' market in the run-up to Christmas. You way want to design a leaflet for customers describing where your honey comes from with a photo of your hives. Or you could make special honey labels as Christmas presents. Your candles and cosmetics would also make unusual products to sell or gifts for family and friends.

December: Oxalic acid, snow clearance, Christmas presents

In our continual struggle with varroa, December is the month to administer some oxalic acid if necessary. The best time to administer this treatment is when the colony is as near to broodless as possible, which should be around the winter solstice on 21 December when the queen will not be laying (see page 192).

If there is snow, clear it from in front of the hive, because on a bright day the reflection of the sky on the white snow will confuse the bees and they will fly upside down. Also clear away any snow that may be blocking the entrance so the bees can bring out their dead or take a flight.

December is a good time to think ahead about equipment you will need for the following year and put it on your Christmas present list.

Epilogue

The future of urban beekeeping

When we started writing this book it was early winter. Our bees were still flying on mild days bringing in pollen from Michaelmas daisies, echinacea and sedums. Outside, we had stacked our supers containing frames that we planned to reuse next year, and inside we were jarring the last of our honey to sell in the run-up to Christmas.

Now it is early spring, the days are getting longer and the bees are again flying when the weather is warm enough. Early flowering cherry trees and hazel catkins in our city landscape are providing much-needed pollen as the brood begins to expand.

Some colonies will not have survived winter. If it is anything like 2010, almost one in five hives will perish: some will have starved; many will have dwindled as the varroa mite reduces the worker bees' life span; others will have been weakened by viruses or disease.

After a few months of silence, bees are suddenly once more in the news. A report by the United Nations Environment Programme showing extensive honeybee losses in Europe, North America and Asia has reignited concerns about the widespread collapse of the species.

Once again urban beekeeping courses are oversubscribed, fuelled by concerned citizens trying to do their bit to protect the beleaguered honeybee's future. The BBKA's membership will continue to spiral, new associations will spring up with urban post-codes and more people will be keeping bees in our cities than since the second world war. More of them will be sharing the workload and responsibilities.

As we write this, as part of a new nationwide Co-op campaign, one of us is staring out from billboards dressed in their bee suit proclaiming how support from the company has helped them to train dozens of urban beekeepers in London. 'My revolution: saving bees in central London,' reads the strapline.

Hardly a day goes by without a query from a company or institution thinking of either keeping bees themselves or dedicating land for hives, from cutting-edge marketing firms to the fire brigade. And a pop-up honeybee shop opening in a trendy part of the capital is selling our books and honey alongside art installations, honey-based cocktails and waggle dance workshops. But isn't the bubble going to burst? Won't people move on to a new fad?

We think the bee craze will continue but it will start to take a slightly different trajectory. After three years of intense focus on honeybees, people will slowly start to become more aware of other types of bees and the perils they too face.

As the UN report made clear, honeybees are part of a *group* of the most important pollinators worldwide. People will begin to appreciate that our western honeybee is only one among 20,000 known bee species. This newfound awareness will be driven by organisations that have hitherto championed the honeybee.

In Newcastle, for example, where initial steps to make the city bee-friendly targeted the honeybee, the council has stated that solitary bees are the priority of its bee strategy in 2011.

And the Co-op, while continuing to support training for new urban beekeepers, has extended its Plan Bee campaign to other pollinators. 'People are well aware of the threats facing honeybees. This has proved a catalyst for getting people interested in what is happening to our other pollinators. Now they are urging us to do more to help other bees and butterflies,' says Naomi Davis, the Co-op's sustainability projects manager.

Dr Adam Hart, scientific director of the Bee Guardian Foundation adds: 'Honeybees can reel people in and then we can get them involved in helping to save other bees.'

A European research project is investigating which nesting

devices, management methods in parks and recreation areas, and plants are best to increase solitary bee populations and is disseminating an action plan to 20 European cities. One of the partners of the Lyon-based project is the Natural History Museum in London, which is helping to design a European awareness campaign. The project is building on initial research in New York that has shown that in densely built-up areas where gardens and green spaces are often in the shadow of tower blocks, sunny, open rooftops may be the best locations to provide food and habitat for wild bee species.

As a result of this increasing awareness of wild bees, many aspiring urban apiarists may decide instead to focus on making their urban environment better for all bees. With local authorities facing severe spending cuts there is no better time to lobby our councilors to ditch expensive annual bedding plants and extensive grass cutting in favour of cheaper, bee-friendly grounds maintenance.

Nailing a bee house to a wall, drilling holes into a piece of wood, or leaving an upturned flowerpot under the garden shed to create nesting habitats for wild bees is a more natural way of helping bees than beekeeping can ever be.

So gradually, over the next few years we expect to see a less frantic rush to keep honeybees in cities and a gradual shift towards the urban guardianship of all bees.

The other trend in urban beekeeping will be keeping bees as a vehicle for social change. This approach has been pioneered by the Golden Company in east London. In Copenhagen, a social enterprise plans to use a similar model to improve the life chances of the city's homeless people. By accident, Kairos Community Trust and Charlton Manor School discovered the therapeutic and rehabilitative qualities of beekeeping. We hope many more organisations working with vulnerable people will keep bees in the future to enable their clients or pupils to enjoy these benefits.

If you are new to urban beekeeping, we hope this book has given you a flavour of the revolution you can become part of, but also practical tips about where you can do it and what's in store, both the highs and the lows.

We hope we have also impressed on you that it is not a hobby to be taken lightly and that there are plenty of other ways you can help bees. With urban beekeeping comes responsibility, not only to your bees, other people's bees, and to your neighbours, but also to the very concept of keeping bees in a city. A few indifferent or lazy beekeepers can give urban beekeeping a bad name.

If you already keep bees in an urban environment, we hope we've given you an insight into the growing and changing movement that you are part of and its potential to change the way we view our cities for ever as sanctuaries for all bee species.

Appendix 1

Sample risk assessment for schools, companies, etc

Who could be at risk?	What is the risk?	Likelihood and measure of risk
Students/staff/ visitors	Bee stings (see British Beekeepers' Association Advisory Leaflet Number B2)	Risk reduced by situating the hive in an isolated part of site where access is supervised. The likelihood of stings can be further reduced by the provision of screening around the hive. This has the effect of forcing the flight path upwards and away from the site. A screen also prevents the accidental arrival of visitors at the hive without suitable clothing. It is also important to keep docile bees to reduce the likelihood of bee stings. Visitors attending the hive must be accompanied by an experienced beekeeper. Visitors with known bee sting allergies should not attend the hive. They should be made aware of the hive site and carry any prescribed medication with them at all times. A regularly updated medical information leaflet should be available at the hive site. If a bee sting occurs, first aid procedures should be carried out. A suitably equipped first aid box should be available near the hive. It is mandatory to have access to a mobile phone/landline in case emergency assistance is required. The exact location of the hive should be provided to ensure rapid assistance.

Who could be at risk?	What is the risk?	Likelihood and measure of risk
		The provision of suitable clothing/headgear/ gloves to those attending the hive will significantly reduce the risk of bee stings occurring. It is recommended that a check is made to ensure that clothes are 'beetight'. A proper hive opening procedure including the use of a hive smoker will also reduce the risk of bee stings. No one should be allowed to stand in the bees' flight path. Anyone attending the hive should avoid the use of strong perfumes, hairspray, aftershave etc. as this may upset the bees. The weather should be suitable for attending the hive. **LOW RISK**
Neighbours/ general public	Swarming (see 'Swarm control for the beginner', British Beekeepers' Association Advisory Leaflet Number B3)	Swarm control describes the measures taken to prevent a swarm from occurring. Factors that will help prevent swarm preparation by a colony of bees include: • using a strain of bee with a low tendency to swarm • using a young and vigorous queen to head the colony • giving the colony ample room in the brood-nest and supers • ensuring good ventilation in the hive (being vigilant regarding the formation of 'queen cells' is necessary and the supervision of an experienced beekeeper is essential). The hotline number for the local beekeepers' association swarm collector should be available. Ground staff should have contact details of staff responsible for the hive as well as the hotline number.

Who could be at risk?	What is the risk?	Likelihood and measure of risk
		A staff rota will operate during holiday times to ensure regular hive inspections are carried out to reduce risk of swarming. (Swarming is a natural occurrence and is something that experienced beekeepers are used to dealing with.) **HIGH RISK**
Neighbours/ general public	Legal and other problems with neighbours (see British Beekeepers' Association Advisory Leaflet Number B1)	Through membership of a local beekeeping association, the beekeeper gains protection of a third-party insurance policy. This provides coverage against all third-party claims arising from beekeeping activities involving injury to persons or damage to property. The BBKA has a legal advisor who can give help on the law in this area. Issues that might affect the neighbours in addition to the above are as follows: **Overflying:** Bees fly about 5 m (16 ft) above the ground, but problems can occur from bees flying out from their hives and returning to them. In windy weather over open ground, bees fly very low because it is less effort. The beekeeper can help by sheltering the apiary site with hedges, shrubs or screening. It helps if the hive is faced away from neighbouring properties. **Cleansing flights:** After winter confinement, bees' early flights can result in anything in the vicinity being spotted with faeces. The position of the hive should take account of this. **Swarms:** See above **Numbers of hives/colonies:** Sheer numbers of colonies exacerbate the above issues. Consider site and suitable numbers. **LOW RISK**

(Adapted from the King Alfred School Beekeeping Risk Assessment, reproduced with permission)

Appendix 2

Sample rules and recommendations for allotments

Best practice rules

Approval: Prospective beekeepers must consult and seek the approval of their own association before commencing beekeeping and agree to follow any rules stipulated. Associations may need to amend their constitution to allow beekeeping.

British Beekeepers Association (BBKA) membership: Full membership of a local BBKA recognised beekeepers association is mandatory. It provides essential third party insurance up to £5m as well many other benefits. Evidence of membership must be made available on request.

Contacts: Beekeepers should ensure that up-to-date contact details are easily available to an association, ideally being posted within the site in case of emergency. In cases of absence, contact details of competent 'cover' should be provided.

Training: Prospective allotment beekeepers should be able to satisfy an association of their competence. Evidence may include completion of a beekeeping course, longstanding experience or supervision by an experienced mentor.

Number of hives: Each association will determine the upper limit of bee colonies per plot and per site based on individual site conditions. Considerations will include equity, availability of forage and minimising inconvenience to others.

Hive location: Entrances should not face onto paths or nearby housing. The site should be agreed with an association and chosen to minimise inconvenience to others. Risks of vandalism and theft should be considered.

Hive management: Bees should be managed to ensure the wellbeing of both the bees and other allotment holders and neighbours. Competent care and control of bees is expected at all times.

Swarming: Beekeepers should monitor and take prevention measures to avoid swarming. Effective arrangements to promptly deal with a swarm are essential.

Disease: Beekeepers should be able to recognise diseased colonies, treat using latest guidance from Fera's National Bee Unit and immediately contact the local bee inspector if a notifiable disease is suspected.

Temperament: Beekeepers should ensure that docile strains are kept.

Water: A water source must be available on each plot keeping bees.

Failure to comply: Non-compliance with an association's rules may result in a request to remove hives from a site.

Recommendations

Mentoring: It is highly recommended that novice beekeepers seek a mentoring arrangement with an experienced beekeeper, especially in their first year.

Number of hives: A recommended maximum limit of two colonies per full plot with the temporary addition of one nucleus colony is suggested. The number of hives per site is recommended at a maximum of three per acre with consideration given to the proximity of other allotment sites.

Hive management:
- When acquiring a colony, local bees are often considered most suitable. Beekeepers should ensure that new colonies are disease-free to prevent cross-infection.
- Potential beekeepers should be aware of the time involved in beekeeping and be able to actively manage hives on a weekly basis between April and September.
- Fencing/screening in order to raise the bees' flight path above head height is recommended.
- When carrying out hive inspections choose appropriate times and weather conditions when other users are least likely to be inconvenienced.
- Registration with BeeBase is recommended. BeeBase is run by Fera's National Bee Unit, and provides free access to the regional bee inspector and other resources.

- Beekeepers should have a clear understanding of the triggers for stinging (weather, clothing and odour can all be factors) and ensure others are aware of this information. Awareness of potentially severe allergic responses to bee stings is needed. Appropriate responses should be clearly understood. However, individuals claiming a severe reaction as a factor in objecting to beekeeping are requested to supply medical evidence of such to an association.
- Risks to bees from spraying herbicides and pesticides should be discussed with association committees.
- Beekeepers should be prepared to work with other plot holders and neighbours to raise interest in beekeeping.

(Excerpted and adapted from the Newcastle Allotments Bee Group Rules and Recommendations, reproduced with permission)

Appendix 3

Sample beekeeping disclaimer for companies

I confirm that I have volunteered to act as a beekeeper for the [name of company] bees. As part of this agreement, I declare that:

1. I understand the restrictions in the lease for the roof terrace and will not go beyond the permitted boundaries.
2. I will attend the training sessions conducted by the professional beekeeper.
3. I will wear the appropriate beekeeping equipment when conducting any work on the beehive.
4. Notwithstanding the provision of appropriate beekeeping equipment, I understand and accept that it is possible I may occasionally get stung.
5. I have read and understand the instructions on 'how to treat bee stings' and am aware of the location of the company bee sting kit.
6. I will record details of any stings in the company beekeeping journal.
7. I do not believe that I have an allergic response to bee stings.
8. I am under no obligation to act in this capacity and have the right to change my mind at any time, by advising _____ at the company.

Signed:_____ Date: _____

Name: _____

(Adapted from the Canopius Beekeeping Agreement, reproduced with permission)

Appendix 4

Bee-friendly flowers, shrubs and trees

FLOWERS

Name	Common name	Notes
Agastache foeniculum	Anise hyssop	Good nectar source from July to September. An urticifolia (nettle-leaf giant hyssop) is also a good nectar plant
Althaea rosea/ Althaea officinalis	Hollyhock/ Marshmallow	Good late pollen source from July to September
Borago officinalis	Borage	Long flowering from mid summer. Visited by all bees for its nectar
Colchicum autumnale	Autumn crocus	Important source of late pollen
Crocus		Important early source of pollen
Digitalis	Foxgloves	Good bumblebee forage in mid-summer
Doronicum caucasicum var. magnificum	Leopard's Bane	Tall, daisy-like flower, provides much-needed early pollen in March and April
Echium vulgare	Viper's bugloss	The most popular bumblebee plant, flowers from July to September
Echinops ritro	Globe thistle	Good nectar source in summer
Endymion non-scriptus	Common bluebell	Good for bumblebees, but cultivated varieties with shorter flower tubes, such as the Siberian squill, are better for honeybees and flower earlier, in February
Eranthis hyemalis	Winter aconite	Can flower in January, so an important early pollen source

Name	Common name	Notes
Geranium pratense	Cranesbill/ Meadow cranesbill	Clump-forming perennial that provides bee forage from June to August. Not to be confused with pelargoniums (bedding geraniums that are not much liked by bees)
Galanthus nivalis	Snowdrop	Flowers in February providing much-needed early pollen and nectar
Lamium album	White deadnettle	Provides year-round forage for all bees
Lavandula	Lavender	Nectar and pollen from July to September. Lots of different varieties including L. angustifolia (English lavender) and hybrid L. intermedia, which are more popular with bees
Leonurus Cardiaca	Motherwort	Widely acclaimed bee plant for its long flowering season from July to October providing late nectar and pollen
Monarda didyma	Scarlet bee balm/ Bee bergamot	Natural source of thymol, which is used by beekeepers to reduce varroa mites in the hive. Nectar and pollen source from June to October
Myosotis	Forget-me-not	Popular nectar and pollen source in May if allowed to flower
Narcissus	Wild daffodil	Provides early pollen for honeybees. A long proboscis is required to reach the nectar, so more suited to bumblebees
Onobrychis viciifolia	Sainfoin/ French clover	Good source of nectar for bees in midsummer
Phacelia tanacetifolia	Lacy phacelia	Good nectar source in mid to late summer
Rudbeckia hirta or fulgida	Black-eyed Susan/ Coneflower	Supplies autumn nectar and pollen

Name	Common name	Notes
Salvia Superba	Blue queen	Flowers from June to September
Solidago virgaurea	Goldenrod/ Woundwort	Good source of late summer nectar and pollen from July to October
Symphytum	Comfrey	Good for bumblebees in May to June
Taraxacum officinale	Dandelion	Provides nectar and pollen throughout the year if allowed to flower
Thymus serpyllum	Creeping thyme/ Wild thyme	A high-yielding bee plant in relation to its size. Ideal for rock gardens. Flowers July to August
Verbascum	Mullein	Good late summer pollen source
Verbena officinalis	Common verbena	Good late summer nectar source

SHRUBS

Name	Common name	Notes
Abutilon vitifolium	'Tennant's White'	Nectar and pollen source in May to July. Fast growing and needs full sun
Buddleia	Butterfly bush	The yellow-flowered buddleia (B. globosa) is reputedly the best for honeybees
Cotoneaster		Great nectar source in May and June
Cytisus scoparius	Broom	Early-flowering Portuguese broom (C. albus) blooms earlier than other varieties to provide pollen and nectar in April

Name	Common name	Notes
Escallonia		Fast-growing evergreen hedging plant with masses of tubular crimson-red flowers from June to October
Hebe spp.		Nectar and pollen for bees. Avoid the smaller species with dark flowers
Ligustrum vulgare/ Ligustrum sinense	Privet/ Chinese privet	When allowed to flower, it provides nectar from June to September, depending on the variety. Can produce dark, bitter honey
Lonicera	Honeysuckle	Shrubby honeysuckles have smaller, more open flowers, with more available nectar than the climbing varieties
Mahonia		Valuable source of pollen in early spring. Mahonia aquifolium (Oregon-grape) is a popular variety for gardeners and bees
Myrtus communis	Common myrtle	Drought-resistant shrub providing pollen and nectar in late summer
Perovskia atriplicifolia	Russian sage	This member of the mint family provides late nectar sources from August to October
Prunus laurocerasus	Cherry laurel	Pollen and nectar in April
Prunus lusitanica	Portugal laurel	Pollen and nectar in May and June
Prunus spinosa	Blackthorn/Sloe	Valuable source of early pollen in February and March
Ribes spp.	Flowering currant	Flowers in April so provides valuable source of early pollen. R. sanguineum, R. odoratum and R. speciosum are all recommended
Viburnum tinus	French White	Valuable source of early pollen. Even known to flower in December

Name	Common name	Notes
Weigela florida		Good source of nectar for bumblebees in June. They often bite holes in the base of the flowers which allows honeybees to get to the nectar

TREES

Name	Common name	Notes
Corylus	Hazel	Wind-pollinated, but early catkins are a valuable source of pollen
Crataegus spp.	Hawthorn/May	Nectar and pollen source in May. C. monogyna and C. oxyacantha are good. Avoid any double-headed flower varieties
Malus spp./ Malus hybrids	Apple trees/ Crab apples	Pollen and nectar when in blossom from April to May
Prunus padus/ Prunus avium	Bird cherry/ Wild cherry	Plentiful supply of nectar and pollen when in blossom in spring
Salix spp.	Willows	Early spring nectar and pollen especially S. apoda, S. boydii, S. hastata, S.lanata, S. melanostachys and S. uva-ursi
Tilia spp.	Limes	Can supply large quantities of nectar. Avoid T. x euchlora (Crimean lime) and T. x orbicularis (Hybrid lime) as the nectar from these species can stupefy bees

(Sources: Brighton and Hove City Council Cityparks; F.N. Howes, Plants and Beekeeping (Faber); Bee Happy Plants Ltd, www.beehappyplants.co.uk; Bumblebee Conservation Trust)

Glossary

Apiary: Place where one or more hives is kept.

Apiarist: Person who keeps bees, otherwise known as a beekeeper.

Apiculture: The science and art of keeping honeybees.

***Apis mellifera*:** Commonly known as the western, or European honeybee, this species of honeybee is native to Europe and is kept for its honey in most parts of the world. There are more than 20 races, or subspecies, of this honeybee.

Bailey method: A method of changing brood comb to remove potentially diseased comb and replace it with clean, healthy comb for the queen to lay her eggs in. Usually takes place in the spring.

Bee space: Space left by bees between the comb and other surfaces in the hive which allows the bees free passage and measures 9.5 mm. Any bigger and the bees will fill it with wax comb; any smaller and they will fill it with propolis.

Bee suit: Full body suit made from cotton and polyester worn by beekeepers to protect them from being stung when opening beehives.

Beeswax: Waxy substance secreted from the bees' wax gland that is used to build comb and cap cells.

Black bee (*Apis mellifera mellifera*): Dark-coloured, hardy member of the western honeybee family that is indigenous to Britain and is kept in the north of England and Scotland.

Brood: Immature stages in the bees' life cycle including egg, larvae and pupa when they have not yet emerged from a cell.

Brood box: The part of the hive where the brood is reared. The queen is usually confined here.

Buckfast bee: A cross-breed of different European honey bees, bred almost a century ago by Brother Adams, a monk at Buckfast Abbey in Devon.

Capped brood: The stage in the bees' development where the cell a larva inhabits is capped, or sealed, with a brown wax cover secreted by the bees. Here it pupates into an adult bee.

Cappings: The beeswax covering over a cell. Cappings over a honey-cell are white because they consist of wax only. The brown cappings covering the brood are porous to allow the pupating larvae to breathe.

Carnolian honeybee (*Apis mellifera carnica*): This race of the western honeybee, originally from the Balkans, has together with the Italian honeybee come to dominate beekeeping worldwide.

Cast swarm: A second or subsequent swarm that leaves with one or more unmated queens after the prime swarm has departed.

Cells: Hexagonal wax compartments making up beeswax comb which are used to store pollen and honey and to rear brood in.

Colony: The group of honeybees living together as a viable, sustainable unit with one queen, brood in all stages of development, and in the summer up to 50,000 worker bees and a few hundred drones.

Comb: The mass of hexagonal beeswax cells in which honey and pollen is stored and brood reared.

Crystallisation: When crystals form naturally in honey to make it hard. Some honeys crystallise quickly, others hardly at all. It can be combated by gently heating the honey.

Crown board (or cover board): A board that separates the brood box or supers from the roof of the hive to prevent bees from building wild comb in the roof or sealing it up with propolis. Can be made of wood with two holes where the porter bee escapes are placed when emptying supers of bees. Perspex versions allow the beekeeper to view the hive without removing the crown board.

Cut comb: Natural comb, or built by the bees on foundation, that contains cells of honey and is cut to a size ready to eat.

Drawn comb: Comb that is built out by honeybees from a sheet of foundation.

Drone: Male honeybee which comes from an unfertilised egg. Its only function is to mate with a virgin queen in the spring or summer, so it doesn't live during the winter.

Drone comb or brood: Comb built to raise drones has larger cells than worker cells and the capping is dome-shaped.

Dummy board: A piece of wood cut to the same size as a frame, but thinner, which is used in the hive to separate areas.

Egg: The first phase in the honeybee's life cycle. Eggs are laid by the queen in the bottom of a cell and look like white grains of rice.

Entrance block: A notched wooden block used to reduce the size of the hive entrance.

Forage: Natural food of bees (pollen and nectar) that comes from flowering trees, shrubs, plants, crops etc.

Forager bees: Worker bees which are at least 21 days old and go out foraging for (collecting) nectar, pollen, water and propolis.

Foundation: Beeswax sheets impressed with the shape of cells that the beekeeper gives the bees to draw out into comb. It can be strengthened with wire.

Frame: Wooden structure designed to hold the foundation and comb that is inserted into hives.

Guard bees: Worker bees of about three weeks old that guard the entrance to the hive from invaders such as wasps, animals or beekeepers. They are the first to attack an invader and give off a danger pheromone if the hive is disturbed.

Hefting: Lifting a hive slightly from its stand to assess its weight.

Hive: A man-made home for honeybees, made of cedar wood, pine or plastic.

Hive tool: The piece of metal that beekeepers use to open hives and prise apart frames.

Honey: A sweet liquid that bees produce by turning nectar from a complex into a simple sugar and reducing the water content to just 19 per cent. The colour, flavour and thickness depend on the flowers from which the nectar is collected.

Honey extractor: A machine that uses a centrifugal force to extract honey from the combs so they can be reused.

Honey flow: A time when there is a heightened influx of nectar into the hive because lots of nectar-bearing flowers are in bloom and the weather conditions are good for foraging.

House bee: An adult worker bee less than three weeks old that stays in the hive and performs domestic duties such as feeding larvae, cleaning cells and receiving food from forager bees.

Italian honey bee (*Apis mellifera liguistica*): A light honey-coloured race of the western honeybee that is popular worldwide for its gentle nature and prodigious honey-making abilities.

Integrated pest management: A combination of bee husbandry techniques and chemical controls to reduce pests in the hive.

Larva: The second stage in the bees' development when a grub-like creature hatches from the egg and eats until it fills the cell.

Mating flight: The flight taken by a virgin queen when she mates in the air with a number of drones.

Mouse guard: A metal strip containing holes that is fitted over the hive entrance in the winter to allow bees in and out but to prevent mice from getting in.

Nectar: A sugary liquid secreted by plants to attract pollinating insects, birds and animals that is turned into honey by bees.

Nucleus: A small colony of about 10,000 bees known as a 'nuc' that is used for beekeeper beginners and usually comes in a nuc box containing five frames.

Nurse bees: Three- to ten-day-old adult worker bees that feed and take care of brood.

Out-apiary: A place to keep bees away from the beekeeper's home.

Pheromone: A scented substance produced by the queen to help the colony to function. It is also produced by other bees to alert the colony to defend itself.

Pollen: The dust-like male reproductive cells of flowers.

Pollen basket: The part of the honeybee's hind legs designed to carry pollen.

Pollination: The transfer of pollen from the anthers (male part) to the stigma (female part) of flowers.

Porter bee escape: Two spring valves allowing bees to pass through one way but not return, which is used to clear bees from honey supers.

Propolis: Resinous substance bees collect from the barks of trees to seal gaps, mummify dead intruders such as mice and use as an antiseptic in their home.

Pupa: Third stage in bees' life cycle when the larvae pupates and metamorphoses into an adult bee in a capped (sealed) cell.

Queen: A mated queen can lay up to 2000 eggs a day in her prime.

She is the only egg-layer in the colony and recognised by the workers and drones by her pheromones.

Queen cups and cells: A cup-shaped cell hanging vertically from the comb into which the queen will lay an egg designed to develop into a queen. When the egg is laid the queen cup becomes a queen cell.

Queen excluder: A device with slots that is usually placed between a brood box and a super and allows workers to pass through but prevents the passage of queens and drones.

Royal jelly: Protein-rich substance secreted from glands of young bees to feed to larvae, especially those being reared as queens.

Scout bees: Worker bees whose job it is to search for new food sources and water and propolis and to find a new home for the colony if the bees swarm.

Sealed brood: See capped brood.

Shook swarm: A swarm-sized mass of bees shaken by the beekeeper from one hive into another with their queen in order to control swarming or disease.

Smoker: A metal container with bellows attached that burns material such as dried grass, hemp or cardboard to produce smoke.

Sting: The organ used by worker bees to defend their colony. Because it is barbed it rips apart their abdomen when used and the bee dies. The queen uses her sting to kill rival queens in a colony during the swarming season.

Supers: Floorless boxes usually placed on top of the brood box and filled with frames for the bees to store their comb containing honey. They are usually separated from the brood box by a queen excluder so the beekeeper can remove honey stores without any brood.

Sugar syrup: A solution of cane sugar and honey in various ratios sometimes used to feed bees.

Swarm: A natural method of propagation when a queen leaves the mother colony with a mass of bees and looks for a new home, leaving behind a new virgin queen and bees to create a new colony of bees. Bees can also swarm to escape disease, or if their home is overcrowded.

Swarm management and prevention: Methods used by beekeepers to stop their bees wanting to swarm.

Uncapping fork: A special fork used to remove the wax cappings that the bees use to seal and store their honey.

Varroa: A parasitic mite that breeds in capped brood cells, feeding on larvae, and lives on adult bees, spreading disease and shortening the lifespan of the western honeybee. It is widespread around the globe apart from Australia and the Antarctic and is implicated in the demise of western honeybees worldwide.

Virgin queen: Unmated queen that emerges in the hive after a swarm and needs to mate with drones to create a new colony.

Waggle dance: A remarkable dance used by forager bees to communicate the distance and direction in relation to the sun of a rich food source. This enables their sisters to go there to collect more food for the colony.

Wax glands: Glands on the underside of worker bees' abdomens that secrete small particles of beeswax.

Winter cluster: A spherical cluster of some 10,000 bees that forms in the hive to generate heat in the winter in order to survive low temperatures.

Workers: Infertile female bees that number around 50,000 in the summer and carry out all the tasks required for the survival of the colony except for laying eggs.

Directory

The British Beekeepeers' Association is the main body for amateur beekeepers in the UK. It provides members with third-party liability insurance and offers training and exams from basic level beekeeping up to Master Beekeeper. The BBKA website will direct you to your local beekeepers' association.

www.britishbee.org.uk

The government's National Bee Unit maintains a laboratory diagnostic service, the bee inspectors' service and a voluntary register of beekeepers called BeeBase, which is also an online resource for beekeepers about disease management.

https://secure.fera.defra.gov.uk/beebase

Beekeeping suppliers

Thorne
Leading manufacturer and supplier of beekeeping equipment and candlemaking supplies
www.thorne.co.uk

National Bee Supplies
Leading manufacturer and supplier of beekeeping equipment including good quality cedar wood hives
www.beekeeping.co.uk

Maisemore Apiaries
Beekeeping equipment and hives
www.bees-online.co.uk/

Stamfordham Bees
Beekeeping equipment and Northumberland bees
www.stamfordham.biz

Bee Thinking
Top-bar hives and Warré hives
www.beethinking.com

BBWear
Polyester/cotton beesuits and protective clothing
www.bbwear.co.uk

Sherriff International
Bee suits and equipment
www.bjsherriff.co.uk/

The Bee Shop
Quality beekeeper clothing at affordable prices
www.thebeeshop.co.uk

Omlet
Manufacturer and supplier of the plastic 'Beehaus' beehive
www.omlet.co.uk

Bee breeders

Contact your local beekeepers' association for names of recommended bee breeders or ask beekeeping suppliers.

Beekeeping training

Your local beekeepers' association will run training courses, but they may not be suitable or may be over-subscribed. City farms and environmental education centres will probably also run courses. Here are some commercial alternatives:

Manchester-based training courses by experienced beekeeper and author Paul Peacock
www.citycottage.co.uk

Northeast-based training courses by Fenwick beekeeper Ian Wallace
www.purehoneycomb.co.uk

Sheffield-based taster sessions by Sheffield Honey's Jez Daughtry
www.buzzy-work.co.uk

Southeast London-based training courses by Capital Bee founder
Camilla Goddard
www.capitalbee.co.uk

Training in Regent's Park by Regent's Park Honey producer Toby
Mason and experienced beekeeper John Hauxwell
www.zootrain.com

A variety of beekeeper training courses by Urban Bees co-founder
Brian McCallum
www.urbanbees.co.uk

A variety of south London-based training courses for beginner
beekeepers
www.eastsurreybees.co.uk

Other useful websites

BeeCraft magazine, www.bee-craft.com
Bee Guardian Foundation, www.beeguardian.org
Bee Improvement and Bee Breeders' Association, www.bibba.com
Bee Part of It campaign,
    www.bbc.co.uk/breathingplaces/beepartofit
BBKA Adopt a Beehive campaign, www.adoptabeehive.co.uk
BBKA leaflets, www.britishbee.org.uk/learn/general_information
Bumblebee Conservation Trust,
    www.bumblebeeconservation.org.uk
Bumblebee.org, www.bumblebee.org
Capital Growth: Capital Bee, www.capitalgrowth.org/bees
City of London Festival, www.colf.org/city-bees.cfm

Co-operative Group's Plan Bee campaign, www.co-operative.coop/
    corporate/ethicsinaction/takeaction/planbee
Defra, the Department for Environment, Food and Rural Affairs,
    www.defra.gov.uk
The Golden Company, www.thegoldenco-op.com
National Society of Allotment and Leisure Gardeners,
    www.nsalg.org.uk
Natural Beekeeping Trust, www.naturalbeekeepingtrust.org
Newcastle City Council's dedicated bee website,
    www.newcastle.gov.uk/bees
Regent's Park Honey, www.purefood.co.uk
River of Flowers, www.riverofflowers.org
Sweet Beginnings (Chicago), www.sweetbeginningsllc.com
The Barefoot Beekeeper, www.biobees.com
The London Honey Company,
    www.thelondonhoneycompany.co.uk
The Sheffield Honey Company, www.sheffield-honey.co.uk
Urban Bees, www.urbanbees.co.uk

Further reading

The Collins Beekeeper's Bible (HarperCollins, 2010)

Benjamin, Alison and McCallum, Brian, *A World Without Bees*, Guardian Books, 2009

Benjamin, Alison and McCallum, Brian, *Keeping Bees and Making Honey* (David & Charles, 2008)

Briggs, Margaret, *Honey and Bees* (Abbeydale Press, 2007)

de Bruyn, Clive, *Practical Beekeeping* (The Crowood Press, 1997)

Flottum, Kim, *Complete and Easy Guide to Beekeeping* (Apple Press, 2005)

Hooper, Ted, *Guide to Bees and Honey* (Northern Bee Books, 2010)

Howes, F.N., *Plants and Beekeeping* (Faber and Faber, 2007)

Louv, Richard, *Last Child in the Woods* (Atlantic Books, 2010)

McIntosh, Alastair, *Soil and Soul* (Aurum Press, 2004)

Owen, Jennifer, *Wildlife of a Garden* (Royal Horticultural Society, 2010)

Reynolds, Richard, *On Guerrilla Gardening* (Bloomsbury, 2009)

Tautz, Jürgen, *et al*, *The Buzz About Bees: Biology of a Superorganism* (Springer, 2008)

Traynor, Joe, *Honey: The Gourmet Medicine* (Kovak Books, 2002)

Waring, Adrian and Claire, *Get Started in Beekeeping: Teach Yourself* (Teach Yourself, 2010)

Weiler, Michael, *Bees and Honey, from Flower to Jar* (Floris Books, 2006)

Wilson, Bee, *The Hive* (John Murray, 2005)

Wilson, Edward O., *Biophilia* (Harvard University Press, 1990)

Winston, Mark L., *The Biology of the Honeybee* (Harvard University Press, 1991)

Index

Index